Stalin in Russian Satire, 1917–1991

Stalin
in Russian Satire,
1917–1991

Karen L. Ryan

The University of Wisconsin Press

Publication of this volume
has been made possible, in part, through support from
the **University of Virginia**.

The University of Wisconsin Press
1930 Monroe Street, 3rd Floor
Madison, Wisconsin 53711-2059

uwpress.wisc.edu

3 Henrietta Street
London WC2E 8LU, England

1   3   5   4   2

Library of Congress Cataloging-in-Publication Data
Ryan, Karen L., 1958 –
Stalin in Russian satire, 1917 –1991 / Karen L. Ryan.
p.   cm.
Includes bibliographical references and index.
ISBN 978-0-299-23444-7 (pbk.: alk. paper)
ISBN 978-0-299-23443-0 (e-book)
1. Stalin, Joseph, 1879 –1953—In literature.
2. Satire, Russian—History and criticism.   I. Title.
PG3026.S3R945   2009
891.7′7009351—dc22
2009012834

For

Katie
Chris
Ben
Pat

Contents

Acknowledgments

Publication of this book was supported, in part, by the College of Arts and Sciences and the Vice President for Research of the University of Virginia. I also owe thanks to many individuals for their confidence in and enthusiasm for the project. My friends and colleagues in the Dean's Office in the College of Arts and Sciences at the University of Virginia were unfailingly encouraging and accommodating for seven years. My students—perhaps unbeknownst to them—were of great help in the writing of this book; they discussed most of the ideas included in it and offered valuable insights in my classes and seminars. I am especially grateful to Gordon Braden for his generous reading of an early version of the manuscript and for his suggestions for revision. My children, to whom this book is dedicated, were my guiding lights throughout.

Note on Translation and Transliteration

All English translations in the text and notes are mine. In some cases, I have included excerpts from the Russian original to demonstrate important stylistic or linguistic features.

The system of transliteration from Cyrillic used in this book is based on that of the Library of Congress. I have, however, omitted diacritics except in notes and the bibliography. I have also chosen to eliminate the soft sign from proper names throughout the text. Proper names that have become standard in common usage are used.

Stalin in Russian Satire, 1917–1991

Introduction

S talinism" refers not only to the repressive political regime developed and sustained by Joseph Stalin; it is a mindset and a mode of behavior that shaped Soviet and Russian culture for three quarters of the twentieth century. Stalinism has been the preoccupation of Russian intellectual life for many decades and remains central today as post-Soviet Russia continues to struggle with the ghost of Stalin. Stalin's specter—his legacy of purges, collectivization, the terror, the gulag, and other great evils—haunts twentieth-century Russian culture. This obsession is reflected in historiography, the press, and political life, and it has been a recurrent theme in art.

Although de-Stalinization was supported following Stalin's death in 1953, it was neither thorough nor genuinely cathartic in the Soviet period. The exorcism of Stalin was not carried through to the end, and he continued to exert an influence, like "a living corpse preying vampire-like upon post-Stalinist, and now post-Soviet, society."[1] Early attempts to repudiate Stalin and Stalinism were limited, cautious, and controlled. Andrei Sinyavsky notes that Stalin's death elicited both grief and jubilation,[2] and by all accounts both reactions were sincere. Khrushchev's so-called Secret Speech, entitled "On the Cult of Personality and Its Consequences," which was delivered at the Twentieth Party Congress in 1956, marked a high point in de-Stalinization. Although the speech was not published, it was disseminated widely, so that Khrushchev's denunciation of the mass arrests, imprisonment, deportations, and executions under Stalin had a significant impact on Soviet culture. However, his condemnation was limited to Stalin, Beria, and a small circle within the People's Commissariat for Internal Affairs (NKVD); the speech signaled the possibility of critical reevaluation of the past but also imposed limitations on its scope. In 1961 more searching, detailed accounts of Stalin's crimes were presented at the Twenty-Second Party Congress as de-Stalinization gained strength and momentum. The removal of Stalin's body from the mausoleum that same year was an important symbolic step toward rejection of the Stalinist legacy. The publication of Evgeny Evtushenko's poem "The Heirs of Stalin" ("Nasledniki Stalina") (1962) and of Aleksandr Solzhenitsyn's *One Day in the Life of Ivan Denisovich* (*Odin den' Ivana Denisovicha*) (1962) intensified debate about the Stalinist past and its meaning for the future. By the time Khrushchev fell from power in 1964, however, no decisive policy on de-Stalinization had emerged. Kathleen Smith notes that Khrushchev strategically implicated the Russian people in the crimes of Stalinism: "He sought to put the Party and the people on an equal footing as victims and unwitting accomplices in the terror. He reminded people that they too had cheered Stalin and supported the death penalty for 'enemies of the people.' The ubiquity of the Stalin cult allowed reformers to try to bind society into the web of complicity."[3] Thus, by the end of the first phases of de-Stalinization issues of guilt and responsibility were far from resolved.

With glasnost Stalinism quickly came to the fore as the central issue in the reevaluation of Soviet history. The reforms carried out under Gorbachev—the lifting of censorship limitations and the granting of the right of association—led to more open and intense debate concerning Stalin's legacy. Initially this meant a flood of revelations about formerly forbidden topics, such as the human cost of collectivization, the purges and deportations, the extent of the gulag system, and the nation's lack of preparedness for the Second World War. Gorbachev's original intent was to discredit Stalin—now securely consigned to the past—and to promote alternatives within the parameters of Leninist socialism.[4] When the examination of Stalinism was permitted, even encouraged, a more probing reassessment of the Soviet past inevitably followed. The establishment of the Memorial Society in the late eighties contributed to popular engagement in the debate over the Stalinist past. This grassroots group, dedicated to investigating and publicizing the terror and to memorializing its victims, was extraordinarily active and vocal during the glasnost period. Although the debate initially focused on Stalinism, it quickly expanded to include Leninism and even Marxism. Stalin's crimes came to be regarded in some quarters not as a distortion of Leninist norms but as the logical continuation of the line he established (an interpretation long accepted in the West). Under attack by historians, politicians, and camp survivors, the foundations of the Communist Party eventually crumbled.

Many Russians were reluctant to confront the revealed crimes of Stalinism. For several decades the regime shielded citizens from the necessity of coming to terms with the past. As Walter Laqueur has noted, "There is a tendency to argue that the old days were not remotely as bad as believed by later generations, that the regime was universally supported, and that, in any case, the worst excesses were planned and carried out by foreigners."[5] The parallels between Stalin and Hitler—obvious to observers in the West—were drawn only in the waning days of the Soviet Union. There were many, however, who from early on were eager to expose the Stalinist past to the light of inquiry. Once this became genuinely possible with glasnost, a flood of material on Stalin and Stalinism ensued. The press carried debates and exposés, literary works and memoirs were published by the dozens, plays and films about Stalinism appeared, exhibitions were mounted, and public events were organized. Adam Hochschild remarks about this period: "It is hard to recall another case where the government and press of a major country were so preoccupied, almost daily, with events that had happened forty or fifty years before."[6] This has led to a more thorough vetting. Russia has been able to look intensively and extensively into her past in order to confront the trauma of Stalinism.

The concept of cultural memory (also known as collective or social memory)[7] is very useful in approaching the process of de-Stalinization or lustration (purification) in Russia. Particularly pertinent is the work of . Maurice Halbwachs; many scholars have built on the theoretical framework he constructed.[8] Individual memories are always formed and experienced within groups or communities. Communities are "constituted by their past,"[9] connected by narratives held in common and retold by their members. There is no collective or group mind separate from individual constituents' memories, but the approach of cultural memory dynamically connects the present with the past. Cultural memory is distinct from history, which preserves the past without sustaining an organic relation to it; an active, living past linked to the present informs cultural memory. Moreover, cultural memory is integral to identity formation and to nationalism. In the case of Stalinist and post-Stalinist Russia, this is complicated by the instability of the question of nationality; it is difficult to identify the self in national terms in the context of a multinational empire (e.g., the Soviet Union). Satirists make this distinction in different ways, so that the locus of cultural memory vis-à-vis these works is sometimes Russians, sometimes Soviets, sometimes a broader community including émigrés. It is this community—however defined by the satirist—that is considered in the literary conversation about guilt, complicity, and the possibility of absolution.

Even before the fall of the Soviet Union and the reckoning that has occurred, the question of responsibility for Stalinism was posed as a moral issue by Russians. Western historians have long debated the causes of Stalinism and its relationship to Leninist socialism. For Russians, however, the issues have often been framed in the context of guilt and repentance. Many of the literary works that have been produced—including works of satire—have been concerned with the question of responsibility rather than with the historical, economic, or social circumstances that brought Stalin to power and supported the terror. Moreover, this ethical debate has often been couched in terms of self and other: "In the end, it is a debate about responsibility. Were the *gulag*, the Purge, the collectivization famine, and all the rest of it things that some alien, outside force—Marxism, Jews, Bolsheviks—did to us? Or was it something that we—Russians living out many centuries of Russian history—did to ourselves? It is a debate, finally, about whether Russians should see themselves only as victims, or as both victims and executioners."[10]

Western scholarship has tended to see Stalin himself—his personality, his character, his pathology—as the primary motive force in the development of Stalinism. This approach can easily become reductive, leading to an underestimation of the importance of the complex circumstances that gave rise to Stalinism. As Derek Spring asks, "Do [historians] not risk creating an image of a superhuman force who manipulated all to his will, unshackled by any other forces and influences?"[11] A competing school of thought holds that Stalinism developed to respond to the particular problems and issues facing the Soviet Union. Moreover, certain groups within society benefited from the Stalinist terror, so that the totalitarian state was the result of "social negotiation."[12] For all his mysterious powers of magnetism and his clever political machinations, Stalin could not have risen to his position of absolute power, nor could he have remained in that position for twenty-five years, without the support of many other people. Stalinism found fertile ground in the Soviet context, took root, and grew; indeed, it turned out to be devilishly difficult to eradicate. These observations have led historians to speculate that Stalinism evolved out of preexisting conditions in Russian political and social life:

> Although certain aspects of Stalinism can be understood only with reference to the personality of the leader (which is also true with regard to Hitler

and Mussolini), it is even more obvious that the system did not develop in a vacuum. It had historical and ideological roots; conditions existed that made the rise and victory of Stalinism possible in the first place. It is unlikely (to put it cautiously) that an outlandish system, which was alien to Russian mentality and tradition and totally opposed to the Bolshevik doctrine and practice, would have generated so much enthusiasm, lasted for so long, and found supporters even decades after the demise of its founder.[13]

Certainly we must question what interests supported Stalinism and which social groups benefited under the conditions it imposed. Yet this approach, which emphasizes the "social contract" over the personal role of Stalin, is also problematic. By focusing on the cultural origins of Stalinism and moving Stalin to the periphery or the background, historians may risk exonerating him.[14] Even within this broader view of Stalinism, it is crucial to acknowledge the responsibility that the dictator personally bears for the crimes of his era and the legacy that he left. Smith argues that the passivity of the Soviet populace (which might be seen as complicity in moral terms) resulted not from this hypothetical social contract but rather from coercion on the part of the state. The state had the power to prosecute, to apply sanctions in the workplace, and to mete out rewards, so that Soviet citizens were induced to turn a blind eye to the evils perpetrated by Stalin's regime. The widespread network of informers established under Stalin cemented the regime's coercive power. It arguably had the effect of making all citizens collaborators as well.[15]

Art has been an important vehicle for exploring questions of complicity, guilt, and responsibility associated with Stalinism. Literature in particular has contributed to the effort to come to terms with the past.[16] Russia has attempted to achieve lustration through writing and reading, through creating and encountering art.[17] These are less official or visible acts than public trials, policy shifts, or statements of apology, but they are nonetheless powerful in the life of a nation. This is especially true of Russia, where art has traditionally played a key role in political and social debates. In addition to Evtushenko's poem "The Heirs of Stalin" and Solzhenitsyn's *One Day in the Life of Ivan Denisovich,* many other literary works have contributed to de-Stalinization. Among these are Solzhenitsyn's novels *The First Circle* (*V kruge pervom,* 1968) and *Cancer Ward* (*Rakovyi korpus,* 1968), his three-volume exposé *The Gulag Archipelago* (*Arkhipelag GULag,* 1973–75), Vasilii Grossman's *Forever Flowing* (*Vse techet,* written in 1955–63 and published in 1970) and *Life and Fate* (*Zhizn' i sud'ba,* completed in 1960 and published in

1985), Varlam Shalamov's *Kolyma Tales* (*Kolymskie rasskazy,* written in the fifties and published in 1978), Anatoly Rybakov's *Children of the Arbat* (*Deti Arbata,* written in the sixties and published in 1987), Yury Dombrovsky's novel *The Department of Unnecessary Things* (*Fakul'tet nenuzhnykh veshchei,* completed in 1975 and published in 1978), Vladimir Dudintsev's *White Robes* (*Belye odezhdy,* 1987), and Aleksandr Bek's *New Assignment* (*Novoe nazna-chenie,* written in the early sixties and published in 1987). Although some of these works were not published in the authors' homeland until the glasnost period, their publication in the West and availability in the Soviet Union undoubtedly had an impact. A number of groundbreaking films fueled the de-Stalinization campaign, raising the level of public awareness and intensifying the debate. Some of these were documentary or quasi-documentary films, such as Semen Aranovich's *I Served in Stalin's Bodyguard* (*Ia sluzhil v okhrane Stalina,* 1989). Tengiz Abuladze's *Repentance* (*Pokaianie*), made in the early eighties but released only in 1987, is a surreal treatment of Stalinism and its legacy of generational guilt; it insistently posed the question of moral responsibility and occasioned an unprecedented degree of collective soul-searching. The visual arts also participated in the debate about Stalinism. Vitalii Komar and Aleksandr Melamid's series "Nostalgic Socialist Realism," painted in the early eighties, is a commentary on Stalinist and anti-Stalinist myths; these paintings are visual explorations of Stalin's character and essence.

Satire has played a significant role in attempts to achieve lustration in the Soviet Union and Russia. Most satirists—certainly all Russian satirists—claim the goal of reform through exposure and criticism. Satire in its literary form provides a "veneer of civilized behavior" that may mask great hostility, even hatred.[18] Stalin is thus made the focus of satire ranging from humorous mockery to vitriolic diatribe. Often blaming Stalin personally but always placing him at or near the center of responsibility, Russian satire has participated directly in de-Stalinization for decades. It is worth pointing out that by its very nature satire is not likely to provide closure or healing of the cultural wounds of Stalinism. Satire "tends towards open-endedness, irresolution, and thus chaos,"[19] rarely permitting the reconciliation promised by lustration. It has instead contributed to the work of de-Stalinization in progress, encouraging and sometimes compelling readers to "look deep into the past and face the very worst, in order to become healed."[20]

Stalin, then, is the focus of many works of Russian satire in the twentieth century. The dictator's central role in the construction and operation of Stalinism is a given in these texts. As we shall see, establishing responsibility for the crimes perpetrated by his regime is the goal of much Russian satire. Satirical works that treat Stalin often emphasize his foreignness, his non-Russian characteristics. We can infer that Stalinism was not a genuinely Russian phenomenon but rather a tragedy visited on Russian culture from outside. Given the wide temporal, geographical, and political range covered, it is not surprising that the authors treated here represent a variety of viewpoints about Russia's culpability. To what degree Stalin was and is "in us" is a central question raised in all of these works. As Hochschild points out, "Of all the stages in coming to terms with oppression, the hardest is realizing how much we internalize our oppressors."[21] These texts struggle with this truth and attempt to bring about cultural catharsis by responding to the question of Stalin's nature. They contribute to the work of coming to terms with the past of Stalinism and achieving cultural lustration.

Critical work on alterity is useful in considering this project of twentieth-century Russian satire. Like satire studies, alterity studies are interdisciplinary and are informed by sociology, psychology, and anthropology as well as by literary theory. Russian culture provides a particularly suitable background against which to think about self and other, for it has retained an "essential polarity, a polarity expressed in the binary nature of its structure."[22] This bipolarity, perceptible in Russia's ideological, religious, and political systems, allows no "axiologically neutral zone."[23] There is thus no gradation between self and other, only distinction and opposition. Indeed, Russia has virtually no tradition of transitional thinking; progressive stages of cultural development have been attained not by evolution and adaptation but by radical reversals, by "changing signs" or "defining the positive as negative."[24] Iurii Lotman and Boris Uspenskii locate the source of this worldview in the medieval period, but it pertains to the contemporary period of Russia's history as well. Yuri Glazov describes this ideological division of the world into self and other (*svoi* and *chuzhoi*) as evidence of Russia's "tribal mentality."[25] Machiel Karskens, following Foucault, suggests that it is a vestige of the premodern era but connects it with the construction of national identity: "In sum, the privative relation and its social practice of exclusion seems to be a subspecies of the general feature of binary conceptual oppositions with their attendant social practices of identity formation."[26] Exclusion—casting Stalin as other in respect to the cultural self—is a particular mechanism supported by Russia's essentially Manichaean worldview.

The subjectification and exclusion of the other is hardly unique to Russian cultural history. This procedure is common in intellectual and political history and has been theorized extensively. Those who are alien and other, who are distinguishable from the self, are frequently separated and excluded. Human types who have been subject to exclusion in many cultures have been foreigners, women, the insane, the uncivilized, and the deformed or diseased. Raymond Corbey and Joep Leerssen assert that "the inferiorization of this type of excluded Others, who fall short of the canonized set of cultural values, remains a constant throughout the development of European thought, up to and including Freud."[27] As I noted earlier, exclusion of the other is often closely connected to identity formation. The other is cast as powerful and threatening so that the self may be unified in opposition and defined as the obverse. "Barbarian," which originally meant only "outsider" or "foreigner," has taken on the connotations of cruelty and savageness.[28] What is not of the self is dangerous and evil, and this projection serves to solidify characterization of the self as normatively healthy and good.

René Girard's concept of the scapegoat is helpful in understanding the mechanism of depicting Stalin as alien and other in satirical texts. The other, according to Girard, is made to serve as a scapegoat in order to restore social order in times of insecurity or unrest. The victim (i.e., the scapegoat) bears signs that suggest his relationship with the crisis (such as drought or famine). In the case of the Soviet Union and Russia, the crisis has been the moral conundrum of Stalinism; society has suffered a crisis of conscience about guilt and complicity. By casting Stalin as other, writers and readers could facilitate the catharsis offered by scapegoating: "The import of the operation is to lay the responsibility for the crisis on the victims and to exert an influence on it by destroying these victims or at least by banishing them from the community they 'pollute.' "[29] Victim's signs are emphasized, exaggerated, and even invented by satirists to make Stalin an effective scapegoat: he was a foreigner who spoke with an accent; he had physical deformities and he was (perhaps) mad. By showing that Stalin could not have been part of Russian culture, by characterizing him as alterior or liminal, satire often functions to affirm the health and soundness of that culture. The evil that Stalin perpetrated did not emanate from existing conditions or circumstances but rather was imported and imposed from without. Of course, satirically focusing on Stalin and Stalinism carries certain risks (and Soviet censorship, while it existed, certainly recognized those risks). As Richard Shusterman notes: "Self-expanding, self-testing encounters with the other are thus not only enriching but can be dangerously destabilizing. What is easy and limitless in theory is often painfully stressful and decapacitating in practice."[30] The satirical works examined here include just such encounters with the other and have been a powerful catalyst for cultural debate and self-examination.

Psychoanalytic theory also offers insights relevant to the dynamic of self and other in Russian satire about Stalin. Freud's most significant contribution to the discourse on otherness is his contention that the other is an essential part of the self. On the level of the psyche, the other is a "screen on which ideals or terrors can be projected, or as [a] location to which problematic feelings about the self can be displaced."[31] Consideration of the other necessarily entails analysis of the self, and this observation can reasonably be extended to pertain to a national self. Moreover, in the process of becoming known and understood, the other necessarily changes the self, the subject that defines the other as other. This hermeneutic relationship has been operative in Russia's attempts to define and perceive Stalin as alien. Considering his liminality and identifying his victim's signs have compelled Russians— sometimes gently and humorously, sometimes forcibly or caustically—to confront the self and the self's role in Stalinism.

Many other philosophers and critics have written extensively on the relationship of the self to the other, and it is worth touching briefly on a few of the ideas that have shaped this study. Emmanuel Levinas's writing on the other is an important source of much twentieth-century philosophy of otherness. For Levinas consideration of the other leads to its appropriation and hence to its destruction. The questions surrounding the relationship of the self to the other are therefore essentially ethical ones.[32] Michel Leiris, an ethnologist, supports and develops the thesis that awareness of the other means contemplation of the self. Thus, the ethnographical study of a foreign culture always entails study of one's own culture.[33] Jacques Lacan modifies Freud's work on the other (as part of the self) to posit the existence of a little other (*autre*) and a big other (*Autre*). The little other is a projection and a counterpart, a specular image or reflection of the self; it is "the other who is not really other."[34] The big other (or Other) is radically alterior, another subject that cannot be assimilated through identification. These concepts obviously have relevance for my study of Stalin's position vis-à-vis Russian culture, for his otherness (established through textual means) can be apprehended in Lacanian terms. Is Stalin as other a mirror image or an Other that is unique and utterly unlike the Self? Although this question will be posed repeatedly, I do not adopt Lacan's nomenclature consistently; it is one of several theoretical systems that shed light on the particular situation of Russian satire about Stalin. Tzvetan Todorov's work on alterity and stereotypes is also very useful in this respect. In particular, he observes that "anxiety arises as much through any alteration of the sense of order (real or imagined) between the self and the Other (real or imagined) as through the strains of regulating repressed drives."[35] We project our anxiety about this balance onto the other, stereotyping and labeling it with signs that reflect our fear of losing control. In this process we perceive the other to possess qualities of good and bad that belong to the self. The associations we make—signs of difference—derive from actual experiences but also from myth.[36] These two sources provide images of the other that are both "real" (based on biography and historical accounts) and fantastical. As we shall see, satirical portraits of Stalin as other in the texts at hand embody this duality.

Satire has often played a part in the process of self-identification by constructing and staging encounters with Stalin as the other. In many cases casting Stalin as the other achieves some degree of exoneration, an affirmation of the health and virtue of the cultural self. However, some of the texts treated here consider Stalin's otherness and provide more ambivalent conclusions. In some cases Stalin's otherness turns out to be part of the cultural self or to illuminate the self in troubling ways. This study covers a wide temporal range, from the Revolution to the fall of the Soviet Union. Some of the works examined were written during Stalin's lifetime, though most were written after his death in 1953. Many were not published in Russia at the time they were written and appeared only in the West until the glasnost period. Others were created by émigré writers living in the West, reflecting on the scars of Stalinism from a distance. This study does not pretend to provide exhaustive coverage; there are many additional satirical works on Stalin and Stalinism that might have been included. The selection of literary texts examined here was based on literary quality, longevity, cultural impact, and—admittedly—the author's personal preference.

Chapter 1 of this study focuses on satirical works in which Stalin is portrayed as insane or psychologically unbalanced. Madness is a marker of otherness in virtually every culture. As Tzvetan Todorov points out, the very idea of pathology reflects the evaluative scale applied in distinguishing the self and the other with respect to mental illness.[37] Nevertheless, Russian culture offers a particular (and decidedly non-Western) context for the literary depiction of madness. Stalin has been portrayed satirically as various kinds of animals, and these portraits are the subject of chapter 2. Animals are always other with respect to the (human) self, so characterization of the dictator as a beast effectively establishes his alterity. There is great variation in the application of this satirical device, however, for animals carry specific literary, cultural, and moral connotations. Chapter 3 considers feminized portraits of Stalin. Sexual categories usually provide clear demarcations of self and other, and in the Russian context the cultural self is definitively male. Thus, blurring the boundaries through transvestism or androgyny is troubling, and several satirists exploit this dynamic in depicting Stalin. Chapter 4 examines satirical portraits of Stalin as a monster. As Girard demonstrates in *The Scapegoat,* the monstrous is an imaginative combination of elements drawn from nature and myth and is traditionally the locus of otherness.[38] Chapter 5 considers satire that casts Stalin as the devil or Antichrist. Stalin's status as a deity (established by socialist realism) undergoes a complete reversal in these works; he is excluded from Russian culture as a demonic other. This procedure depends on the premise—accepted by these satirists—that the Russian cultural self is Christian. Finally, chapter 6 treats images of Stalin as the unquiet dead, a spirit that continues to haunt Russia. Both superstition and literary tradition inform these treatments of Stalin; they convey metaphorically the protracted struggle of de-Stalinization.

Satire has made a significant contribution to the serious, often agonizing, process of cultural de-Stalinization. The works analyzed in this book offer us images of Stalin that are both radical, absolute other and internalized, integral parts of the self. They attempt lustration through radical exclusion of Stalin as well as through the more open-ended consideration of his otherness in relation to the self. All of the images of Stalin present in these texts— madman, monster, devil, beast—lead back to the familiar and the known and can teach us about the self precisely because they are other. Satire has played—and continues to play—a role in coming to terms with Stalinism by addressing painful question of guilt, complicity, and responsibility.

1

The Insanity Defense

Russian satirists have sometimes portrayed Stalin as a madman, based in part on his actual psychological pathologies. Casting him as insane, however, has ramifications for his position vis-à-vis Russian culture (insider, outsider, liminal) conditioned by literary conventions. Madness has historically often led to exclusion; the insane have frequently been marginal members of their communities. In considering Russian satirical practice, one must take into account Russia's particularized cultural perception of madness; the *iurodivyi*, or holy fool, is a central figure of Russian culture—indeed, its conscience. Moreover, as Michel Foucault has shown, since the Renaissance madness has functioned as a mirror that reflects an inner, essential truth: "Madness deals not so much with truth and the world, as with man and whatever truth about himself he is able to perceive."[1]

The texts treated in this chapter share the conceit that Stalin's madness characterizes and differentiates him; his insanity or mental aberration offers the reader a rationale for his reasoning and his behavior and hence for Stalinism. These works also present broad variations on the general theme of Stalin's madness, both in terms of the nature of this madness and its consequences for the society he controlled. Vladimir Nabokov's 1936 short story "Tyrants Destroyed" ("Istreblenie tiranov") paints a picture of Stalin (or perhaps a composite picture of dictators) as an unbalanced egomaniac whose most frightening power is the ability to drive his subjects mad. Aleksandr Solzhenitsyn's detailed psychological portrait of Stalin, extended over four chapters of *The First Circle* (*V kruge pervom*), portrays the dictator as disconnected from reality, paranoid, and megalomaniacal. Aleksandr Zinoviev's 1980 novel *The Madhouse* (*Zheltyi dom*) reverses this pattern, depicting Soviet society as an asylum and Stalin as a disturbingly sane warden.

14

Vladimir Maksimov's *Ark for the Uncalled* (*Kovcheg dlia nezvannykh*), published in 1979, humanizes Stalin; in Maksimov's account he is unbalanced and unpredictable, but the Soviet people are willingly complicit in supporting Stalinism.

Stalin's Madness

Stalin's actual psychological state is not a matter of trifling interest. It certainly affected—perhaps warped—the trajectory of Russian history in the twentieth century. Biographical sources, though often based on anecdote and rumor, have shaped literary accounts of his mental aberrations and eccentricities. Though madness is a most imprecise term, it is safe to say that Stalin was not clinically mad or insane.[2] Nevertheless, as Roy Medvedev concludes, he displayed pathological elements in his personality and behavior: "Morbid suspiciousness, noticeable throughout his life and especially intense in his last years, intolerance of criticism, grudge-bearing, an overestimation of himself bordering on megalomania, cruelty approaching sadism—all these traits, it would seem, demonstrate that Stalin was a typical paranoiac."[3] Critics such as Robert Tucker and Daniel Rancour-Laferriere have attempted a psychoanalytical analysis of Stalin based on biographical and historical evidence, concluding that he engaged in repression, rationalization, and projection as "internal security operations."[4] D. Jablow Hershman and Julian Lieb have developed an elaborate theory that Stalin (and other dictators) exhibited a manic-depressive personality.[5]

In assessing Stalin's actual sanity or insanity, one must distinguish between the stages of his long political career. Unhealthy elements in his personality were certainly exacerbated by aging and perhaps by stress; the last decade of Stalin's life was particularly fraught with evidence of mental imbalance. We see in these satirical works an emphasis on his old age, which is not surprising; these writers share the popular assumption that personality traits are exaggerated with age. Gustav Bychowski cites the observations of George Kennan and Milovan Djilas to speculate that Stalin became increasingly senile in his later years.[6] It is also worth noting in this regard that Stalin purposefully engaged in obfuscation and mystification. Andrei Sinyavsky suggests that he had an artistic side, and that he "thickened the brew with his own dramatizations and embellishments."[7] According to his biographers, Stalin was smart and cunning; these qualities do not, of course, exclude mental aberration.

Although information about Stalin's early life is scant, there is solid evidence that a traumatic childhood and a difficult youth distorted his psyche. Suppressed hostility toward his brutal father probably developed early in his childhood, as he and his mother suffered violent beatings at his father's hands. Psychoanalytical critics have suggested that Stalin displayed the syndrome of "identification with the aggressor," which made him as violent and vindictive as his father toward perceived authority figures.[8] Stalin's biographers agree that the death of Stalin's first wife devastated him and solidified the tendencies of mercilessness and ruthlessness already present in his personality. Stalin's mother—by all accounts a strong, determined woman—also had a formative influence on his character. Charles Prince, writing in 1945, suggested that it was to her the dictator owed "his ambitions and repressions."[9] His experiences at the theological seminary where he was educated also shaped and determined his personality. The rigid, repressive discipline of the seminary and the spying and informing it encouraged intensified the young Stalin's hatred of authority and (most likely) his paranoia.[10] His physical defects—a pockmarked complexion, a weakened arm, a slight limp—may have damaged his ego and led to overcompensation for an inferiority complex. Finally, he considered his Georgian ethnicity to be a significant handicap and probably regarded it as a mark of his own second-class status, for which he had to compensate.

Stalin's basic (and unconscious) sense of inferiority may also have been rooted in his weak education and his lack of intellectual training. In comparison to Lenin, Bukharin, and Trotsky, Stalin was indeed an intellectual primitive. His envy manifested itself in extreme suspiciousness and resentment of those who were better educated or more articulate. In this respect, Stalin's narcissism was insatiable; his vengeful wrath was visited upon almost everyone who displayed talents or abilities superior to his own.[11] His narcissism was also expressed in his extreme sensitivity to criticism or insult. Possibly stemming from the humiliations he suffered at the hands of his father in childhood, it may have been intensified by social slights he experienced later in life: "Social humiliations naturally increased his general feeling of inferiority and his desire for revenge and compensation. In addition to social humiliations there were mortifications engendered in the domination of Russian officials over the Georgian population."[12]

Stalin's behavior suggests that he perceived any kind of opposition or disagreement as a sign of disloyalty, which he interpreted as criminal. Stalin's mind-set was essentially Manichaean, so that people were either friends or enemies, completely good or utterly evil. Transforming the latter into

class enemies was a necessary rationalization. In order to justify their destruction, they were cast as enemies of the people and not just of Stalin.

Stalin's inferiority complex was accompanied by megalomania, a not
infrequent combination of psychological traits. The title he preferred—
genial'nyi Stalin, or the Genius Stalin—apparently expressed his own esti-
mation of his gifts.[13] Rancour-Laferriere speculates that Stalin's megalomania was a consequence of his mother's blind adoration of her son in his
childhood.[14] His creation of an image of unsurpassed and unsurpassable
genius was conscious and purposeful. Moreover, it was crucial to his psyche
to have his superiority and his grandeur acknowledged by others; he needed
praise and adulation—probably to strengthen his fragile ego. Given his sensitivity to educational pedigree, it is understandable that Stalin would lay
claim to brilliance as a theoretician. He needed to be recognized as an original and profound thinker precisely because intellectual prowess was for Stalin a point of great insecurity. As Bychowski notes, "Ideas of grandeur are
usually determined in their content by the specific elements which originated the sense of inferiority."[15] Any evidence to the contrary Stalin firmly
rejected. Adam Ulam puts forth the intriguing theory that the praise Stalin
demanded helped him to retain his sanity: "Stalin's need for the chorus of
adulation to grow louder the deeper he waded in blood was due to his own
inability to believe the whole monstrous web of lies which he had loosed on
the country. Adulation was a barrier keeping him from stepping over into
actual insanity. It was . . . a constant and much needed reassurance that it
was not one man's irrational whim and suspiciousness but the interests of
Russia and of the new social order that were exacting these appalling sacrifices."[16] At the same time, Stalin maintained a facade of modesty that became part of the cult of the dictator. His spartan style of dress, simple tastes
in food, and apparent indifference to personal comfort all helped to conceal
his enormous vanity. Like medieval saints, Stalin exhibited to the Soviet
people an appearance of asceticism.[17] He was able to create and maintain
an image of himself that was "group-centered,"[18] selflessly devoted to the
collective rather than the self. The trope of asceticism that Stalin appropri-
ated powerfully echoed the myth of Lenin as well as the tradition of Russian sainthood.

Stalin's paranoia was a major feature of his personality and exerted a
tremendous influence on his behavior. "Paranoiac" was the term applied to
Stalin by a Soviet psychologist who saw him in 1927.[19] Of course, paranoia
describes a spectrum of mental conditions and not a single, consistent

state. Stalin's paranoia was largely functional; he was not incapacitated by his delusions but rather motivated by them to take action and formulate policy. Increasingly, as he consolidated his power, Stalin grew to suspect everyone of disloyalty and conspiracy, and he became more calculating and shrewd as the years passed. His political strategies—the elimination of his rivals and playing off factions against one another—were certainly shaped by paranoia. What is recognizable as a "warfare personality"[20] was actually advantageous for Stalin in the years when he was building his power base and strengthening his hold on the party. When internal political opponents and external threats to the new Soviet state actually existed, Stalin's paranoia fit the needs of the party. After the war, however, circumstances no longer favored a paranoid leadership model and Stalin's behavior became more pathological than pragmatic.

The logic that Stalin followed was irrational and often seemed to border on madness. For example, his reasoning about wreckers infiltrating Soviet society is absurd: some enemies only operated destructively some of the time, and the most dangerous enemies were so cunning that they did not wreck at all but rather presented themselves as heroes of labor.[21] According to Stalin's logic, the more an enemy professed loyalty and good will, the more perfidious he really was. Whether Stalin actually believed this reasoning is perhaps unknowable. Sinyavsky asserts that Stalin's artistic nature was such that he could simultaneously believe and disbelieve his own imaginary constructs.[22]

As he aged and his power became absolute, Stalin's fear of those around him intensified. He became what psychologists term a "persecuted persecutor" ("[un] persécuteur persecuté"),[23] a ruthless dictator terrified of everyone. His extreme isolation and loneliness is conveyed in satirical portraits through his fantasies about a loyal friend, someone he could trust. Stalin's acute insomnia, which is described in many texts, may well have been linked to his paranoia. Biographical accounts agree that he was most active at night, often only falling asleep at dawn.

Another psychological trait that shaped Stalin's regime was his sadism, attested by many who knew him personally and witnessed his behavior. While Stalin's sadism was certainly pathological—or would have been regarded as such outside the political context he created—it was nonsexual or "characterological."[24] Inflicting pain and humiliation on others may have been satisfying to Stalin, but these were primarily a means of control rather than a source of titillation. Another relevant insight offered by psychoanalysis is that punishing others for our own actual or latent crimes is pleasurable.

Stalin's pathologies might well have excluded him from a position of leadership in a different political and historical context. Instead, within the nascent totalitarian system emerging in the Soviet Union his psychopathology exerted a decisive, formative influence. His "private affects" (i.e., his mental aberrations) were "displaced upon public objects" (the party, the military, Soviet society).[25] According to this theory, the purges and trials were not a system need but rather a consequence of Stalin's paranoid delusions. This does not satisfactorily explain the lack of resistance to Stalin's methods of terror, but the willingness of the Soviet leadership to accede to Stalin's irrational logic may have intensified his pathology. Prince analyzes the situation as follows: "Psychoanalysts point out that lack of hindrance from the external world to a person's complex of omnipotence results in a subconscious feeling of guilt with an accompaniment of strange and terrible reactions, often in opposition both to the instinct of self-preservation and to the demands of the ideals concentrated within the ego. In Stalin's case the result is his undeniable ruthlessness."[26] Ironically, the people's faith in Stalin provided him with reassuring evidence that he was not mad, and this dynamic likely contributed to still more extreme measures of repression.

It is not surprising that biographers and historians have attributed Stalin's behavior to madness. Communist Party apologists, in particular, have advanced the theory that Stalin suffered from mental illness.[27] Others less inclined to pardon his crimes have insisted that Stalin's masterful strategic planning and his realization of his goals belie an insanity defense. For example, Anton Antonov-Ovseyenko asserts that Stalin suffered from neither schizophrenia nor paranoia but was simply malicious by nature.[28] If Stalin were indeed mad, he could be absolved of responsibility for his enormous crimes, and most witnesses and victims find this idea unacceptable. However, demonstrating Stalin's madness has the collateral effect of exculpating the Russian people as well, and this is appealing to some commentators. As we shall see, the four satirists alluded to earlier confront the question of Stalin's madness in their work and interrogate this issue of guilt.

Madness, of course, is a capacious term that can be applied to a broad range of psychological conditions, from whimsicality to psychosis. Moreover, it has somewhat different connotations in the Russian cultural context than in the West. Russian taxonomy concerning sanity and insanity is tripartite rather than binary and oppositional. In addition to normal and abnormal mental states, Russian tradition recognizes paranormal states, such as *iurodstvo*, or holy foolishness.[29] As Ewa Thompson notes, the mentally ill were historically cared for in Russia (as in the West) as long as they did not traffic with the devil. In the West, beginning in the Enlightenment, treatment of the mentally ill deteriorated to contempt and cruelty, while *iurodstvo* assumed a separate status in Russia. The European taxonomy of mental illness was introduced in Russia in the eighteenth century by Peter the Great through his edicts discouraging the veneration of *iurodstvo*.[30] The number of hospital-style asylums in Russia increased markedly under Catherine the Great; these were places of confinement rather than of treatment, modeled on Western institutions. Nevertheless, the vast majority of the mentally ill—both the "abnormal" and the "paranormal"—were not confined in prerevolutionary Russia. Thus, despite the Westernizing reforms of Peter and Catherine, the tripartite taxonomy of mental illness and the concomitant toleration of holy foolishness persisted in Russia until the Revolution.[31] Of course, both before and after the Revolution it was possible to accuse one's political enemies of insanity; the Soviet practice of declaring dissidents insane probably has its roots both in Nicholas I's denunciation of Chaadaev and in Belinsky's attack on Gogol.[32]

A special case of madness often referenced with regard to Stalin is that of Ivan the Terrible. According to his biographers, Stalin admired Ivan and perhaps modeled his own career on that of his tsarist predecessor.[33] The development of the secret police under Stalin bears a striking resemblance to Ivan's creation of the *Oprichniki,* and Stalin's insistence on blind, unquestioning loyalty echoes Ivan's absolute authoritarianism. Stalin measured his own successes against those of the tsars and aimed to surpass their achievements. Ulam notes that in Russian cultural history great cruelty and ruthlessness are associated with leaders such as Ivan the Terrible and Peter the Great, who, "for all their savagery, contributed to the strength and glory of the Russian State."[34] This fact may help explain Stalin's acceptance as a popular leader, for barbaric cruelty has ample precedent in Russian history. Indeed, popular support for Stalin during the thirties and forties and even into the fifties suggests the construction of a folkloric image not unlike that of Ivan the Terrible:

> The problem which arose for the party faithful under Stalin was identical to that which faced Orthodox Christians in sixteenth-century Muscovy: how to reconcile the presumed goodness of the ruler with the manifest horror of his reign of terror. And similar answers were provided: the victims of the terror were real traitors, genuine counter-revolutionaries and enemies of the people who were being correctly punished; alternatively, the victims were innocent, but Stalin genuinely believed them to be guilty, since he had been misled by evil agents such as Ezhov and Beria who had infiltrated the NKVD.[35]

Historians have speculated (though there is no proof) that Ivan himself was insane. Whether or not this is true, Stalin seems to have admired and emulated Ivan's effective use of ruthless power and his exercise of sadistic revenge.

Nabokov's "Tyrants Destroyed"

Vladimir Nabokov's biography, and particularly his antipathy toward Stalinism, are very well documented. Born in 1899, Nabokov spent his early life in Russia but emigrated in 1919 in the aftermath of the Revolution. After attending Cambridge University, he spent the years 1922–37 in Berlin, where he wrote nine novels, roughly fifty short stories, and many poems. Dating from this period, the short story "Tyrants Destroyed" was first published in 1936. In 1937 Nabokov emigrated to France to escape nazism, then departed Europe for America three years later. There he established his career as an English-language author while teaching. With the success of *Lolita* in 1958, he devoted himself entirely to writing. Nabokov spent the last years of his life in Switzerland and died in 1977.

Nabokov's virulently anti-Soviet sentiments surfaced frequently in his writings and public statements. He eloquently expresses his hatred of the Communist regime in his autobiography *Speak, Memory*. Lenin is not only implicated in the violent excesses of Bolshevik rule but is directly culpable: "When, at the end of the year, Lenin took over, the Bolsheviks immediately subordinated everything to the retention of power, and a regime of bloodshed, concentration camps, and hostages entered upon its stupendous career."[36] Nabokov chastises Western sympathizers, concluding that they do not know enough about "the bestial terror that had been sanctioned by Lenin—the torture-house, the blood-bespattered wall."[37] Stalin is pronounced "no less ghastly" than Lenin.[38] Nabokov's disdain for communism as a theoretical system is made clear in an article written for the tenth anniversary of the Revolution: "I despise communist faith as an idea of low equality, as a boring page in the festive story of humanity, as the negation of earthly and unearthly beauty, as something that stupidly infringes on my free 'I,' as a supporter of ignorance, dullness and self-satisfaction."[39]

"Tyrants Destroyed," with its portrait of a Stalinesque dictator, finds an echo in other works by Nabokov. It is related thematically to both *Invitation to a Beheading*, a novel published in 1938, and to *Bend Sinister*, which appeared in 1947. *Invitation to a Beheading* dates from the same period as "Tyrants Destroyed" and presents a similar vision of madness empowered absolutely. *Bend Sinister*, written after the horrors of the Second World War and another decade of Stalinist atrocities, portrays an even more horrific picture of the consequences of dictatorship. "Tyrants Destroyed" appears to be a prototype for *Bend Sinister*; there are many stylistic as well as thematic similarities. Both are set in a recently established absolutist state and in both the dictator figure is a composite portrait. The first-person narrator in both works opposes the dictator personally and politically, bringing about his own ruin. The theme of madness pervades both works, though it is (as one would expect) more fully developed and elaborated in the novel. "Ekwilism," the theory propounded by the dictator Paduk in *Bend Sinister*, is a parody of communism. According to Ekwilism (or equalism), all people's talents and gifts must be restrained at a common, low level in order to establish justice. This idea is only nascent in "Tyrants Destroyed," which focuses on the character and personality of the tyrant. *Bend Sinister* gives us a more fully realized vision of the world created by the mad dictator, while "Tyrants Destroyed" lingers on the nature of the madness that drives the dictator's ascension.[40]

In a 1975 translation of this short story Nabokov prefaces the text with the statement that his fictional dictator is a composite and a precursor of Paduk in his later novel: "Hitler, Lenin, and Stalin dispute my tyrant's throne in this story—and meet again in *Bend Sinister*, 1947, with a fifth toad."[41] He (as he is referred to in the text) has a number of features that link him closely with Stalin, which are of particular interest here. Nabokov begins by describing his character: "But when a limited, coarse, little-educated man—at first glance a third-rate fanatic and in reality a pig-headed, brutal, and gloomy vulgarian full of morbid ambition—when such a man dresses up in godly garb, one feels like apologizing to the gods."[42] It was Stalin's vulgarity or coarseness (*grubost'*) that Lenin found so objectionable in his "Testament," in which he recommended that Stalin never be permitted to hold significant power; it is telling that Nabokov uses the adjective *grubyi* to describe his fictional dictator. His eyes, which Stalin's biographers frequently comment upon, are "unbearably eerie" (*neterpimo zhutkie*) (4, 166) and are "night-bird eyes" (*nochnye sovinye glaza*) (12, 174). His manner of speaking is ponderous and repetitive. He pauses frequently to let his words sink in, but then "repeats verbatim what he has just disgorged, but in a tone of voice suggesting that he has thought of a new argument, another absolutely new and irrefutable idea" (29, 193).

Nabokov's dictator has psychological features reminiscent of Stalin's pathology. He writes letters that "hinted at the machinations of mysterious enemies" (14, 177), suggesting a streak of paranoia. He lives behind many walls and doors, guarded by locks and bodyguards. The degree of suspicion and fear he experiences is conveyed in Nabokov's description of an old woman's audience with him. She is granted a brief meeting with the dictator because she has grown an eighty-pound turnip; she is, it turns out, the heroine of the fairy tale "The Turnip" ("Repka"). Before she can tell her story, she is led through a labyrinth of rooms and corridors, then told to wait until the dictator enters, accompanied by a half dozen bodyguards. Nabokov's narrator speculates that his cruelty may stem from the tragedies he has suffered in his life but also notes that this cruelty is unalloyed and absolute: "I myself once had the fleeting impression that he was capable of mercy; only subsequently did I determine its true shade" (15, 178). The narrator cites rumors that the dictator pays personal visits to the torture chamber but dismisses these as unconvincing not because the tyrant is not sadistic but because it seems more credible that he is content to delegate torture to his minions. An inflexible will is a psychological feature that particularly distinguishes him and helps to account for his rise to power. It is "the kind of somber, concentrated will deeply conscious of its sullen self, which in the end molds a giftless person into a triumphant monster" (10, 173). Nabokov's dictator has an unshakable belief in his own destiny and in his power to shape that destiny. His protagonist, then, has psychological abnormalities— paranoia, sadism, megalomania—but is functional and, indeed, able to convince his followers of his superior abilities as a leader.

Through its satirical portrait of the Stalinesque dictator, "Tyrants Destroyed" explores the dynamic of infectious madness. The narrator ostensibly knew the dictator in their youth and recalls their relationship during those years. He cannot forgive himself for not foreseeing his evil and banality and (by implication) preventing his rise to power. Now obsessively following every thought and action of the dictator, he identifies with him to such a degree that his own independent personality is eradicated. He pursues him mentally, eating breakfast with him, reading the newspaper with him, carrying out the duties of a political leader with him. His madness— for it is madness—becomes indistinguishable from the dictator's madness; the narrator believes that if he can successfully establish their complete identification, he will be free: "[I] whisper, gesticulate, and ever more insanely hope that at least one of my thoughts may fall in step with a thought of his—and then, I know, the bridge will snap, like a violin string" (31, 195 – 96). Nabokov erases the opposition between self and other in this near-identification of the narrator and the dictator. This is very significant, for it suggests that the dictator merely reflects the insanity of those he oppresses.

Eventually the narrator despairs of eradicating the dictator through the exercise of his powers of concentration and decides to kill himself. He reasons that by doing so, he will also kill the tyrant, for "he was totally inside me, fattened on the intensity of my hatred" (33, 197). As he prepares to commit suicide, however, he suddenly experiences a complete change of heart and realizes that he has been ungrateful and stubborn. He renounces his former resistance to the kindness and mercy of the "Master" (variously *Gospodin* and *Khoziain* in the Russian text) (34, 198) and begins to praise his enemy in the most fulsome terms.

The narrator's madness is more palpable than the dictator's in "Tyrants Destroyed," but they are essentially linked; what we experience directly of the narrator's growing insanity reflects the mind of his alter ego. It is important to recognize that madness does not bear entirely pejorative connotations for Nabokov.[43] Creativity and genius are tinged with insanity, and some of his most positive literary protagonists (e.g., Adam Krug in *Bend Sinister*) are mentally unstable. Donald Morton interprets this as a kind of holy madness[44] perhaps related to *iurodstvo*. Madness is also an escape offered to a character so traumatized by the evil of tyranny that sanity is unbearable. At the end of *Bend Sinister* Adam Krug is released from the horror of his son's brutal murder when the authorial narrator bestows madness upon him. In "Tyrants Destroyed," however, a more insidious and dangerous kind of madness prevails in the personality of the dictator. Like Stalin, he is mad to the extent that he justifies despotism and terror through his goal of building a utopia. This is the other side of madness in Nabokov's oeuvre, a "'malignant' lunacy which warps perception into delusion and makes of its victims an instrument of self-torture and a menace to others."[45]

Madness in "Tyrants Destroyed" is an infectious disease rather than a source of creativity. The dictator, who is characterized by delusional reasoning, is not positioned outside the collective by Nabokov. Rather—and more frighteningly—his madness comes to define the collective. Nabokov resists the role of apologist for Russia, focusing instead on the dictator: "Then again, let me repeat that I am no good at distinguishing what is good or bad for a state, and why it is that blood runs off it like water off a goose. Amid everybody and everything it is only one individual that interests me. That is my ailment, my obsession, and at the same time a thing that somehow belongs to me and that is entrusted to me alone for judgment" (6, 168–69). Nabokov's satiric goal is less absolution of Russian culture than exposure of the madness that has enveloped it. Laughter saves the narrator of "Tyrants Destroyed" as he moves from adoration of the tyrant to liberation;

laughter effectively restores the opposition between self and other and rees-tablishes the dictator's alien nature. Having destroyed the dictator by ex-posing his banality, the narrator recommends this approach as a general antidote against tyranny: "This is an incantation, an exorcism, so that henceforth any man can exorcise bondage" (36, 201). Indeed, his verbal por-trait of his nemesis—at least partially based on Stalin—constitutes a kind of personal exorcism that he recommends to his countrymen.

Solzhenitsyn's *The First Circle*

Aleksandr Solzhenitsyn's career was ineluctably shaped by Stalin and much of his work is a response to Stalinism. Born in 1928 in Kislovodsk, Solzhe-nitsyn spent his early childhood and youth in Rostov-on-Don and entered the university there to study mathematics and physics. His performance at the university earned him a Stalin Scholarship, which he used to enroll in a correspondence course at the Moscow Institute of Philosophy, Literature, and History. In 1941 Solzhenitsyn was called up to serve in the military and the next year was commissioned as an artillery officer. By all accounts his service at the front was exemplary, but in 1945 he was arrested for criticizing Stalin in letters he had written to a school friend. Sentenced under Article 58 to eight years of hard labor, Solzhenitsyn spent a few months working on construction sites near Moscow and was then sent to a *sharashka,* a special facility where prisoners worked on scientific projects, an experience that became the basis for *The First Circle.* Four years later he was transferred to one of the newly established labor camps for political prisoners and spent the last three years of his term there. Released in March 1953, Solzhenitsyn was consigned to exile in Kazakhstan, but he was allowed to return to Euro-pean Russia in 1956 thanks to the amnesty accompanying the first de-Stalinization campaign.

Solzhenitsyn's rise and fall in Soviet literature occurred in a little over a decade. The publication of *One Day in the Life of Ivan Denisovich* in 1962 was a watershed event of Khrushchev's Thaw and established Solzhenitsyn's reputation as a writer. Several more of his short stories appeared in the So-viet Union in 1963, but by the time of Khrushchev's fall from power the next year Solzhenitsyn had effectively ceased publishing. Under increasing offi-cial opprobrium, he began to circulate his work in samizdat and openly spoke out against the control of literature exercised by the party, the Soviet Writers' Union, and the censorship apparatus. Solzhenitsyn was expelled from the union in 1969 and was compelled to reject the Nobel Prize that he

was awarded in 1970. In 1974 he was forcibly exiled from the Soviet Union
and stripped of his citizenship. Within a few years Solzhenitsyn had become
a controversial figure in the West as well. He continued to write and publish
prolifically, but his vociferous criticisms of Western democracy and the
weakness of the West were problematic for European and American audiences. For example, in his commencement address at Harvard University in
1978 he charged the West with a failure of courage vis-à-vis the global threat
of communism:

> The Western world has lost its civic courage, both as a whole and separately,
> in each country, in each government, in each political party, and, of course,
> in the United Nations. Such a decline in courage is particularly noticeable
> among the ruling and intellectual elites, causing an impression of a loss of
> courage by the entire society. . . . Political and intellectual functionaries ex-
> hibit this depression, passivity, and perplexity in their actions and in their
> statements, and even more so in their self-serving rationales as to how re-
> alistic, reasonable, and intellectually and even morally justified it is to base
> state policies on weakness and cowardice.[46]

Following the fall of the Soviet Union, Solzhenitsyn returned to Russia in
1994 with great fanfare and initially enjoyed the status of a public intellectual and moral authority. However, with time and exposure his reputation
waned; his pronouncements and editorials came to seem irrelevant or
anachronistic. He died in 2008 in Moscow.

From his young adulthood Solzhenitsyn had regarded Stalin as his political and personal enemy. Even when he still professed faith in Marxism, he
seems to have been acutely aware of the extent to which Stalinism represented a distortion of its ideals. Certainly by the time of his incarceration in
the *sharashka* Solzhenitsyn had come to loathe Stalin as the architect of a
vast system of repression and tyranny. This is not to say that he held Stalin
solely responsible; for him the regime as a whole was pernicious. In his
memoir *The Oak and the Calf* (*Bodalsia telenok s dubom*) he sarcastically
dismisses the claim that the Twentieth Party Congress started a "purifying
process": "In what sense was it a purifying process? In heaping all the
regime's evil deeds on Stalin's head?"[47] Nevertheless, Stalin is positioned at
the center of corruption and is a primary target of Solzhenitsyn's attack.

Solzhenitsyn's depiction of Stalin in *The First Circle* is one of the most
vivid and extended satirical portraits of the dictator. Most critical studies
focus on the three chapters devoted to Stalin in the eighty-seven-chapter
version of the novel, first published in 1968.[48] This version of the text was
written while Solzhenitsyn was still in the Soviet Union, before he had access

to Western sources on Stalin's biography or psychology. Moreover, in 1963, while writing this novel, Solzhenitsyn had reason to hope that the extended passage on Stalin might be published in *Pravda* as part of Khrushchev's de-Stalinization campaign;[49] it is plausible that he wrote it with an eye toward the censor. He has maintained that *Circle-87* was subject to self-censorship, that the "real" text was too explosive to circulate even in samizdat.[50] Aleksandr Tvardovsky, who was editor of *Novyi mir* at that time, probably rejected the manuscript because the "camp theme" had become extremely sensitive after the Manège affair of 1962. It is likely that at this point Solzhenitsyn made changes to the manuscript he had given Tvardovsky, making it less cautious and intensifying its critical tone.[51] It was this edited manuscript that he sent abroad by means of a trusted courier and that was subsequently published in 1968 as *Circle-87*.

Solzhenitsyn's *Collected Works*, published in 1978 following his departure from the Soviet Union, includes an expanded version of *The First Circle* with ninety-six chapters in all. The portrait of Stalin is reworked significantly in this edition, and the author claimed that this constituted a restoration of the original, uncensored text.[52] A major addition is the chapter "Study of a Great Life" ("Etiud o velikoi zhizni"), which includes "an imaginative reconstruction of Stalin's complete biography."[53] This expansion of the satirical portrait of Stalin makes his presence even more central in the novel. Georges Nivat suggests that the major difference between the treatments of the dictator in *Circle-87* and *Circle-96* is the quantity of material.[54] However, there is also a detectable shift in tone between the earlier version and the later one, namely, from pathos or tragedy to vitriolic condemnation of Stalin.[55] It is possible that in 1963, when *Circle-87* began its life in samizdat, Solzhenitsyn had actually come to pity the decrepit, aging dictator. In any case, it is clear that in the new version there is little to move the reader to compassion or understanding of Stalin. Rather, we are presented with a detailed picture of his psychological aberrations, the pathology that shaped his outlook and behavior.

Set in 1949, *The First Circle* portrays an elderly Stalin fully in the grip of madness. According to Michael Scammell, these last years of Stalin's life reflected the most intense period of paranoia, megalomania, and sadism.[56] Solzhenitsyn's portrait is a powerful satirical exposé that takes the reader progressively deeper into Stalin's psyche. Although fictional, it is based on historical and biographical accounts of those who knew Stalin or observed him closely. Solzhenitsyn's treatment of Stalin has been problematic for some readers because he claims to serve as both artist and historian.

Rosalind Marsh notes that he does not aim at complete objectivity but instead shapes historical facts artistically: "Solzhenitsyn resembles a medieval chronicler rather than a modern historian; in the definition of the German critic Walter Benjamin, the historian writes history, but the chronicler narrates it."[57] Khrushchev had begun the work of demystification of Stalin's persona, but Solzhenitsyn aims at a complete reversal of the image. To accomplish this, he needs to delve into the recesses of Stalin's mind, "to invade its privacy."[58]

The markers that Solzhenitsyn employs to identify and characterize Stalin are traditional and are used intensively. The narrator is initially objective and omniscient, offering us insights into Stalin's condition that the dictator himself does not recognize. As Marsh notes, this method is very effective in emphasizing the contrast between Stalin's public stature and his "personal insignificance."[59] This technique, which he employs to introduce the frail and senile dictator, resembles Tolstoy's "removing the wrapping" (*sniatie pokrovov*)[60] and may well be the result of conscious literary imitation. Solzhenitsyn's initial description of Stalin is devastating in its unflinching directness; the satire is enhanced by the narrator's ironic parenthetical asides: "And he was simply a little old yellow-eyed man with reddish hair (always depicted as black) that was already thinning (they depicted it as thick); with a sprinkling of pockmarks here and there across his graying face, with a desiccated pouch of skin on his neck (not depicted at all); with dark, uneven teeth, partially inclined backward, into his mouth, and smelling of tobacco leaves; with fat, moist fingers which left traces on papers and books."[61] His pockmarked skin, the smell of tobacco that clings to him, and his greasy fingers are all unattractive features typically emphasized by satirists. The soft Caucasian boots he wears, "like smooth stockings" (115), are standard issue in literary portraits, as is his vaguely Napoleonic-style coat (116). Of course, these descriptors are also meaningful; his soft boots suggest feline slyness and his coat implies imperial aspirations. Stalin's eyes are described as yellow (the color of the demonic and of madness), and once as "yellow unhealthy eyes" (123). Solzhenitsyn loads his satirical portrait of Stalin with the various grandiose titles that were applied to him. He is called "the Boss" (*Vozhd'*), "the Almighty" (*Vsesil'nyi*), "the Master" (*Khoziain*), "the Absolute Ruler" (*Edinoderzhets*) and "Little Father" (*Bat'ka*).

Unlike many satirists who portray Stalin, Solzhenitsyn replicates the dictator's Georgian accent extensively. He provides phonetic renderings of Stalin's speech, with accent marks and hyphens to indicate misplaced stress and incorrect vowels inserted to show the absence of palatalization: *Pá-smotrym, Né znaiu, Idý-poka* (123–24). When Stalin is agitated, his accent becomes more pronounced, which is the case even in passages of interior monologue: "When it was already clear to everyone that communism was on the right path and not far from completion—that cretin Tito thrusts himself forward with his Talmudist Kardelii and announces that communism must be built differently!!!" (*Kogda vsem uzhe iasno, chto kámunizm návernoidoroge i-nédalek át-versheniia,—vysovyvaetsia etot kretin Tito sá-svoim talmudistom Kardelem i zaiavliaet, sh'tó-komunizm nado stroit' né tak!!!*) (146). Solzhenitsyn reproduces Stalin's speech habits, especially his fondness for turns of phrase such as "it is clear to everyone" (*vsem iasno*) and "it is not by chance" (*ne sluchaino*).[62] Stalin's litanies and repetitions are mimicked not only in passages of direct discourse and in interior monologue but also in passages of authorial narration.[63] Stalin's linguistic mannerisms reflect qualities of his mind; his intellectual rigidity and clumsiness come through in his verbal style. Solzhenitsyn also carefully traces how Stalin writes; the process by which the written word becomes an instrument of control clearly fascinates him.[64] His mental wrestling with Marxism is for Solzhenitsyn a sham, for the dictator lacks the intellectual grounding to engage seriously with philosophy. The focus of Stalin's energy is power, not ideas.

As Gary Kern notes, Solzhenitsyn's satirical portrait demonstrates "the paucity—perhaps the complete absence—of ideas and principles."[65] Solzhenitsyn portrays Stalin's mind as mediocre and banal, but he credits his obsessive thirst for power with propelling him to a position of absolute authority. He suggests that Stalin had the mind of an agent provocateur, then draws the conclusion that he served as a tsarist spy while working in the revolutionary underground. This is the most problematic element of Solzhenitsyn's portrait of Stalin, for there is no solid historical evidence to support this allegation. His portrayal of Stalin as a double agent follows from the reasoning that his amorality and his will to power would lead him to assume this role.[66]

In his literary portrait Solzhenitsyn attempts to provide access to the inner workings of Stalin's psyche and to probe the question of his sanity. It is important to acknowledge that Solzhenitsyn's strategy is that of the satirist: his goal is not to understand the origins of Stalin's aberrant psychological behavior but rather to fully expose these traits. Thus, Solzhenitsyn's Stalin is endowed with a number of pathologies, identified by Rancour-Laferriere as "paranoia, hyperdeveloped narcissism, megalomania, agoraphobia, obsessive power hunger, sadism (with associated masochism), and defective conscience (underdeveloped superego)."[67]

Stalin's agoraphobia is complex, for he fears both space and time. In a passage of quasi-indirect discourse he muses: "It cost no great effort to isolate oneself from worldly *space,* to not move in it. But it was impossible to isolate oneself from *time*" (116). Because he fears assassination attempts, he has had several apartments and shelters built and prefers his suburban dacha, located away from the "surroundings of the dense city" (159). His agoraphobia ironically renders him weak and vulnerable. Solzhenitsyn stresses the physical effect of this mental condition through repetition: "Only when it was necessary to enter that objective reality on his own legs, for example to go to a big banquet in the Hall of Columns, to cross the frightening space from the car to the door on his own legs, and then to go up the stairs on his own legs, to cross the excessively wide foyer and to see on all sides the rapt, respectful, but too numerous guests—then Stalin felt ill and didn't even know how to use his arms, long unsuitable for real defense" (174–75). Stalin's habit of working at night in his closed office and his dislike of daylight underscore his fear of space and time. Like Dante's Satan, he is imprisoned in his omnipotence,[68] made helpless by his own phobia.

Solzhenitsyn also endows Stalin with pathological narcissism,[69] a firm conviction that he is irreplaceable. That he believes in the mendacious biography he has helped to author suggests that he suffers from delusions. Accounts of his close relationship with Lenin, his important role in the civil war, his masterful leadership in the Second World War, his love of the Soviet people, his modesty—all of these strike him as true and convincing (117). He approves of the tendency in recent films and plays to show him warning and correcting Lenin, who tended to make rash decisions (119). Displays of adoration in public celebrations of Stalin's birthday are conclusive proof that the people are devoted to him (120). Evidence that agriculture is thriving on Soviet collective farms is provided in films and novels, and Stalin's narcissism persuades him that these portrayals are accurate (121). His self-love is fueled by his nocturnal habit of listening to recordings of his own speeches (153). Solzhenitsyn may have borrowed some of the details pointing to Stalin's narcissism from Khrushchev's so-called Secret Speech of 1956. His belief that he was irreplaceable, his love of public adulation, and his habit of rereading his biography were adumbrated by Khrushchev as evidence of the cult of personality.[70] In Solzhenitsyn's version, Stalin is so thoroughly steeped in his delusions that he is no longer psychologically

capable of seeing the truth behind the facade. The self-deception he practices on his own psyche spreads out in ever-widening circles of corruption,
encompassing all of Soviet society.

Megalomania is central to Solzhenitsyn's satirical portrait of Stalin. The
dictator firmly believes in his superior powers of perception and insight
and measures himself against his political rivals: "He clearly saw his own
vital superiority, their instability, his own firmness. Among all of them he
was distinguished by the fact that he *understood people*" (134). He is convinced that no one can reason or act as flawlessly as he (156), and that there
is not his equal in world history (166). In one passage of interior monologue, Stalin muses that God, too, must be lonely, for He, like Stalin, stands
above all of humanity (167). Still, he frets that his contemporaries do not
adequately recognize the profundity of his genius and worries that they
underestimate him (171). All of this evidence of megalomania is, of course,
Solzhenitsyn's fictional creation. He constructs passages in quasi-indirect
discourse and implies that these thoughts are the products of Stalin's own
mind. This is a devastatingly effective satirical device and much more powerful than direct criticism. Stalin's megalomania reaches its apogee in his
stated aspirations to conquer Europe and, finally, the world: "The path to
world communism is generally simplest through a Third World War: first
unite the whole world, then establish communism" (177). While some critics have found this extrapolation unfair and excessive,[71] it is consistent with
the delusional, megalomaniacal character Solzhenitsyn has created.

Another trait that shades to madness in Solzhenitsyn's satirical portrait of Stalin is paranoia. He distrusts the people in whose name the Revolution was fought and blames his isolation on the "constant insincerity and
treachery of people" (119). Stalin considers it a strength never to trust anyone's word and lives in perpetual fear of betrayal. Solzhenitsyn employs the
technique of the list to emphasize the degree of Stalin's paranoia: "He didn't
trust his own mother. Nor God. Nor revolutionaries. Nor the peasants (that
they will plant grain and collect the harvest if you don't force them). Nor
the workers (that they will work if you don't set a norm). And especially not
engineers. He didn't trust soldiers or generals, that they will fight without
penal battalions and guard detachments. He didn't trust those close to him.
He didn't trust his wives and lovers. Nor did he trust his children. And he always turned out to be right!" (155). Stalin devises many strategies to ensure
his security, trying to anticipate plots and conspiracies. He has his residences
reinforced, eliminates curtains and other possible hiding places, and has
multiple beds prepared so that no one knows where he is sleeping on any

given night. He is a victim of his own insecurity, incapacitated by suspicion and dread. Though it may appear exaggerated, Solzenitsyn's portrait on this score corresponds quite closely to Khrushchev's and to Medvedev's accounts of his extreme paranoia.[72]

In Solzhenitsyn's text Stalin is motivated by envy in his search for acclamation. This is especially true with respect to Trotsky, who Stalin despises for his "self-importance" and his "pretensions to eloquence" (136). Stalin's extreme sensitivity leads him to remember every slight, and he never forgives anyone who has offended him. Thus, he nurses a grudge against Trotsky and other Old Bolsheviks for their insolent mockery (133) and waits for an opportunity to destroy writers who depicted his role in the civil war as less than singularly heroic (143). All those under enemy occupation during the Second World War betrayed not just the Soviet Union but Stalin personally (144) and cannot be forgiven. Anyone who contradicted him in his policies or strategies has long since been destroyed in the present of the novel, but he has collected their writings during his night study "in order to be more malicious at night when making decisions" (169–70). Another aspect of Stalin's extreme jealousy toward those he perceives as rivals is projection. In Tito he sees a "vain, proud, cruel, cowardly, disgusting, hypocritical, base tyrant" (147). His mental state is such that he locates all these objectionable qualities (which Solzhenitsyn certainly intends to apply to Stalin) in the person of Tito, who has resisted his authority.

Stalin's cruelty, his delight in the suffering of others, is expressed in passages of direct discourse in Solzhenitsyn's text. In his meeting with Viktor Abakumov, his minister for state security, Stalin orders that students should be given full prison sentences of twenty-five years, concluding in strongly accented Russian: "They're young! They'll survive!" (*Máladye! Dá-zhivut!*) (161). He forbids the delivery of food packages to political prisoners, lamenting the "sanitorium conditions" (*sánitornye usloviia*) (162) permitted by the prison authorities. Responding to Abakumov's impassioned plea for the return of the death penalty, Stalin promises to restore it, declaring that "this will be a good educational measure" (*Ét-ta budyt khareshaia vospitatel'naia mera*) (163). He then jokes sadistically that Abakumov will be the first to be shot. Solzhenitsyn depicts Stalin sitting in an adjacent room at the show trials of his political opponents, reveling secretly in their destruction.[73] Rancour-Laferriere suggests that Stalin's sadism is linked to masochism. Resigning himself to suffering for another twenty years for the sake of the Soviet people, he identifies on some level with the object of his sadism and sentences himself to a term analogous to those of typical inmates of the gulag (121).[74]

Having made himself the unchallenged arbiter of life and death, Stalin experiences complete isolation that exacerbates his psychological instability. He longs for a true friend like the fictional character depicted in a film about him (119) and laments the impossibility of trusting anyone at all. Late at night, alone in his study, he is filled with terror and doubts the reality of the world around him. In passages of interior monologue, he expresses self-pity; he must sacrifice himself for the people and for posterity by not sleeping and working constantly. Stalin's conception of his own sacrifice resembles martyrdom: "And through the remaining hours [when he is not sleeping], he has to crawl, as on sharp rocks, to drag himself along with his weak, no longer young body" (121). Insomnia torments him, and his thoughts sometimes do not crystallize completely; Solzhenitsyn suggests that dementia has begun to affect Stalin's mind. He hears an inner orchestra, and his nocturnal, insomniac musings are accompanied by music.[75] A fleeting reference to Richard III suggests a comparison with the English king's isolation, fear, and madness.

Solzhenitsyn depicts Stalin in the grip of multiple psychological pathologies and the cumulative effect is a portrait of empowered madness. However, he does not employ this satirical strategy in order to absolve the Russian people. Stalin is presented as a scapegoat for the evils engendered by the communist experiment in Russia. He is endowed by Solzhenitsyn with a complex of mental aberrations, but these did not cause the horrors of Stalinism. Stalinism was rather the expression of "the pathological features of the people around [Stalin], or collective aberrations of the entire Soviet society . . . which harmonized nicely with the personal psychopathology of Stalin."[76] His mental illness is given license and eventually controls Soviet society because the ground has been made fertile. For Solzhenitsyn the real cause of Stalinism was Marxism as it took shape in the Soviet Union; it is "the lie" of Marxism that engendered and supported a regime based on paranoia, sadism, and extreme egotism.[77] Marxist ideology enabled Stalin's megalomania, allowing insanity to shape and define Russian culture for a quarter of a century. In Solzhenitsyn's vision Stalin's madness is thus symptomatic and serves to implicate rather than absolve the Russian people.

Zinoviev's *The Madhouse*

Aleksandr Zinoviev was originally trained as a philosopher and has been extraordinarily prolific as a scholar. Since 1958 he has published over two hundred books and articles on logic, specifically the logical structure of scientific language. While only quasi-literary, his numerous novels, written since the

seventies, are certainly satirical and reflect his study of Soviet society following Stalin's death. Zinoviev is also a visual artist; he draws and paints, creating memorable and striking cartoons. His tendency to make controversial,
sometimes contradictory generalizations in his writing is even more pronounced in his interviews and public remarks. In short, Zinoviev has been a
maddeningly inconsistent yet keen and vociferous analyst of Stalinist and
post-Stalinist Soviet culture whose satiric voice demands our attention.

Born in 1922 in Kostroma, the sixth of eleven children, Zinoviev was
raised according to explicitly Christian values. He became an ardent communist in his youth, influenced by collectivist ideals, his mother's teachings
about mutual responsibility, and the revolutionary zeal of his teachers.[78]
His embrace of disparate doctrines is an early example of Zinoviev's intellectual eccentricity. For example, in a 1984 interview he claimed that although he was bitterly anti-Stalinist, he was willing to "put [his] life on the
line for Stalin . . . without hesitation."[79] In 1933 Zinoviev went to Moscow to
join his father and grandfather, who were working in the capital. He lived
there in a damp basement room in extremely cramped and uncomfortable
conditions; firsthand acquaintance with social and economic hardship
apparently strengthened Zinoviev's communist convictions. Disillusioned
by the discrepancy between his ideals and the reality of life in the Soviet
Union, he also considered suicide in this early period.[80]

Zinoviev maintains that he was anti-Stalinist throughout Stalin's reign
and up until the Thaw, when he claims that anti-Stalinism lost its meaning.
His early hatred of Stalin grew out of his own experiences:

> My anti-Stalinism was born of the unbearably difficult conditions of the
> lives of the people among whom I grew up. My personal hatred of Stalin
> was only the embodiment of my protest against these conditions. But very
> early I began to think about the reasons for this monstrous (so it seemed to
> me then) injustice. Toward the end of school I was already convinced that
> the reasons for this evil are rooted in socialism (communism) itself. My per-
> sonal hatred of Stalin began to give way to purely intellectual curiosity—a
> desire to understand the hidden mechanisms of socialist society that pro-
> duce all those negative phenomena which I had already seen too much of.[81]

Although it was replaced by hatred of communism and the Soviet system,
this revulsion toward Stalin informed Zinoviev's youth to a very unusual
and significant degree. He considered assassinating Stalin and even discussed this plan with a friend. Ultimately they abandoned the plot not because it seemed practically impossible but because they could not overcome
"the moral-psychological barrier."[82]

Since he was quite open about his anti-Stalinism, Zinoviev attracted the attention of the authorities in 1939 while studying at the Moscow Institute of Philosophy, Literature, and History. He recalls that he was expelled "for speaking out against the Stalin cult" at a party with friends,[83] where he also declared himself a neoanarchist.[84] After being examined at a psychiatric hospital, he was found unfit to continue his studies and was subsequently arrested. In a rather bizarre turn of events, he was left momentarily unsupervised by his NKVD guards, so he simply walked away, fled Moscow, and spent a year traveling to avoid apprehension. Eventually Zinoviev enlisted in the military (although he had no official papers) and served with distinction for six years in the cavalry, tank forces, and the air force. He participated in the liberation of Prague and Berlin and was decorated several times. In 1946 he resigned from the military and enrolled in the Faculty of Philosophy at the University of Moscow. He defended his dissertation for the *kandidat* degree in 1954, but his work on the logical structure of Marx's *Das Kapital* aroused a scandal since it demonstrated that Marx used ideological rather than scientific argumentation.[85] The Higher Examination Board withheld the degree for several years, while the dissertation reportedly circulated in samizdat.[86]

In 1954 Zinoviev was invited to work at the Institute of Philosophy attached to the Academy of Sciences and remained there for twenty-two years, first as a technical assistant, then as a junior research fellow, and finally as a senior research fellow. Part of his job in his early years at the institute was to evaluate the mental conditions of people whose manuscripts had been sent to the KGB and who were suspected by the authorities of being insane. These encounters form the basis of many accounts included in *The Madhouse*. Despite his own dissident tendencies, Zinoviev successfully defended his dissertation in 1962 and four years later became a full professor. In 1967 he was named head of the Department of Logic at Moscow University and the next year was named to the editorial board of *Voprosy filosofii*, the premier Russian journal of philosophy. However, his principled refusal to write from a Marxist viewpoint led to various clashes and confrontations and he was eventually dropped from the journal's editorial board. Over the next few years Zinoviev experienced increasing pressure and criticism, leading to his almost complete isolation by 1974.

The publication in 1976 of his novel *The Yawning Heights* (*Ziiaushchie vysoty*) in the West exacerbated the already deteriorating situation and elicited strong negative responses from virtually all Russian constituencies, from the Soviet authorities to the liberal intelligentsia. The novel was, as

Michael Kirkwood puts it, "a kind of interminable suicide note as far as his career as a Soviet academic was concerned."[87] *The Yawning Heights* was quickly translated into French and German and enjoyed considerable success abroad. In 1977 Zinoviev was fired and stripped of all his degrees and titles; he had already been formally expelled from the Communist Party the previous year. The next two years proved exceedingly difficult since Zinoviev had no source of livelihood and he and his family were subjected to continual harassment and threats. Upon his emigration in 1978, he was deprived of his Soviet citizenship. Unfamiliar with life outside the Soviet Union, Zinoviev also experienced significant problems adjusting to life in exile. He continued with both his scholarly and artistic work, publishing (among other volumes) *The Radiant Future* (*Svetloe budushchee*) in 1978 and *The Madhouse* in 1980. At the same time, he succeeded in alienating much of the third-wave émigré community with his public statements and interviews; he also managed to create enemies among Sovietologists by repeatedly asserting that Western scholars could not possibly understand Soviet culture. His claims of superior insight sometimes sound ludicrous: "I am probably the only man in the world who has developed his own sociological framework for the comprehension of Soviet society based on the experience of having lived in that society."[88] Thanks to his publications, interviews, a televised debate with Boris Yeltsin in 1990, and the restoration of his citizenship, Zinoviev reentered Russian cultural life. He became a vociferous advocate of Great Russian nationalism and remained a profoundly polarizing figure until his death in 2006.

One of the greatest sources of controversy in Zinoviev's work has been his views on Stalin and Stalinism. In particular, his book *Flight of Our Youth* (*Nashei iunosti polet*), published in 1983, has been widely interpreted as an apologia for Stalinism. Here Zinoviev develops ideas about Stalin that he had only hinted at earlier; the result is what one reviewer calls "a poem of nostalgia for Stalin's time."[89] He claims the right to examine the period objectively because he was opposed to Stalin as early as 1939; he disdains his compatriots, who condemned Stalin only after the Twentieth Party Congress. In *Flight of Our Youth* Zinoviev asserts that it is senseless to assign blame or assess guilt for the crimes of Stalinism. He expresses deep loyalty to the society that shaped him and defends the culture of his youth: "Now time has passed and I have come to understand that this epoch deserves comprehension. And defense. Not justification, I repeat, but defense. Defense from superficiality and triviality of judgments."[90]

Zinoviev insists that Stalin was the right person in the given historical circumstances and that he was compelled by those circumstances to take on the role of dictator. Stalinism was historically conditioned and the situation in the Soviet Union following the Revolution—a low level of economic development, weak governmental rule, the vulnerability of the new regime—necessitated his rise to power. Moreover, he argues, there were no norms to violate when Stalin came to power; those norms were, in fact, created during the process of the regime's consolidation of power,[91] and it is only in retrospect that Stalin's behavior seems criminal. He observes that when terror was no longer necessary, power passed into the hands of lawful party functionaries and the youthful stage of Soviet history ended. The Soviet system remained Stalinist not because of Stalin's personal qualities but because people had been shaped by the system and came to support it out of personal interest: "The Stalinist epoch in its most essential substance entered into our flesh and blood forever; it gave rise to our present reality and to the bearers of that reality. It gave rise to the future."[92] Stalin's persona, then, was not a decisive factor in the creation of Stalinism. Zinoviev typically asserts this as an irrefutable fact: "An evaluation of Stalin's personality is meaningless without an evaluation of the epoch indissolubly linked with his name—the epoch of Stalinism. What is Stalin without Stalinism? A short man. A semiliterate, incompletely educated seminarian. Pockmarked. With a Georgian accent. He was sly, vengeful, and cruel. His fingers left greasy spots on the pages of books. . . . Isn't this just too flimsy for the characterization of the man who controlled and still continues to control the hearts and minds of millions of people?!"[93] In Zinoviev's view, Stalin was not even particularly evil by nature but only became evil when he accepted the role of dictator created for him by historical circumstances. His thirst for power was not a motivation for his assuming absolute power but rather a consequence; anyone else in his place would have acted in the same way.[94] Zinoviev's analysis of Soviet culture rests on the premise that Stalinism cannot be blamed on Stalin.

According to Zinoviev, Stalin's era was a period of true popular power (*narodovlastie*). Stalin himself was a genuinely popular leader insofar as he understood the Soviet people and possessed the qualities necessary to lead them. The system of denunciation fostered under Stalinism was a natural outgrowth of popular power, for it represented authentic participation by the masses. Millions of people took part in constructing and maintaining Stalinism: "The same people often played the roles of executioner and victim."[95] Zinoviev asserts that the vast majority knew what was happening under Stalin and believed it was necessary and just. Stalinism was effected not by a small elite but by the broad masses, who saw in it an opportunity to improve their standard of living. Stalin himself was a symbol of the ideal of collectivity and the possibility of a more comfortable future. Ordinary Soviet citizens were willing to become victims and to destroy their fellow citizens in order to seize the opportunity (however dangerous) of advancement and promotion. Moreover, according to Zinoviev the mass arrests and executions of the purges and the millions of deaths resulting from the collectivization of agriculture were justified. He insists on viewing this bloody history through a value-neutral lens, concluding that it occurred in accord with "social laws."

Zinoviev began writing *The Madhouse* in 1978 and completed about half of it before his exile from the Soviet Union. He completed the novel the next year in Munich and it was published in 1980. The original Russian text is very long, running to two large volumes; the single-volume English translation is heavily cut. In a 1980 interview Zinoviev stated that the division of the text into two volumes was a purely practical matter and that he worked on both parts simultaneously.[96] To call the work a novel is to use the term in the loosest sense, applying mainly the metric of length. *The Madhouse* is subtitled "A Romantic Tale in Four Parts, with a Warning and Edification."[97]

JRF, the protagonist and sometime narrator of the text, is a junior research fellow chosen by Zinoviev precisely because he is a nonentity; he certainly has autobiographical characteristics. JRF has multiple egos that take turns expressing their views and conversing with the author. One of these voices is identifiable as Stalin; others are Lenin, Marx, Beria, and Dzerzhinsky. A character vaguely named He (*On*) fulfills the role of JRF's mentor and may well be Stalin or Stalin's ghost. This figure—it is never clear whether he exists outside of JRF's head—explains and justifies the Soviet system to JRF. Finally, Stalin appears in Zinoviev's text as the subject of the Scoundrel's manuscript and as the subject of Petin's play. Stalin is thus a character created by other characters; he figures within texts that exist within the text of *The Madhouse*. The distancing of Stalin's persona and the expression of his character through a variety of dissonant voices allow Zinoviev to present conflicting and contradictory ideas. While this procedure is common in Zinoviev's texts,[98] it is particularly effective in his evocation of Stalin in *The Madhouse*, for the contradictions he expresses about the dictator are clearly ones that bedevil him personally.

Zinoviev's characterization of Stalin in *The Madhouse* includes physical, psychological, and biographical aspects. The physical description he provides is clipped and telegraphic, suggesting that these details are already clichés: "Stalin is small, with a pock-marked face, moustache, smokes a pipe, speaks with a baboon accent" (1:335). Typically Zinoviev coarsens and exaggerates the point about Stalin's pronunciation, interpreting his Georgian accent as nonhuman. In a much later passage narrated by Stalin himself, Zinoviev satirically treats his foreignness as a calculated political ploy:

> Moreover, the Russian people form the heart of this country and are used to having a tsar over them—and they are longing for a new tsar. And not one of their own Ivans, but a foreigner. But not a Jew. And not a German. A Georgian—now *there's* someone a Russian can get on with and yet he's more or less foreign. That circumstance has to be brought to the fore. I'll have to speak with an accent; otherwise I'll be taken for a Jew. From this moment on I will have to get everyone used to the fact that Stalin speaks with a Georgian accent. (2:292)

The biographical details Zinoviev provides grow out of rumors and anecdotes about Stalin's life. Like Solzhenitsyn, he accepts the premise that Stalin was a double agent, that is, that he worked for the tsarist *Okhrana* while a member of the Bolshevik Party in the prerevolutionary period. He includes in his text a lengthy dialogue in which Stalin informs on Lenin to a colonel in the *Okhrana* (2:219–21). Stalin is also involved in "expropriations"—specifically bank robberies and bombings—in Zinoviev's account of his youth. This aspect of Stalin's biography is widely accepted, but Zinoviev depicts him plotting a bank robbery with conspirators whom he fully intends to betray once the deed is done. In fact, his plan involves two consecutive betrayals, first of the criminals who will carry out the robbery and subsequently of the innkeeper who arranges their arrest. Stalin rationalizes his plan to a shady accomplice whom he enlists to murder the innkeeper: "The interests of the revolution demand it. And, as Lenin says, you don't make revolution wearing white gloves. Get on with it! Deliver every last kopeck of that money" (2:232). Perhaps the most shocking allegation Zinoviev includes in his fictionalized account is Stalin's direct and active involvement in Lenin's death. Reasoning that Lenin dead is more valuable to the cause of the Revolution than Lenin alive, Stalin arranges his murder by Chekists (2:265). Following Lenin's death, he ensures that Trotsky will be informed too late to return to Moscow for the funeral, seriously damaging his chances of becoming Lenin's successor (2:269–70). Stalin is also charged by Zinoviev with intentionally causing the famine during the collectivization campaign. He directs Molotov and Voroshilov to confiscate all of the grain in "M district"—"down to the last kernel" (2:293)—fully aware that this will destroy the local populace.

Zinoviev's Stalin is not mad but rather clear-sighted and rational in the extreme. He is utterly pragmatic and knows the Soviet people, the inhabitants of "the madhouse," intimately. Devoid of abstract ideals (which he disdains), he is free ruthlessly to follow what he calls "the fundamental law of historical reality: the one who wins is the one who does the deed, no matter how dirty it might seem" (2:293). Sounding very much like the Grand Inquisitor, he envisions consolidating his power on a fundamentally corrupt basis: "They regard us as a necessary but temporary evil. Oh you naïve dreamers! It's you who are a necessary but temporary . . . let's say, good. Life, however, is based not on good but on evil, because the good is ephemeral, but evil is solid and unshakable. If the revolution triumphs, we shall decide who shall enter the radiant edifice of communism and who shall not" (2:215). Perhaps with Lenin's "Testament" in mind, Zinoviev depicts Stalin as vulgar, blunt, and cynical, uninterested in engaging in philosophical debate. Everything worthwhile in Marxist thought has been condensed by Stalin in *On Dialectical and Historical Materialism,* and all the rest is dismissed as "nonsense for blabbermouths" (1:103).

Stalin is an effective leader since he is not hampered by idealism or philosophical subtlety. Lenin, Zinoviev argues, was a historical figure and acted according to historical laws; Stalin was a sociological phenomenon and shaped the future of Soviet culture beyond the Revolution: "The historical froth was carried away by the current, but the roots of sociology put forth shoots and then bore fruit" (2:247). The Soviet system is the result of the collective efforts of millions of people. Stalin should be taken seriously insofar as "he belongs to our ant heap" (2:242), but his unique psychology is of limited interest and importance. Petin tells JRF that he will only solve the riddle of Stalin when he realizes that it resides in him—and, by implication, in all those complicit in Stalinism (2:332). The Soviet people loved and still love Stalin because they perceived order and justice in the system of denunciations he fostered; you could be sure that denunciation would result in arrest and that the punishment would fit the allegation. A character named Dobronravov delivers a discourse on the Russian people and paints them as brutal and semicivilized. Dobronravov's name echoes that of Dobrosklonov, one of the protagonists of Nekrasov's poem "Who Is Happy in Russia" ("Komu na Rusi zhit' khorosho"). Based in part on Dobroliubov, Grisha Dobrosklonov is Nekrasov's spokesman for the lyrical strength and beauty of Mother Russia.[99] He expresses faith in the Russian peasant's capacity to achieve social justice:

> Enough! This accounting with the past is done.
> This accounting with the master is over!
> The Russian people are gathering their strength
> And learning to be citizens.[100]

Zinoviev is responding parodically to Nekrasov's model, for Dobronravov's view of the sovietized Russian peasant is that he is self-centered, materialistic, and amoral. It would seem that Zinoviev locates the basis of the "social laws" that gave rise to Stalinism in the lower level of social and moral development of the Russian people.

Although Stalin appears as several different personae in *The Madhouse*, the portraits share important characterological features. Moreover, these depictions of Stalin collectively anticipate Zinoviev's publicistic treatment of the dictator in *The Flight of Our Youth*.[101] Zinoviev denies that his literary characters are intended as "historical caricatures."[102] In *The Madhouse* and elsewhere he asserts that Stalin cannot be a comic figure, that he does not inspire jokes. Portraying Stalin as a character certainly offers Zinoviev ample opportunity for satire and criticism, but we never simply laugh at Stalin: "'If you can laugh at someone, it means he's still a person,' said JRF. 'But if you can't laugh at someone, then he's not a person but a superperson or a nonperson. Which is essentially one and the same thing'" (2:344). Zinoviev regards Stalin as a preeminent Marxist who successfully reduced Marxism to its essence. On some level Stalin's talent for theatrical performance and spectacle (e.g., the show trials, Stakhanovism, collectivization) is admirable for Zinoviev. While Trotsky asserts Stalin's ignorance, Zinoviev uses many of his characters to refute this idea, suggesting that Stalin was shrewd and quite intelligent. He is portrayed as practical and focused, willing to use any means to achieve his ambitions.

The Madhouse is an allegorical satire on Soviet culture: the country is a vast asylum and madness is its core defining quality. Stalin himself, however, is not mad but is rather the perfectly sane and rational keeper of the asylum. Through his examination of Stalinism Zinoviev demonstrates that history created the conditions that put Stalin in power and kept him there for a quarter of a century. Millions of people contributed to the construction of Stalinism and no single individual—not even Stalin—can be held responsible. Paradoxically, faith in Stalin may have provided a link with reality for many Soviet citizens, for the world must have seemed increasingly mad:

> The psychological element that made it possible for Stalin to get away with the Purge trials was their sheer absurdity. The inclination of the man in the street was to say: "There must be something in it," for the only alternative conclusion he could draw from the laughable plots and abject confessions was that the world had gone mad and Russian society was in the throes of some gigantic St Vitus's dance. His own sanity demanded that he should

give credence to Stalin's fabrications. This was the horrible paradox. . . . It was, if you like, an irrational way of making sense of something that yielded to no rational explanation. No madhouse could have been madder.[103]

While madness characterizes Soviet society under Stalin and may explain the complicity of the Russian people, it does not provide exculpation. G. R. Urban takes this point a step further and supports Zinoviev's point of view when he asserts that Soviet culture induced psychosis and was a natural breeding ground for psychopaths because it denied the obligations imposed by morality.[104] Zinoviev provides a devastating satire of Stalinism, but madness fulfills a quite different function in this text. Ironically Stalin stands apart because he is preeminently sane, whereas the madness of Stalinism is endemic to the system.

Maksimov's *Ark for the Uncalled*

Vladimir Maksimov, whose real name was Lev Alekseevich Samsonov, was born in 1930 or 1932 (there is some discrepancy in biographical sources) into a working-class family in Moscow. Brought up in a series of orphanages and reform schools, he received only a rudimentary education and then traveled around the Soviet Union for several years. At twenty-one he landed a job working for a newspaper, which marked the start of his career as a writer. He first published poems and plays but was dismissive of his early efforts.[105] Like many artists of his generation, he wrote a laudatory poem on the death of Stalin, which was later used to discredit his liberal credentials. Maksimov's first prose work, a short story called "We Make the Earth Livable" ("My obzhivaem zemliu"), appeared in 1961 in the anthology *Pages from Tarusa* (*Tarusskie stranitsy*). A second story entitled "A Man Survives" ("Zhiv chelovek") was published the following year in *Oktiabr'* and was subsequently adapted for the stage in 1965. Maksimov was invited to join the Soviet Writers' Union in 1963 and served as an editor of *Oktiabr'* between 1967 and 1968.

As early as 1958 Maksimov clashed with Soviet authorities and was sent to a mental hospital, where he was compelled to undergo a course of treatment.[106] His two major novels, *Seven Days of Creation* (*Sem' dnei tvoreniia*) and *Quarantine* (*Karantin*) circulated in samizdat in the sixties and appeared in the West in the early seventies. By this time he had become persona non grata in the Soviet Union and attacks began to appear in *Literaturnaia gazeta, Izvestiia,* and elsewhere. In 1973 he was expelled from the

Soviet Writers' Union and within a year he was granted permission to leave the Soviet Union. He went to France, ostensibly for one year, but was stripped of his Soviet citizenship while living there. Maksimov did not regard his exile as either heroic or voluntary: "The choice was whether to travel to the West or to the East."[107] Having settled in Paris, Maksimov became editor in chief of *Kontinent* and thus played an exceedingly powerful role in Russian émigré culture for seventeen years. His quarrels with Solzhenitsyn and Sinyavsky—played out on the pages of émigré journals and newspapers—were scandals within this insular world. He publicly criticized Solzhenitsyn of hypocrisy, of the "Tolstoyan sin" of "Preaching one thing and living differently."[108] Sinyavsky's penchant for blurring the line between personal antipathies and literary disagreements was also a source of irritation to Maksimov.[109] However, Maksimov was a vociferous participant in these journalistic fracases and his statements about his compatriots were often insulting. After the fall of the Soviet Union, Maksimov frequently visited his homeland, attending conferences and granting radio and television interviews. His articles often appeared in journals and newspapers in post-Soviet Russia. He died in 1995 in Paris.

Ark for the Uncalled, a novel that features a detailed portrait of Stalin, was published in the West in 1979. Maksimov's portrayal of the dictator has been called "a *lubok*-like caricature,"[110] and it is certainly true that the author selects standard details to characterize Stalin. As Violetta Iverni notes in her review of the novel, there is an inherent risk in any attempt to depict a historical figure like Stalin: one is easily drawn to schematic representation because it is impossible to know the true character of such a figure and because one must create his image in reverse, proceeding from the results of his actions to his personality.[111] Before leaving the Soviet Union, Maksimov reportedly sought out people who had known Stalin personally and collected details that he would later use in his satirical portrait. However, he is ultimately less interested in the details of Stalin's appearance or behavior than he is in his internal, moral life; the rather clichéd descriptors he includes merely serve as markers of the familiar.

The physical sketch of Stalin Maksimov provides renders him extremely unattractive, and this is meaningful in the context of this novel, which reads like a parable. As Petr Ravich notes, "His mediocrity, the boredom emanating from him, the grayness of this man who was deified like no other in his life, are all the more striking because of the biblical rhythm of the work."[112] His eyes are "heavy, sclerotically veined,"[113] and he is pockmarked, with red hair and long arms (36). He walks with a limp, "slightly dragging his left leg" (66). Stalin's manner of speaking is of particular interest to Maksimov. His "Caucasian accent" (35) tends to emphasize the weightiness of every utterance, yet it also fuels his inferiority complex. Here we move from external description to psychological characterization:

> Since childhood he had disliked his Georgian accent, which reminded him vividly of his plebian origin. With envy he listened to the fluent speech of his peers from noble families, where Russian was considered colloquial, noting with what ease they moved from the rolling Georgian "e" to the almost soundless Russian "e," pronouncing the foreign "sh" and "ch" without a single whistling sound [*ot raskatistogo gruzinskogo "e" k pochti bezzvuchnomu russkomu "e" proiznosia chuzhie "sh" i "ch" bez edinogo svistiashchego zvuka*]. His childish envy of them, of their appearance, of their air of superiority—although almost all of them suffered the same penurious existence as he (in Georgia, as is well known, there are three noblemen for every beggar)—in time turned into burning, almost insuperable hatred. (226–27)

Stalin repeats himself and overuses proverbs; he clearly enjoys turning a phrase and takes pleasure in his own cleverness. In his audience with Stalin Zolotarev, the careerist protagonist of the novel, is struck by the fact that he employs language as a barrier against the world, suggesting his psychological isolation: "He fences in, protects, barricades with words what's going on inside him against penetration or interference from outside" (37). In Maksimov's literary portrait Stalin listens only to himself; he has willfully separated himself from external reality. Internally he dwells on past insults and betrayals and seethes with murderous rage.

Maksimov devotes many pages to a satirical exposé of Stalin's pathological character traits. He is profoundly paranoid, trusting no one—including Beria—and allowing no one to become intimate with him. His dislike of doctors is partly based on his fear of assassination but more generally on his unwillingness to permit anyone access to his inner life: "Medicine sickened him with the danger of penetration from outside into his concealed life" (58). He experiences a terrible feeling of vulnerability "in this huge and furious world" (60) and longs for a burrow in which he can hide. This passage certainly suggests agoraphobia, described by Solzhenitsyn as well. Megalomania is another key feature of his psyche. False modesty conceals his grandiosity, but it occasionally makes itself known, as when he decides to go to the outer office to receive the Patriarch of the Russian Orthodox Church: "It can't be helped; the mountain will go to Mohammed if necessary" (76). Stalin indulges in fantasies of anonymity and friendship reminiscent of passages in both Solzhenitsyn's and Iskander's works. His fondness for films and his extreme emotional reaction to them have been attested by a number of his biographers.[114] These details in Maksimov's text support the conclusion that Stalin's grip on reality was tenuous.

Maksimov's Stalin is a sadist and enjoys degrading and humiliating his underlings. The novel includes a fairly detailed account of Stalin's destruction of Poskrebyshev's wife, a well-known case of his cruelty. Poskrebyshev, who Maksimov calls a "gnome," a "shadow" (65) and a "parchment statue" (73), crawls on all fours while beseeching Stalin to show mercy but cannot prevent his wife's arrest. Stalin supplies him with a new wife and mocks his grief, advising him that "it's easier for the horse with the woman out of the cart [*Baba s vozu—kobyle legche*]" (73). He despises any sign of weakness in others yet paradoxically encourages sycophancy. Maksimov provides a kind of explanation for Stalin's pathological cruelty, repeating the legend that he became inhumanly pitiless when Keke, his first wife, died (74).[115] Her death also motivates his hatred of Iakov, his first son, for Iakov's existence constantly reminds Stalin of his loss.

Stalin's misanthropy is particularly harsh toward Jews, and Maksimov devotes considerable attention to his anti-Semitism.[116] He hates Jews because he believes they are contemptuous of him and react to his speeches with irony and laughter (70–71). His inferiority complex also feeds his envy of Russians, though this is expressed perversely: "Despising Russians and everything Russian generally in the deep-rooted Caucasian manner, he thirsted to be taken by outsiders for a full-blooded Russian, so that he would have the right to look down on foreigners and their pitiful attempts to imitate a grandeur alien to them" (227). He does not miss Georgia, where he was treated like an interloper and an outsider. A joke made long ago in prison by a fellow inmate suggesting that Stalin was an Ossetian Jew is remembered and punished by the dictator with particular viciousness in Maksimov's text.

Now old and infirm, Stalin is obsessed with his mortality and the possibility of extending his life. His memory is failing, which torments him, for it points to a diminution of his omnipotence. Memories of his childhood and youth increasingly disturb him, making him furious and irrational. The past pursues him relentlessly, and he is tortured by inner voices: "'You are the son of the town strumpet, who bore you of her rich neighbor Revaz Ignatoshvili in revenge on her drunken husband; you are illegitimate and your mother is a whore!'" (63). As Iverni notes, it does not matter whether or not this story about Stalin's illegitimacy is true. Through his psychological characterization of the dictator Maksimov attempts to explain how he became vengeful and pitiless.[117] Stalin is also haunted by a fear of punishment, which the author implies might be viewed as divine retribution: "His seminary education made itself felt: somewhere in the depths of his soul he couldn't manage to shake off the fear of possible punishment" (67). In his old age he is terrified by the thought of suffering a stroke and having the contents of his secret safe disclosed. Ironically, as Iverni points out, Stalin is consumed by the same fear (Maksimov uses the word *strakh*) as those around him.[118]

Stalin's madness in Maksimov's text is humanized and explained, in a sense, by the context of his life and revolutionary culture. Maksimov has said that his work is influenced by religion,[119] and this is most relevant to a reading of this satirical portrait. He is profoundly concerned with the question of guilt—specifically the guilt that passes from generation to generation.[120] We are held responsible for the sins of our parents and our grandparents, so that Stalinism is still very much an active force in Russian culture. *Ark for the Uncalled* is an apocalyptic novel, setting out in chapter and verse the wages of the sins of Stalinism. Maksimov is at pains to understand and analyze Stalin's personal demons, the sources of his psychological pathology, but his intention is not pardoning the Russian people. Rather, his satirical depiction of the dictator serves as a warning that Russia has let herself be lured into the madness of self-destruction. In Maksimov's view it still remains for Russia to cleanse herself from the sins of Stalinism.

Conclusion

Casting Stalin as a madman is effective satirically, for it offers a way of understanding how Stalinism was established and supported in the Soviet Union for a quarter of a century. While psychological aberration is a strong characterological marker, and while it has a firm grounding in biographical evidence, it does not automatically make Stalin other vis-à-vis Russian culture. The dynamic is complicated by the perception of madness in Russia. The madman is distinctly alien in Western terms, but he may occupy a liminal position that evokes admiration or sympathy in Russian culture. Psychological abnormality is not prima facie negative, nor does it necessarily result in ostracism. The issue of guilt and complicity in Stalinism on the part of the Russian people is, in fact, problematized when Stalin is rendered as mad.

Nabokov's "Tyrants Destroyed" provides a composite portrait of mad tyrants, with Stalin figuring heavily in the mix. Writing from outside the collective madness of Stalinism even as it reached its climax, Nabokov offers a means of inoculation or—should that fail—of exorcism; art created in freedom can serve as an antidote to the poison of madness represented by his dictator. In *The First Circle* Solzhenitsyn provides an extraordinary depiction of Stalin's psychological pathologies, including paranoia, megalomania, narcissism, and sadism. His madness does not absolve the Russian people of culpability in Stalinism. Rather he demonstrates that Stalin's madness gained ascendancy because Marxism as it developed in the Soviet Union provided a fertile ground. Thus, Solzhenitsyn's portrayal of Stalin as at least slightly mad serves to indict his countrymen for supporting the excesses of Stalinism. The title of Zinoviev's novel promises direct engagement with the question of madness and, indeed, insanity figures centrally in his text. Stalin, however, is characterized as quite sane, if cold-bloodedly ruthless. *The Madhouse* is actually less a novel than a long publicistic exercise in philosophical argumentation, Zinoviev's point being that Stalin was an effective leader in the cultural and political context of the period. He charges that millions of Russians—virtually everyone—were complicit in Stalinism and that they contributed actively in building the asylum that was the Soviet Union. Maksimov's *Ark for the Uncalled* presents a mentally unbalanced yet humanized Stalin. We can understand his pathologies, and Maksimov warns us that understanding should lead to repentance. For this religious author, the sins of the fathers will be visited on the children until there is a full reckoning. Stalin's madness is an important feature of his personality, but it does not provide any excuses for those who participated in his reign.

Stalin's psychological aberrations are detailed and demonstrated in the literary portraits examined here. All four of these authors show us a Stalin isolated and cut off from the society he controlled (a situation that has a strong grounding in biography and history), but his madness does not simply make him alien to that society. Instead, his madness shapes and distorts Russian culture in terrible ways that must be seen in the clear light of retrospection. These authors interrogate the issue of whether Stalin's madness was infectious or whether the Russian people willingly (and self-interestedly) accepted its mad logic. Thus, these texts contribute significantly to the work of self-examination, which can lead to cultural absolution.

2

A Bestiary of Stalins

S talin sometimes appears in the guise of an animal, and the beast metaphor turns out to be very productive in satirically characterizing the
dictator. This chapter considers three works of anti-Stalin satire that
feature animal villains. Kornei Chukovsky's poem "The Big Bad Cockroach" ("Tarakanishche"), written in 1921 and published in 1923, is an early
consideration of coercive terror and possible responses. Bulat Okudzhava's
song-poem "The Black Tomcat" ("Chernyi kot"), published in 1966, portrays Stalin as a threatening feline presence living off the fear of those who
dwell in the house he inhabits. Fazil Iskander's tale *Rabbits and Boa Constrictors* (*Kroliki i udavy*), published in the West in 1980 and in Russia in
1987, is an elaborate beast allegory that casts Stalin as a python ruling a tribe
of boa constrictors.

On the one hand, depicting Stalin as nonhuman—an animal or insect—
tends to liminalize him. Portraying him as bestial may emphasize his otherness, his not belonging to the collective (which is both human and Russian).
However, the beast metaphor is nuanced, and this dynamic is qualified.
After all, humans have animal qualities; the line between the human and
the nonhuman is not distinct and clear. Moreover, a rich tradition of art—
fables, allegories, fairy tales, and so on—anthropomorphizes animals. The
conventions that underlie these genres also shape satirical portraits of Stalin as an animal.

Animal Satire

Theriomorphism, or portraying humans as animals,[1] does not always function satirically and usually has didactic import. For example, the Bible is

replete with animal characters but is not satiric. Fairy tales are a particularly rich source of animal characters representing humans or human qualities. Animals found in fairy tales are often enchanted and may change from animal to human or vice versa.[2] This blurring of the boundary between the human and animal worlds does not, however, function satirically in the fairy tale. Closer to satire—indeed, often within its realm—is the fable. From the fable's inception with Aesop in the sixth century B.C. to its apogee with La Fontaine (and, in the Russian context, Krylov), it has presented animal characters speaking and behaving as humans do. Its purpose has often been to satirize individuals or human foibles, thereby providing moral instruction.

The bestiary is a good example of nonliterary satire that utilizes this device.[3] As we shall see, topoi that originate in these collections of animal descriptions are found in satirical works up to the present day.[4] A specifically Russian source of theriomorphic satire is the *lubok*, folk pictures (woodcuts or copper engravings) mixing illustrations and text, that have been circulating since the seventeenth century.[5] Theriomorphism is also operative in political cartoons, a satirical form popularized in the West in the nineteenth century and widespread in the twentieth-century Russian press. Literary satire featuring animal characters may be traced to Aristophanes' *Birds* and *Frogs*, through Chaucer's "Nun's Priest's Tale," to Orwell's *Animal Farm* and Ionesco's *Rhinoceros*.

In utilizing the beast metaphor, satirists choose a powerful weapon of criticism. When we recognize ourselves or other human targets in animals speaking and acting, the effect is likely to be strong, for incongruity is inherent and considerable when men appear as beasts. Moreover, how we regard animals that represent humans largely depends on how we perceive the animals themselves. Use of the beast metaphor implies a rejection of the Enlightenment notion that animals are innocent creatures with souls. Rather, they are creatures positioned lower than humans on "the great chain of being"[6] and are intellectually and morally inferior to us. If this premise is accepted, then depicting a human as an animal is indeed a disparaging critical gesture. By drawing a comparison between people and animals, the satirist suggests that humans are no wiser than nonrational creatures and that they are no more worthy of respect. Indeed, the vision of human society or human nature created through the agency of the beast metaphor is frequently bleak, tending to misanthropy.

Different animals represent different aspects of the human condition or embody different human traits. The extent to which a theriomorphic satiric portrayal is effective depends on the reader's apprehension of the meaning connected with a particular animal. This meaning is often a matter of convention: the fox is sly; the bear is slow-witted; the pig is greedy; and so on. When we look for the source of these associations, we can trace their evolution back through fairy tales, through the bestiaries, to the *Physiologus*.[7] Of course, contemporary theriomorphic works derive their satiric power from a variety of sources—literary, mythological, folkloric—based on these conventions. Unraveling the fabric of symbolism woven by Chukovsky, Okudzhava, and Iskander in their creation of animal characters is part of the aim of this chapter.

For animal satire to be effective, the writer must sustain a dual level of perception: the characters must be felt both as animal and human. If there is slippage in either direction (i.e., if the characters lose their dual and balanced beast/human quality), the satire will sacrifice some of its force (both aesthetic and didactic). Orwell's pigs are power-hungry and increasingly totalitarian, but they do not cease to be swine; they have hooves and snouts and they squeal. A second prerequisite of effective animal satire is the clear establishment of the author's point of view vis-à-vis the beast characters. The author's tone may range from gentle mockery to bitter vituperation, but the reader must understand where the author stands. Ionesco's *Rhinoceros* makes its point clearly because the reader readily grasps that the rhinoceros has strong negative associations (brutishness, mindless loyalty, ideological rigidity) for the author.

Rendering human beings as animals in satire is effective not only because of the conventional associations we make with various animals but also because it establishes the individual or individuals targeted as other. Indeed, animals constitute an important category of beings that we perceive as alterior. Tzvetan Todorov notes that certain Spanish writers equated American Indians with animals. This identification was based on what was for the Spaniards a clear difference: animals are unlike human beings in that they are animate but lack souls.[8] Since humanity was defined for them as having qualities belonging to the self (an emphasis on the written word, the habit of going about fully clothed, Christianity, etc.), people who did not possess those qualities were animalistic, subhuman. Being essentially beasts, they "enjoyed no claim to moral consideration."[9]

The attitude toward animals underlying such reasoning (which is certainly shared by modern Russians) contributes to a definition or redefinition of human society. What is brutish, unreasoning, or violent is cast out, relegated to the status of other to affirm the health of the self: "By embodying the antithesis of all that was valued and esteemed, the idea of the brute was as indispensable a prop to established human values as were the equally unrealistic notions held by contemporaries [in early modern England] about witches or Papists. 'The meaning of order,' it has been well said, 'could only be grasped by exploring its antithesis or 'contrary.'"[10] Animals present a convenient locus for projections of antisocial human impulses precisely because of the unique position they inhabit in relation to humans. They are in many ways similar to humans but are not the same; biologically closely related, they are nevertheless amoral. In Girard's conception of the other, it would not be the dissimilarity of the beast that compels us to banish it but rather "its unutterable contrary, the lack of difference."[11] The beast, in short, represents both continuity and discontinuity with humanness, and this disturbing ambivalence underpins a reliance in satire on theriomorphism.

Chukovsky's "The Big Bad Cockroach"

Kornei Chukovsky (born Nikolai Korneichukov, 1882–1969) was a gifted literary critic, sensitive translator, and author of numerous children's poems. "The Big Bad Cockroach" has often been read as a satirical exposé of tyranny, and a convincing case can be made for interpreting it as a portrait of Stalin. Chukovsky's biography and his autobiographical statements suggest that an ad hominem reading is quite plausible. While he was never an overt dissident, Chukovsky was certainly a liberal thinker who quietly resisted Stalinism. After beginning his career as an anti-tsarist satirist, over the years he went on to express his opposition to Trotsky, Lenin, Stalin, Khrushchev, and Brezhnev.[12] Even before the Revolution, he had aroused the displeasure of Lunacharsky by insisting on the principle of artistic freedom. Politically he allied himself with the Constitutional Democrats and wrote for the Cadet newspaper *Rech'*. Chukovsky's attitude toward Stalinism is less clearcut. While Nadezhda Mandelshtam accuses him of complicity with the regime,[13] more objective critics regard him as a courageous figure: "His defense of those in distress during the Stalinist years speaks for itself."[14] In a 1931 diary entry Chukovsky speaks of himself, Platonov, and Pilniak with typical understatement as "writers constrained by the epoch."[15] It is also worth noting that Chukovsky was a scholar and translator of Walt Whitman and expressed great admiration for the American poet's ideals of democracy and egalitarian individualism.[16]

Chukovsky's worldview, then, would certainly incline him toward antiauthoritarianism. The fact is, however, that the poem was written in 1921 and published in 1923. Stalin was not particularly prominent at this time; he was certainly not as well known as Lenin and not as visible as Trotsky. He was, by the time of publication of "The Big Bad Cockroach," general secretary of the party and a member of the ruling triumvirate (with Lenin and Trotsky). Perhaps a perceptive observer—which Chukovsky was—could have detected distinctive signs of megalomania and ruthlessness in Stalin even as he was jockeying for power. Lev Loseff argues that Chukovsky's poem is allegorical and particularized: "Although Stalin had only just put out feelers at the time Chukovsky was composing his verse narrative, the work intended a specific target: it took aim not at a concrete ruler so much as at that authoritarian system of rule which later in the century would be designated 'Stalinism.'"[17]

Given the historical context, Marsh suggests that the poem should be regarded as prophetic rather than specifically aimed at Stalin or Stalinism.[18] M. Petrovskii, a leading Russian commentator on Chukovsky's work, notes various attempts to link the poem with specific events and people but feels that these have resulted in strained interpretations.[19] Chukovsky's own account of the composition of the poem would seem to support the view that it is a generalized satirical portrait of tyranny. In an autobiographical introduction to a 1961 collection of poems, he recounts researching and writing an article on Nekrasov for the journal *Byloe*. He recalls that "The Big Bad Cockroach" intruded on this process, almost writing itself in the margins of his manuscript on Nekrasov.[20] Although this seems to characterize the poem as whimsical and spontaneous (to the point of being unintentional), the connection Chukovsky draws between the poem and the scholarly essay is significant. The article on Nekrasov is one of a series of essays Chukovsky wrote on the poet, the most well known being "The Poet and the Hangman" ("Poet i palach"), which was published in 1922. Its subject matter is the relationship between Nekrasov and Count Mikhail Muravev, the infamous Petersburg gendarme who was responsible for brutally suppressing the Polish uprising of 1866. Two brief examples from this essay will suffice to illustrate the point that it, too, may be Aesopian, that the *palach* of the title may point to more contemporary executioners. The first passage defends Nekrasov's notorious poem urging the suppression of Poland on the grounds of collective responsibility:

> But it is curious: this betrayal [the reading of the poem] seems such a great crime only when we scrutinize it outside of the context of the public life of the time, artificially divorcing it from the totality of social and historical phenomena. On the other hand, if one relates the whole affair as it occurred

then, without isolating Nekrasov from his epoch and his environment, he immediately appears justified, if not completely, then in part. Not a single prosecutor in all of Russian society would dare accuse him, for the Russian society of the time was just as guilty as he.

The second passage elaborates on the nature of the terror felt by Russian intellectuals before Muravev and attempts to explain their behavior:

> Everyone who wore blue-colored glasses or long hair or subscribed to *The Contemporary* or had read the novel *What Is to Be Done?* felt himself an outlaw and terrifiedly expected some sort of monstrous retribution, and thus hastened to insure himself against all suspicion, by exaggerated shouts of hurrah. Anyone not shouting hurrah was nearly considered a state criminal.[21]

If Chukovsky's scholarly work related to the genesis of "The Big Bad Cockroach" is itself Aesopian, it seems reasonable to entertain the possibility that this poem, which arose in the author's mind, is polyvalent. Perhaps more important, the poem has been widely read as Aesopian after the fact. Independent of the author's design, readers have tended to see Stalin in Chukovsky's strutting cockroach, and for later generations (of adults) this ad hominem reading will probably remain compelling. It is this fact rather than any tentative conclusions one might draw about Chukovsky's intentions that justifies a serious examination of the cockroach as Stalin.

Complicating the reception of this poem by Soviet readers is the fact that Stalin himself referenced it—both its characters and plot—in his 1930 address to the Sixteenth Party Congress. Denying the failure of radical collectivization in the agricultural sector, he used the fairy-tale motifs of "The Big Bad Cockroach" to mock and denigrate the right opposition:

> A cockroach has begun to rustle somewhere, it hasn't even managed to crawl out of its hole. But they're already rushing backward in terror, wailing about a catastrophe, about the demise of Soviet power. . . . We calm them down and try to reassure them that there's nothing really dangerous here, that after all it's just a cockroach, that it's nothing to be frightened about. How could that be! They keep wailing—"What cockroach? That's not a cockroach, but a thousand furious beasts! That's not a cockroach, but the abyss, the demise of Soviet power."[22]

Chukovsky noted Stalin's "plagiarism" in his diary entry of 9 March 1956 even as he refuted the popularly held idea that his poem satirizes Stalin.[23] In his retelling (without ever naming Chukovsky as the author), Stalin cast himself as the brave sparrow who destroys the threatening cockroach, as well as the kangaroo who points out that the cockroach is a mere insect. Mark Lipovetskii notes that in his quotation from Chukovsky's poem Stalin demonstrated his power to create discourse, to compel his listeners to replace observed reality with his fairy-tale version.[24] The poem thus gained what Lipovetskii calls a "dual permit" (*dvoinaia propiska*) and subsequently belonged both to official Soviet culture and to the culture of opposition.[25] Paradoxically, Stalin's appropriation of the poem for his own rhetorical and political purposes may have deflected the censor's detection of anti-Stalinism; this explanation would seem to account for the poem's repeated publication in full during the Soviet period despite its popular interpretation as targeting Stalin.

Chukovsky endows his villain with physical and behavioral characteristics that enhance the specificity of the satire. Though small of stature, the despot is a "frightening giant" (*strashnyi velikan*).[26] The rhyming juxtaposition of this phrase with the word "cockroach" (*tarakan*) results in humorous deflation. This effect is enhanced by hyphenating the syllables, indicating that the word is to be drawn out and emphasized in an oral reading: "A terrible giant, / With red hair and a mustache / The Cock-Roach!" (*Strashnyi velikan, / Ryzhii i usatyi / Ta-ra-kan!*) (174). The suffix -*ishche* appended to *tarakan* in the next line is similarly incongruous. Both augmentative and pejorative, the suffix gives the word the added nuances of "big" and "bad," neither of which typically apply to an insect. Loseff suggests that the term reflects "the political situation in a nation brought to heel by the dictatorship of a trifling political faction,"[27] namely, the Bolsheviks.

Chukovsky's cockroach is repeatedly characterized by references to his mustache. (Russian cockroaches conveniently have "mustaches" [*usy*] as the popular equivalent of "antennae.") The villain is "mustached" (*usatyi*), he "wiggles his mustache" (*usami shevelit*), he is "the one with a mustache" (*usach*). Stalin was commonly referred to as "the Mustache" (*Us*) or "the Mustached" (*Usatyi*), and variants on these forms are found in many sources.[28] Marsh suggests that Stalin's nickname actually originated with Chukovsky's poem,[29] but this seems unlikely. Like many nicknames, it probably derived from a distinctive physical characteristic. Stalin's mustache was so much a part of his persona that biographers mention his being clean-shaven (when he was traveling incognito before the Revolution) as a notable exception. In "The Big Bad Cockroach" it is precisely this feature, the mustache (or feelers), that the cockroach waves at the other animals to bully them into submission. This verbal caricature emphasizes Stalin's defining

attribute and—irrespective of Chukovsky's original intention—has encouraged an ad hominem reading.

The cockroach consumes or threatens to consume the other animals in
the poem. On one level this is absurd and humorous, given that many of
these animals (e.g., wolves, bears, hippopotamuses) are large and powerful
and all are much larger than the cockroach. On another level Chukovsky's
satire is quite pointed, for the kangaroo's remonstrance to the other animals
rings true:

> Aren't you ashamed?
> Isn't it offensive?
> You have teeth,
> You have claws,
> But you cringe before a tiny thing,
> You've submitted to a little bug!
>
> [*I ne stydno vam?*
> *Ne obidno vam?*
> *Vy—zubastye,*
> *Vy—klykastye,*
> *A maliavochke*
> *Poklonilsia,*
> *A koziavochke*
> *Pokorilsia!*]
>
>   (178)

Once the cockroach has become a despot, he demands that the animals
offer up their young to him. Chukovsky heightens the pathos of this idea by
cataloguing the kinds of baby animals he eats: "baby bear, wolf cub, baby
elephant" (*Medvezhonka, volchonka, slonenka*) (177). The epithets applied
to the cockroach are very strong for a children's poem; he is an "evil glut-
ton" (*zloi obzhora*) and an "insatiable scarecrow" (*nesytoe chuchelo*) (177).

The cockroach not only eats other animals but causes them to consume
one another as well. He initiates a purge mentality whereby his victims turn
on one another: "The wolves from fear / Ate one another up" (*Volki ot is-
puga / Skushali drug druga*); "The poor crocodile / Swallowed up the toad"
(*Bednyi krokodil / zhabu proglotil*) (174). Along the same lines, the hippo-
potamus makes an offer to the crocodiles and whales that involves consumption of their fellow animals; whoever will do battle with the cockroach, he promises, will receive as a reward two frogs (presumably to be
eaten). Given that all of Chukovsky's animals are anthropomorphized, this

consumption is equivalent to cannibalism or anthropophagy, the eating of like by like. Stalin-the-Cockroach's inciting the peaceful animals to break this taboo enhances his alterity, for cannibalism is a feature often associated with an exotic other. It implies "a short circuit in the culinary circle," a failure to discriminate between the similar and the different.[30]

Additional details support a reading of "The Big Bad Cockroach" as ad hominem satire. The other animals and insects in the poem are of various types; in the first part we are introduced to bears, a cat, mosquitos, crabs, a dog, wolves, lions, rabbits, and a toad. In short, we have a community comprised of disparate groups moving along together, albeit by various means of transportation: "They're driving and laughing, / They're munching gingerbread" (*Edut i smeiutsia, / Prianiki zhuiut*) (174). Prior to the appearance of the cockroach, the atmosphere is harmonious, even festive; the animals are laughing and eating *prianiki* (gingerbread cookies), which represent abundance and prosperity. Without warning—"Suddenly from beneath the gate" (*Vdrug iz podvorotni*)—the cockroach enters the scene and immediately alters the mood of the poem. His origin is rather vague, for *podvorotnia* means either the space between a gate and the ground or a board attached to the bottom of a gate. Most important, he comes from elsewhere and is clearly an outsider. In considering the cockroach's behavior, it is noteworthy that by this time Stalin had established a reputation for himself as Commissar of Nationalities; his job was to effect (by whatever means necessary) the unification of the diverse nationalities comprising the fledgling Soviet Union.

The animals in "The Big Bad Cockroach" inexplicably acknowledge and bow to the power that the cockroach wields. Chukovsky indicts his compatriots' failure to resist the growing threat of totalitarianism by ironically cataloguing their reactions to the cockroach. The bulls and rhinoceroses decline a confrontation, saying: "We would get the enemy / With our horns / But our skins are precious, / And horns are also not cheap these days" (*My vraga by—/ Na roga by, / Tol'ko shkura doroga, / I roga nynche tozhe ne deshevy*) (175). The crocodiles and elephants hide, their teeth chattering in fright. The monkeys pack their suitcases, "And as fast as their legs can carry them / Take to their heels" (*I skoree so vsekh nog / Nautek*) (176). Although the animals pay obeisance to their new ruler, they secretly loathe and curse him under their breath. The cockroach's unmasking by the kangaroo and his demise are thus cathartic. The kangaroo points out that the king is naked, that he is merely a tiny insect; the diminutive suffixes she uses— *tarakashechka* and *koziavochka-bukashechka*—emphasize the incongruity of the situation (178). Ignoring the animals' terror at the kangaroo's insolence, the sparrow makes short work of the cockroach, gobbling him up and liberating them all.[31] However, at this point in the poem we are already in the realm of the fantastic and the prescriptive.

There are several reasons why a reading of Stalin as a cockroach is effective satirically. The cockroach is widely considered to be an obnoxious pest that arouses abhorrence and distress.[32] It is regarded as an unwelcome interloper, an outsider. Germans colloquially call the insect "Russe" and Russians call it *prusak,* or "Prussian."[33] Because it is associated with conditions of poor hygiene, its intrusion is at least partly the fault of its hosts. Most important, the cockroach has no positive role or function to balance its nastiness; it has exclusively negative connotations.

The word *tarakan* is etymologically linked with the concept of the tyrant. Loseff notes that it is derived from the Turkic *tarkan,* meaning "dignitary," and Jakobson attests to its pejorative nuance.[34] While these details may not be obvious to the casual reader of "The Big Bad Cockroach," one may assume that they are part of the subtext and that they influence our perception of Chukovsky's villain on some level.

Folkloric sources also offer good evidence for interpreting the cockroach as an evil character. *Usy* is rooted in the Russian folk consciousness as a slang term for "thief."[35] Several satiric folk songs utilize this metaphor. In the following example *Usy* is a thief who robs the foolish peasants:

> Oy, here is that big bad mustache-ataman
> He comes into the hut, sits down in the front,
> He says nothing, just wiggles his mustache,
> He looks around on all sides from time to time,
> The hut is packed full of mustaches,
> Oy, mustaches on the stove and mustaches under the stove,
> Mustaches on the benches, mustaches on the crib,
> Oy, cried the mustache in his loud voice:
> "Oy, come on master, turn around,
> Turn around, open up your purse,
> Give us breakfast, master."[36]

Chukovsky's innovation is to expand the symbolic equation *usy* = thief to cockroach = *usy* = thief = Stalin. The last step in this equation depends on widespread anecdotal tales claiming that Stalin was a thief in his youth. His ruthless acts of "expropriation" before the Revolution enriched the party coffers but often involved mayhem and murder.[37] Indeed, his propensity for terrorism in his early life also figures in Iskander's tale *The Feasts of Belshazzar* (see chapter 5).

Among pertinent literary sources of the image of the cockroach, Franz Kafka's *Metamorphosis* (*Die Verwandlung*) comes immediately to mind. Published in 1912, this tale offers an explicit description of Gregor Samsa's transformation into a giant insect. (Whether he is a cockroach is the subject of debate, but his appearance and behavior certainly suggest this identification.) Gregor's transformation into an insect expresses his alienation from his family and his coworkers in a very vivid manner. On one level he embodies the other that is cast out. Although Kafka's use of the insect image to express his hero's alterity prefigures Chukovsky's, the effect is quite different. Kafka creates a highly sympathetic character in Gregor; his otherness sets him apart from a base, venal society. Whereas the appearance he takes on is paradoxical, Chukovsky's characterization is straightforward. The allegorical significance of the image in "The Big Bad Cockroach" is direct; Stalin is effectively represented as a cockroach because he shares its abhorrent features.

Chukovsky's use of the image of the cockroach also seems to echo an important passage in Gorky's *Childhood* (*Detstvo*), published in 1913. Gorky's grandmother is extraordinarily close to nature and loves all living things—with the notable exception of cockroaches. She loathes cockroaches passionately and instinctively because they have no purpose. She explains her fear of them to Aleksei as follows: "'I can't understand what use they are, for the life of me. . . . They do nothing but crawl about, and they're all black. God gave the lowest creature some appointed task; the woodlouse shows a house is damp. A bedbug means the walls are dirty. A louse means that someone's going to be ill—it all makes sense! But these things—who knows what evil power lives in them or what they're here for?'"[38] In his grandmother's view, cockroaches exist outside of the divine scheme of life and are therefore evil. It is significant that the grandmother is almost a fairy-tale character in Gorky's text; the good/evil dichotomy is particularly pronounced in her case, and she embodies the former.[39] Chukovsky, one should note, had an ambivalent relationship with Gorky. From their published polemics and memoirs describing the first decade of the century, we know that Chukovsky strongly disagreed with Gorky's ideas concerning the function of art.[40] Yet Gorky was instrumental in securing Chukovsky a position at his publishing house Parus in 1916. Given the complex literary and ideological ties between the two men, a reading of Chukovsky's cockroach as a literary response to Gorky's model is plausible. In contrast to Gorky's (relatively abstract) cockroach, Chukovsky's totalitarian cockroach has a definite—and most malign—purpose.[41]

Okudzhava's "The Black Tomcat"

Bulat Okudzhava (1924–1997) enjoyed enormous stature and credibility as
a poetic spokesman of his generation. The experiences of his youth were
shared by many Russians: his father and mother were arrested in 1937; his
father was shot and his mother was sent to a camp in the Far East. He vol-
unteered for the army two years later and served in the infantry; he was
wounded several times. After his parents were rehabilitated in 1955, Okudzhava began building a successful literary career in Moscow, writing poetry
and later prose. Beginning in the late fifties, he wrote and performed guitar poetry (*avtorskaia pesnia*), first privately and then for an increasingly
large audience through the medium of *magnitizdat*. In its early stages guitar poetry met with considerable official resistance. Press reviews of his
concerts as banal and philistine were probably veiled attempts to diminish
his popularity.[42] Reflecting on the phenomenon of guitar poetry in a 1987
interview, Okudzhava said: "It was written by thinking people for thinking
people. We tried to talk to people not in the language that held sway for
many years but in the language that was concealed within them. We tried to
wake people up."[43] With the advent of glasnost, Okudzhava raised his public profile, appearing frequently on television and in published interviews.
Having lived through almost the entire Soviet period, he articulated the experience of the failure of communist idealism. In a poem published in
1994, Boris Chichibabin expresses his generation's admiration and respect
for Okudzhava:

> The nest is destroyed,
> And brother is pitted against brother,
> But all the same
> We are admirers of Bulat.[44]

Despite some difficulties resulting from his samizdat and *tamizdat* ac-
tivities, Okudzhava was largely an apolitical poet; he was certainly not a dissident in the ordinary sense of the word. By his own and others' accounts,
he strongly believed in communism "as the incarnation of truth, justice,
and the meaning of life"[45] and was a member of the party. Although his
poetry was often tendentious, it was indirect and metaphorical. This feature may have been a concession to the censorship, but it may also have
given his work broader relevance and longevity. In any case, the song-poem
"The Black Tomcat" is an important exception to this rule of indirectness.
The piece was first published in 1966 in *Sel'skaia molodezh'*. Presumably

affected by the atmosphere of the Thaw, the editor of the paper decided to turn it into a vehicle for new voices and took the rather daring step of publishing Okudzhava's poem.[46] He was consequently fired and the editorial board of the paper was reshuffled. The poem itself was consigned to a samizdat and *magnitizdat* existence within the Soviet Union until it was finally republished in 1988.[47]

As we shall see, although the widespread interpretation of "The Black Tomcat" as an allegorical treatment of Stalinism is well grounded, Okudzhava's own relationship to Stalin was complex. In some published statements he suggested that Stalinism was historically determined, that is, that Stalin's rule was necessitated by historical circumstances. He called himself a Stalinist and explained that the terror entailed forcefully suppressing doubt.[48] Yet the issue of the assignation of guilt clearly unsettled him, for he repeatedly returned to it in his poetry and prose. Particularly interesting in this respect is a cycle of twelve poems published in 1988 in *Druzhba narodov*. While all of these poems treat Stalinism and the effects of the purges, in one he questions the nature of the dictator himself:

> To Dorogomilovo from the shadow of the Kremlin,
> Wiggling his smoky mustache,
> My fellow tribesman flies past.
> He is small, unwashed, and pockmarked
> and looks confused and drink-sodden,
> but his essence is wide open space and brigandage
> in the bloody fight of the past with the future.[49]

Stalin's defining characteristics are quintessentially Russian: "wide open space" (*prostranstvo*) and "brigandage" (*razboi*) link him to the traditions of Stenka Razin and Pugachev. Okudzhava seems to conclude that his own life is inextricably interwoven with Stalinism: "I love the mustached man of the Kremlin, / and for that I love myself."[50] In his final autobiographical prose works Okudzhava ponders the question of responsibility more explicitly by revisiting the events of his own youth and reexamining the effects of the terror. In the story "Girl of My Dreams" ("Devushka moei mechty") he argues against quietly shutting the door on the past. In "The Art of Sewing and Life" ("Iskusstvo kroiki i zhit'ia") he emphasizes his own resemblance to Stalin and exorcises that aspect of his self. The novel *The Cancelled Theater* (*Uprazdennyi teatr*) recounts the many losses suffered by his extended family in the Stalin years.

All of these frank examinations of Stalin had to wait for the glasnost period, however. One can assume that similar sentiments motivated Okudzhava to compose "The Black Tomcat," but his manner in this earlier evocation of Stalin is purposefully Aesopian. The cat in the poem has been interpreted as the embodiment of the contemporary philistine, as Soviet power, as generalized tyranny, and as a satirical portrait of Stalin himself.[51] The text of the poem offers good evidence for an ad hominem reading. The cat's whiskers—or mustache (*usy*)—are mentioned twice, both times in connection with concealing a smile: "He hides a smile in his mustache" (*On v usy usmeshku priachet*); "he grins into his mustache" (*usmekhaetsia v usy*).[52] He has yellow eyes, a feature that is frequently associated with Stalin.[53]

Utterly silent, the cat uses darkness "as a shield" (*kak shchit*). While this phrase certainly refers to Stalin's habit of working in isolation at night, it also illustrates Okudzhava's satiric strategy: this Stalin-cat is a creature with whom no dialogue can occur; hence no acknowledgment of him as a subject (comparable to the author) can be made.[54] We know that the cat does not catch mice (its natural food) and that "each person brings him something / and thanks him" (*Kazhdyi sam emu vynosit / i spasibo govorit*). This act sounds very much like sacrifice and what is offered up is left unspoken; sacrifice—especially human sacrifice—is usually associated with an exotic other.[55] Okudzhava tells us that the cat "only eats and only drinks. / He touches the dirty floor with his claws / As though scraping along a throat" (*tol'ko est i tol'ko p'et. / Griaznyi pol kogtiami tronet—/ kak po gorlu poskrebet*). Consumption is thus linked with violence in the poem and Stalin's "appetite" is made to seem unnatural.

The cat of the title is individuated and consistently juxtaposed against collective groupings in the text. First he is spatially isolated: he lives in an entranceway (*pod″ezd*) "as on an estate" (*kak v pomest'e*), while the collectives are linked with the courtyard (*dvor*) and the house (*dom*). It is noteworthy that the term *dvor* is often used by Okudzhava in his poetry to signify communality.[56] The cat is referred to repeatedly in the poem as "He" (*On*); in fact, four out of the six stanzas begin with this word. His singularity is contrasted with both "All cats" (*Vse koty*) and forms of "we" (*nas, my*). The latter collective—perhaps the Russian intelligentsia—is indicted for its apathy, but it retains its unity vis-à-vis the cat, which is powerful and alien.

Klaus Dieter Seemann has convincingly demonstrated that "The Black Tomcat" is on one level a parody of Lebedev-Kumach's 1938 song "The Gardener" ("Sadovnik").[57] Given that the model is an adulatory hymn to Stalin's beneficence, the anti-Stalin force of Okudzhava's parody is enhanced through this reversal. There are also folkloric sources of the image of Stalin as a black tomcat. Many superstitions surround black cats in Russian culture, as in the West. A black tomcat may be lucky or unlucky, depending on the context in which he is encountered.[58] It is, however, essential to take a stray black cat into one's home to avoid bad luck, and under no circumstances should one kill a cat; a folk saying warns that seven years of bad luck will ensue. These superstitions may partially account for the paradoxical necessity of putting up with the tyranny of the tomcat in Okudzhava's song. The cat is a sly and resilient animal; it has nine lives and always lands on its feet. Speaking of Stalin, Okudzhava noted in an interview: "Stalin was not, after all, intelligent; he was cunning [khitr]."[59]

The religious and allegorical symbolism of the cat as a concomitant of evil has a long and solid history. Particularly interesting for a reading of Okudzhava's cat as Stalin are traditions that originate in medieval Christian thought. The devil was thought to take the form of a black tomcat and heretics were accused of worshiping him in this form.[60] Cats were consistently associated with darkness and the occult. This correlation has persisted in our century; it is certainly the basis for Bulgakov's characterization of Behemoth in *The Master and Margarita*. Okudzhava strengthens the diabolical symbolism of the cat in his work both through the yellow color of his eyes and his association with fire: "His yellow eye burns" (*zheltyi glaz ego gorit*). The reference to mice in the poem is also significant, for since the medieval period the cat chasing the mouse has been interpreted as Satan seeking to catch souls.[61]

> He hasn't caught mice for a long time —
> he grins into his mustache,
> catches us at our word,
> on a piece of sausage.
>
> [*On davno myshei ne lovit* —
> *usmekhaetsia v usy,*
> *lovit nas na chestnom slove,*
> *na kusochke kolbasy.*]

In light of the cat's connection with Satan, Okudzhava's Stalin has already "caught the mice" (i.e., souls) and now exploits and manipulates them. Another medieval association of the cat was with the wicked priest who wanted to devour his parishioners.[62] For Okudzhava Stalin is a corrupt, evil interpreter of dogma (here Marxism-Leninism). A distorted product of the seminary himself, he "consumes" his subjects like the medieval cat-priest.

Another source of the image of the cat is fairy tales, which frequently feature feline characters. These are sometimes wise and helpful, as in "The Enchanted Ring" ("Volshebnoe kol'tso") and "The Cat, the Cock, and the Fox" ("Kot, petukh i lisa"). Often, however, fairy-tale cats are cruel and deceitful. Indeed, the protagonist of "The Cat and the Fox" ("Kot i lisa") could well serve as a model for Okudzhava's satiric version.[63] This cat is so mischievous (*shkodlivyi*) that the peasant who owns it decides to abandon it in the deep woods. There it assumes the identity of Kotofei Ivanovich, takes the fox as wife, and proceeds to terrorize the other animals. Although the bear and the wolf are much larger and stronger, they fear the cat and bring it food. For its part, the cat attacks the food—a ram and a bull—ferociously, complains that it is too little, and turns on the other animals. Here we see those fairy-tale characteristics that underpin Okudzhava's creation: Kotofei Ivanovich is sly, manipulative, tyrannical, and insatiable.

A final important source of the image of Okudzhava's tomcat is the *lubok*. *Lubki*, which often had secular, satirical themes, circulated widely in many versions and achieved considerable currency. They have influenced the poetry of such modern writers as Esenin and Gorodetsky, and their impact can be felt in Mayakovsky's ROSTA Windows.[64] Okudzhava's imagery may derive in part from "The Kazan Cat" ("Kazanskii kot"), a very popular *lubok* depicting a demonic cat with prominent whiskers and claws.[65] This work, in turn, served as the model for another well-known *lubok* called "The Mice Bury the Cat" ("Myshi kota pogrebaiut"). The cat in this case represents a deposed tyrant (originally the satirical referent was Peter I) and the mice are the Russian people. This symbolism also resonates in Okudzhava's poem.[66]

Iskander's *Rabbits and Boa Constrictors*

Fazil Iskander (b. 1929) is best known as the chronicler of Chegem, the mythical village in Abkhazia that is the locus of his *Sandro* tales. *Rabbits and Boa Constrictors*, published in the West in 1982 and in Russia in 1987,[67] is probably not Iskander's most outstanding work in aesthetic terms. Concerned with limning an allegorical portrait of tyranny, Iskander sometimes sacrifices artistry to edification in this tale, which is not to say that the work is insignificant. In grappling with the image of Stalin, it makes an important

contribution to the ongoing effort to come to terms with the dictator's legacy. Some critics have stressed the global nature of the satirical targets in
Rabbits and Boa Constrictors. Iskander himself has insisted on the general
quality of the allegory, calling it "an attempt to tell, in a very abstract form,
what power is based on."[68] Most commentators, however, have discerned
the particularized target of Iskander's satire as well.[69] This was certainly the
interpretation endorsed by the editors of *Iunost*', who published the tale
with a drawing of the Great Python (*Velikii Piton*) clad in a military service
jacket and endowed with Stalin's typical expression and posture.

A reading of *Rabbits and Boa Constrictors* as a particularized satire of
Stalinism and of the Great Python as an allegorical portrait of Stalin is not
definitive or exclusive, but it is firmly grounded. There is a plethora of extratextual evidence suggesting that Stalin looms large in the author's imagination. In considering Iskander's attitude toward Stalin, it is important to
keep in mind his relatively successful coexistence with the Soviet regime. A
ranking member of the Soviet Writers' Union, he was published widely and
frequently (although his prose often suffered heavy cuts at the hands of the
censor). Iskander has asserted that he did not subject himself to self-
censorship: "I have never known what the 'internal censor' is. Not because I
was so fearless—I am simply made that way. In the process of working you
comprehend the truth, and the joy of recognition is many times stronger
than the desire 'to stay within the boundaries.'"[70]

Beginning with glasnost, Iskander's statements about Stalin as an
individual—his nature, his personality, his relationship to Russian culture—
became increasingly outspoken.[71] He has described Stalin as a vampire and
compared his ascension to power with that of other ambitious but "morally
backward" leaders, such as Hitler, Mussolini, and Franco.[72] In a series of
essays published in 1991 entitled *Poets and Tsars* (*Poety i tsary*), Iskander
examines Stalin's psychology and behavior. These musings are particularly
germane to the portrait he creates in *Rabbits and Boa Constrictors*. Recalling
Lenin's famous "Testament" in an essay called "A Letter to Friends" ("Pis'mo
druz'iam"), Iskander concedes the omission of positive traits in his remarks
about Stalin; there were, he implies, none to be noted. Furthermore, he
freely reinterprets Lenin's statement that Stalin was "coarse" (*grub*) and
"capricious" (*kaprizen*): "There is something childish in these definitions.
He probably was thinking: despotic, perfidious."[73] In the essay called "Poets
and Tsars" he considers Stalin's reaction to Mandelshtam's poem about him
and conjectures that he probably liked it; its very existence, he notes, con-
firmed the terrible power wielded by the dictator and this confirmation

must have been satisfying. Typical of Iskander's inquisitive attitude toward Stalin, an approach that abjures simple condemnation, is a 1994 statement made in an interview in *Moscow News*: "Is it really possible to determine the point at which a tyrant becomes a tyrant? Writing my book 'Sandro of Chegem' and, naturally, without any hope that some day it would be published in my country, I mostly feared lapsing into speculations on hatred for Stalin."[74]

In his artistic prose—and especially in *Sandro of Chegem*—Iskander has frequently revisited questions pertaining to Stalin and Stalinism. The tale *The Feasts of Belshazzar* features a detailed psychological portrait of Stalin as a demonic tyrant (see chapter 5). Stalin is also portrayed directly in the story *Uncle Sandro and His Pet* (*Diadia Sandro i ego liubimets*). Iskander's narrator recounts the dictator's vacation fishing trip in Abkhazia, where he is accompanied by numerous NKVD agents and where he catches fish already stunned with explosives. Treating his bodyguards to roasted chicken, Stalin jokes: "Eat up the chicks, or else they'll grow up."[75] Issues connected with Stalinism are again treated in *Pshada,* a later contribution to the *Sandro* cycle.[76] The protagonist of this story is a retired general who finds himself morally adrift in the post-Soviet world. In analyzing General Mamba's relationship to Stalinism, Iskander may be suggesting a model for comprehending a whole generation's behavior:

> General Mamba was never an outstanding Stalinist, but he felt the charm of the leader's incredible power for a long time. And after the war, when he clearly understood that some serious matter or other in the country was being handled incorrectly, in his reveries he would suddenly appear in Stalin's office and would tell him about the mistakes his comrades were allowing to happen. Stalin would listen attentively to him and, using his fantastic power, would pick up the telephone and order the mistake corrected. At these moments the general experienced great human happiness. What can be more beautiful than limitless power which is tirelessly directed toward the correction of mistakes. No red tape. Oh, the sweetness of terrible authority![77]

In this thoughtful, rather gloomy story Iskander applies what Lesley Milne calls the "device of subsequent understanding"[78] to assess Stalin's role in his country's history. As always, his goal seems to be reconciliation rather than indictment.

Returning to *Rabbits and Boa Constrictors,* one finds ample textual evidence to support a reading of the Great Python as a satirical portrait of Stalin. His speech clearly echoes Stalinist aphorisms. He cautions the boa constrictors: "Hiss in a whisper; don't forget that the enemy is inside us."[79]

Here the humor derives from the application of this abstract turn of phrase to a most concrete situation; a rabbit who has been swallowed but not yet digested is listening to the boas' discussion. The Great Python subsequently blames the boa who swallowed the unruly rabbit for failing to suppress him: "A boa from whom a rabbit speaks is not the kind of boa we need" (13). Although Natal'ia Ivanova supports Iskander's assertion that his tale should not be read as simple allegory, she notes: "In the speeches of the Python, in his lexicon and phraseology Iskander is parodying the style and the iron logic of Stalin."[80]

The Great Python displays paranoia and carries out ruthless acts of retribution against his enemies, both real and imagined. It becomes apparent that his spies are omnipresent and denunciation is a way of life. When a young boa finds himself engaged in a dubious conversation with an older boa, he hesitates to denounce him only because he might incriminate himself as a willing listener. The Great Python demands a ritual show of obeisance: "A boa who heard his greeting but did not raise his head was considered a traitor and deprived of his life" (6). He regards his kills as trophies and keeps models of them mounted on the walls of his underground palace, where he is attended by his personal physician, his aides, and his bodyguards. Most significantly, he arranges a mortal struggle between two boas as an instructive demonstration (a sort of show trial). Although it is obvious that the old boa named Squinter is not strong enough to put up a fight, the Great Python urges him on: "'Resist, resist,' shouted the tsar. 'We need experience under jungle conditions'" (136). After Squinter has been killed, the Great Python praises him: "He died for the good of the cause" (136). The Great Python's procedure certainly alludes to Stalin's destruction of Bukharin, Zinoviev, and other Old Bolsheviks in the purges.

A megalomaniac, the Great Python encourages mythmaking and demagoguery. He feigns modesty yet compels the boas to listen to the silly riddles and banal anecdotes that he relates. When necessary, he organizes "spontaneous" exchanges for the edification of his subjects. Iskander grants us access to the Great Python's thought processes in his ironic account of one of these meetings: "He wanted someone to ask him about this punishment, but no one asked. Then he whispered to one of his helpers that he should organize a question from among the rank-and-file boas" (10). The myth about the Great Python having swallowed a native is particularly pertinent to Iskander's evaluation of Stalin. It is on the basis of this feat that the Great Python was chosen tsar of the boas, whereas in actual fact (as the narrator reveals to us) the native was inebriated and incapacitated. Not only does the

Great Python fabricate the story of his having hypnotized his victim, but he himself comes to believe this version. As Iskander notes, this is perfectly understandable since "he had seen the sleeping native only once, but he had heard about his hypnotizing him hundreds of times, at first from himself and then from others" (94). Iskander's analysis demonstrates the mechanism of inflation and exaggeration of Stalin's biography in a humorous yet satirically effective manner.

A number of historical markers in the tale are allusions to events that occurred during Stalin's reign. The shift in strategy for catching rabbits from hypnosis to smothering may refer to Stalin's movement from ideological means of control to arrest and physical destruction of his enemies (what Iuliia Troll' calls the "metamorphosis of Stalinism").[81] There is more than a hint that the Great Python's death is not entirely natural (i.e., that he was murdered when he showed weakness). He is mummified by his successor, the Great Hermit, following his death, and his body is displayed "with vigilant eyes, which created a terrible ambiguity, a rather frightening hint that this was his most brilliant kill" (138). The words Iskander chooses to describe the mummy—its eyes are *bdiashchie*; it creates ambiguity that is *groznaia*; the hint it provides is *strashnovatyi*—are all coded references to Stalin. He urged *bditel'nost'*, or vigilance; he encouraged the parallel drawn between himself and Ivan *Groznyi*; he instituted the period known as *strakh*, or the terror. Following the Great Python's death, some of the boas and even some of the rabbits express nostalgia for the relative stability of his reign. One of the rabbits sighs: "In a word, what can you say . . . there was order" (146). "Order" (*poriadok*), of course, is a euphemism for Stalinism.

A particularly interesting historical allusion to Stalinism in *Rabbits and Boa Constrictors* is the phenomenon of self-consumption, or *samopoedanie*. This method of punishment (now abolished) relied on the boas' appetite being stronger than their reason: "They gave [the boa] nothing to eat for two months, and then stuck his own tail in his own mouth. It's difficult to imagine anything more instructive. On the one hand, he understands that this is his own tail and he is sorry to swallow it. On the other hand, as a boa he cannot help swallowing whatever falls into his mouth. On the one hand, he is destroying himself by eating himself. On the other hand he prolongs his own torments by feeding upon himself" (10). This procedure obliterates the difference between the boas and their usual victims, the rabbits; both may be consumed in the same manner.[82] In this passage Iskander is probably allegorizing the mechanism of Stalin's purges; the parallelism is underscored by the grotesque quality of the description.

Textual evidence for a reading of the Great Python as Stalin is thus abundant. Moreover, Iskander's procedure in rendering Stalin as a giant snake is not Aesopian; the task of establishing allegorical meaning in the text is not very challenging. As Troll' notes, "The book *Rabbits and Boa Constrictors,* despite its allegorical quality, is completely devoid of camouflage."[83] A more interesting project is to consider the significance of Iskander's characterization of Stalin as a python. The python's effectiveness as a satirical embodiment of Stalin is based on a rich complex of associations, and these function together to shape Iskander's portrait of the dictator.

Iskander's depiction of Stalin as a python draws on a common phobic response to snakes. The reaction experienced by people to snakes ranges from extreme revulsion to mild discomfort, but most of us are instinctively repelled by them. Jung's explanation of this phenomenon is helpful in understanding the mechanism of Iskander's satire. Because snakes are cold-blooded reptiles, according to Jung their psychology is definitively nonhuman: "One can establish a sort of *rapport* with almost any warmblooded [*sic*] animal but with snakes there is no parallel feeling."[84] Their reptilian nature enhances their alterity, which partially accounts for why we find them repulsive.

The fact that the Great Python rules over the kingdom of boa constrictors is significant with respect to Stalin's otherness. Pythons are both like and unlike boas; considering the actual relationship of these species helps to delineate the satiric dynamic operative in the text. The two families of snakes are actually very closely related and differ only slightly in terms of their anatomical features and behavior. Their geographical distribution, however, varies considerably; most boas occur in the New World, while pythons are for the most part Old World species. Thus Iskander's fictional situation of a python ruling boas approximately parallels the relationship of Stalin (a Georgian or Ossetian)[85] leading the majority Russian population of the Soviet Union. Moreover, Iskander suggests that nationalist sentiment was a significant force in shaping Stalinism. The Great Python ostensibly punishes a young boa for failing to hypnotize the rabbit Ponderer (*Zadumavshiisia*), but in reality (as Iskander reveals) it is for questioning his right to rule: "At a sign from the Great Python the boas began to slither off. The young boa was dragged out in the direction of the desert by two guards. 'The boas should be ruled by a boa,' he heard the mumbling of the tsar behind him, 'and do you think I'm a piece of stinking log, or what?'" (100).

Pythons are chiefly distinguishable from boas by their enormous size and strength. The giant African python is especially huge, sometimes reaching a length of twenty feet. Despite Iskander's assertion that the specifically African setting of *Rabbits and Boa Constrictors* "plays, of course, no role whatsoever" in an interpretation of the tale,[86] it would seem its placement is in fact significant. Size, however, should probably be regarded as a metaphor in the text; the Great Python is positioned far above the boas he rules in the hierarchy of power and prestige. They are characterized and addressed as *pitomtsy Pitona*, which Ronald Peterson translates as "disciple" but which also carries the meanings of "foster-child," "pupil," or "ward."[87]

It is worth noting that both pythons and boas kill their prey only by constriction. The technique of hypnosis discussed in the text derives from the popular ascription of hypnotic powers to these families of snakes.[88] Of course, the term *gipnoz*—cultural and social hypnosis—is often used to explain the phenomenon of Stalin's rise to authoritarian power as well. In describing Stalin's physical appearance, Roy Medvedev refers to his "brownish hypnotizing eyes."[89] That this force is illusory is certainly meaningful in an interpretation of Iskander's satire. Indeed, the plot of the tale turns on the rabbits' discovery that hypnosis is a chimera arising out of their own fear. *Davit'*, which describes the alternate means of killing rabbits in the tale, is also a satirically rich term. Its primary meaning is "to press" or "to squeeze," but it is also used to refer to the behavior of the state, hence "to oppress."[90] The notion of rabbits continuing to talk from the stomachs of the boas who have swallowed them is a purely fantastic detail that facilitates cathartic humor. Having nothing to lose, a rabbit can speak the truth about the Great Python:

> "Yes, me!" screamed the daring rabbit from the boa, who had turned to stone from terror. "You're the number one scoundrel among your scoundrels and a blockhead to boot!"
> "I'm a scoundrel?!" repeated the Great Python, at a loss for words from anger.
> "Yes, you're a scoundrel!" joyfully shouted the daring rabbit. (12–13)

Derivations of the image of Stalin as a python may be traced to biblical and literary sources as well. The symbolism connected with serpents in general has an obvious origin in Genesis.[91] The image of the "perfidious serpent" is based on the Old Testament account of Satan assuming the shape of a serpent to tempt Eve to taste the forbidden fruit. Snakes are thus linked with Satan as tempter and deceiver. It is significant that as a result of his deceit the serpent in Genesis is cursed by God "above all cattle"[92] and doomed to eternal enmity with man. Iskander's casting of Stalin as a snake certainly derives from this Judeo-Christian tradition, which differs markedly from that of some Eastern civilizations, where snakes are venerated.[93] A related literary source for Iskander's version of the "perfidious serpent" might be the evil python Kaa from Rudyard Kipling's *Jungle Book*. An animated film adaptation of Kipling's work was produced in the Soviet Union in the mid-seventies and was very popular with audiences.[94]

Iskander's representation of Stalin as a python is enriched by details derived from mythology. In classical myth the snake often represents destruction because of its chthonic nature.[95] The destructive quality of the serpent is sometimes emphasized by juxtaposition with the eagle, which represents "lightness or good overcoming darkness or evil."[96] This particular contrast is meaningful, given that Stalin was popularly characterized in adulatory songs and poetry as an eagle. Frank Miller cites a *novina* (or new folk song modeled on *byliny*) about the First World War and the Revolution in which "two eagles, Lenin and Stalin, see to it that the old order does not return. They call together their eaglets (the Red Army) to defend the country against the White generals and the foreign powers backing them."[97] Iskander's depiction constitutes a reversal of official twentieth-century Soviet mythology and benefits from a more deeply rooted associative relationship of the snake and the eagle.

The Greek myth of Python and Delphi sheds light on Iskander's choice of species for his satirical portrait. According to this myth, Python (for which the family of snakes was named) was a serpent who arose from the mud following a devastating flood. This flood killed all human beings except for one couple, a man and a woman, from which the human race regenerated itself. Python crept forth from the slime left over from the flood. Ovid gives the following vivid account of the creature's genesis:

> So when earth
> After that flood, still muddy, took the heat,
> Felt the warm fire of sunlight, she conceived,
> Brought forth, after their fashion, all the creatures,
> Some old, some strange and monstrous.
> One, for instance,
> She bore unwanted, a gigantic serpent,
> Python by name, whom the new people dreaded,
> A huge bulk on the mountain-side.[98]

Python lived in the caves near Mount Parnassus and terrorized the people living in those parts for many years. The god Apollo eventually slew him, liberating the populace and earning the name "Pythian Apollo."

Many variants of this myth of Python and Delphi provide a kind of template for reading Iskander's satirical characterization of Stalin. Joseph Fontenrose has researched the myth exhaustively and the typology he develops in his work is useful in the present analysis.[99] Iskander's Great Python is, on some level, a descendent of the mythological Python and shares some of his monstrous characteristics. In the first place, the enemy (the serpent) is of divine origin, usually the son of a primordial mother and/or a god father. The Great Python (and his subjects) are described as "descendents of the dragon" (*potomki drakona*) (97). The identity of the dragon is not specified, but he is certainly a supernatural entity. Fontenrose's second generic feature is that the enemy has a distinct habitat that is exotic, a site where monsters and demons customarily dwell. Iskander's Great Python rules a kingdom in Africa, a place that is decidedly foreign for the Russian imagination. To emphasize its exoticism, the narrator tells us that his tale takes place "in a certain very southern country" (1). Third, according to Fontenrose, the enemy has an extraordinary appearance and supernatural abilities. In some variants of the Python myth the serpent takes on enormous proportions and transcends the boundaries of the natural world. Moreover, it can cause the death of its victims with a mere glance or with its breath. As was previously noted, the Great Python is distinguished by his literal and figurative size; he is larger than the boas by virtue of his species and he enjoys greater stature and prestige. He is especially adept at hypnosis; indeed, he is renowned for his "outstanding swallowings" (94) carried out when his victims are hypnotized. Iskander's attribution of this power to his antihero (illusory though it is) gains credence through its link to the myth of Python. It also connects him more firmly to Stalin, whose death-dealing glance was infamous. Fontenrose's fourth theme is the enemy's viciousness and greed. The serpent in the Python myth was "a despotic ruler or master who oppressed his subjects and imposed tribute."[100] The orders of Iskander's Great Python are carried out by his henchmen without question, and he brutally punishes those subjects whom he suspects of treason or even of exercising free thought (e.g., the vegetarian boa Stubby). A related feature established by Fontenrose is the serpent's conspiring against heaven to take control of the world. The Great Python, we are told, is an amoral, soulless creature who recognizes no authority higher than himself. His soul is located at the bottom of his stomach (i.e., he is motivated by base physical appetites, not spiritual concerns). He is mystified by the rabbits' notion of a vow of silence and is satisfied with the explanation offered by his grand vizier: "'What's a vow of silence?' 'An after-dinner nap,' answered [the grand vizier]" (97).

Beyond these five characteristics of the enemy serpent delineated by
Fontenrose, the model of the myth of Python as a template for reading
Iskander's satiric portrait of Stalin breaks down. The additional five themes
adumbrated are all connected with the appearance of a champion who
challenges the enemy and ultimately slays him. No champion emerges in
Rabbits and Boa Constrictors; if the Great Python is slain, it is by covert
means. Moreover, he is replaced by another ruler nearly as tyrannical as he
was. This departure from the mythological model is significant, for it suggests that Stalin's power was uniquely invincible. Though it is called for by
the myth that underlies Iskander's characterization, the intervention of a
serpent slayer is not realizable when the serpent is Stalin.

The historical referent of Stalin's purges contained in the notion of self-
consumption (*samopoedanie*) has already been mentioned. This punishment is also rooted in the symbol of the Ouroboros, the "tail eater" or the
"encircled serpent." In alchemy it is represented as a winged serpent and
wingless serpent devouring each other; each is eating the tail of the other,
forming a ring. The symbol may be traced back to late antiquity; the fifth-
century *Hieroglyphica* lists its three meanings as "eternity," "the universe,"
and "power."[101] In general, the self-consuming serpent is "an obvious emblem of the unity of the cosmos, of eternity, where the beginning is the end
and the end is the beginning."[102] Jung explicates the symbol of the encircled
serpent as representing the relationship of man's consciousness to darkness
or, more broadly, the relationship between good and evil. The alchemistic
emblem, he suggests, finds an analogue in the figure of Yin and Yang, "the
transformation into each other, being conceived and born of each other,
the one eating the other, and the one dying becoming the seed of itself in
its own opposite."[103] Here darkness and light, good and evil are present in
equal and eternal balance. The cyclical, eternal, and interdependent quality
of Ouroboros is important to an understanding of Iskander's evaluation of
Stalin. Stalin, the dark side of the self, may be a manifestation of cosmic
evil, inevitable and necessary as darkness is to light. There is more than a
hint of symbiosis in this arrangement, which Ivanova has called "a special
type of monstrous coexistence."[104]

Iskander's *samopoedanie* also echoes Nietzsche's vision of the "heavy
black snake" in *Thus Spoke Zarathustra*. The following horrific passage has
been the subject of considerable analysis: "And truly, I had never seen the
like of what I then saw. I saw a young shepherd writhing, choking, con-
vulsed, his face distorted; and a heavy, black snake was hanging out of his
mouth. Had I ever seen so much disgust and pallid horror on a face? Had

he, perhaps, been asleep? Then the snake had crawled into his throat—
and there it had bitten itself fast."[105] The only way that the shepherd can
save himself is to bite off the serpent's head. These two acts of biting in
Nietzsche's text suggest mutual consumption; the serpent and the shepherd
significantly bite each other's throats. Iskander's description of the snake
swallowing itself as punishment may derive part of its force from resonance with this model. Jung has interpreted Nietzsche's black snake as the
shepherd's own shadow, his "other side" or "second self."[106] He must bite
the snake's head off to recognize and accept the darker side of his nature.
This loathsome, repulsive creature (the other) must be consumed and integrated into the self. Stalin, the serpentine, monstrous other, must be recognized and reconciled with the self through an act that is on some level a
form of punishment. Though it will cause the shepherd great disgust ("Had
I ever seen so much disgust and pallid horror on a face?"), this consumption is necessary for survival. Iskander implies that to recognize Stalinism
as a part of Russian/Soviet history and culture proper will induce self-
loathing, but that it is essential for the restoration of health.

Conclusion

It is interesting to note the relationship between the beast metaphor and
other conventional forms of alterity thus far considered. As we shall see,
Antichrist is the Beast and the devil often takes on animal forms in popular
lore (especially the guises of cat, pig, and rat). Witches' familiars are animals capable of changing their appearance. Shape-shifters such as werewolves and vampires also combine animal and demonic elements (though
these cases are complicated by the admixture of human features). Animality is also closely linked to insanity; lunacy is (or historically was) regarded
as the ascension of the bestial in man. The amorality of insanity renders the
madman nonhuman and alien: "Through animality, madness does not join
the great laws of nature and of life, but rather the thousand forms of a
bestiary."[107] Regardless of advances in understanding the nature of madness, this association will continue to be exploited in satire. Thus, Stalin
portrayed as a beast is related to Stalin as the devil or Antichrist, as well as to
Stalin as a madman.

Consideration of the sources—psychological, mythological, literary,
folkloric—from which these animal portraits of Stalin are derived provides us with a richer, fuller interpretation of the images. Certainly equat-
ing Stalin with a cockroach, a cat, and a snake achieves the satiric effect of

diminution. To picture the dictator as a beast is to deflate his grandiose and terrible reputation. The reader experiences some degree of catharsis when the characters' identity is established.

As Girard has demonstrated, the other may be made to serve as a scapegoat; the other is defined and expelled to preserve or restore social order. We may see these portraits of Stalin—pernicious insect, evil feline, odious reptile—as gestures of expulsion and purification. Rejecting Stalin as a foreign interloper affirms the health of the self (i.e., Russian culture). However, the other may be a location (or, as in this case, an animal being) to which problematic feelings about the self are displaced. Indeed, these beast portraits of the dictator may represent parts of the self that the self finds intolerable. All of this suggests that these writers' interrogation, definition, and exclusion of Stalin as alien have profound implications for their relationship with Russian culture. Chukovsky, Okudzhava, and Iskander are self-consciously moral writers. In these texts they are engaged both in exorcising Stalinism and in questioning the essence of the culture that permitted its encroachment.

Redefinition of the self is a dynamic closely connected with the process of exclusion of the other. Demonstrating what Russianness is *not* in these animal characterizations of Stalin contributes to the ongoing dialogue about what Russianness *is*. As we shall see, this assertion of identity is often implicit; in portrayals of the antithesis of the self (or what the authors perceive the self to be), an image of that self emerges. Here we are presented with an illustration of the dual function of satire: on the one hand, exposing, blaming, excoriating, and, on the other, affirming, defending, championing.

3

Stalin in a Dress

One of Russian satire's most productive means of exorcising Stalin is casting him as a feminine or androgynous entity, other in relation to a cultural self that is decidedly male. Despite the mythology of "mother Russia" and a purported matriarchal prehistory (reaching back to the Amazons),[1] Russia has been a male-dominated society for many centuries. Alongside a cult of motherhood, a fear of woman as temptress characterizes Russian Orthodoxy; women have been associated with sin and the occult since the Middle Ages. Moreover, scholars have identified a revulsion expressed toward the maternal body that coexists with the veneration of motherhood in Russian philosophy and art.[2] The tradition of the *terem*—the isolation and restriction of female members of the upper classes—in Muscovite Russia instantiated the idea that women were best kept invisible.

In this chapter I examine two works of satire that establish Stalin's alterity by blurring gender lines. Vladimir Voinovich's *Life and Extraordinary Adventures of Private Ivan Chonkin* (*Zhizn' i neobychainye prikliucheniia soldata Ivana Chonkina*), written in 1963–70 and published in 1975, includes a dream sequence where Stalin is depicted in a dress. An embedded story in Iuz Aleshkovsky's novel *Kangaroo* (*Kenguru*), written in 1974–75 and published in 1981, portrays Stalin's leg as an independent (feminine) character who confronts and defies the dictator. As we shall see, regendering Stalin is a very effective technique of diminution and mockery given the fact that he is an exaggeratedly male cultural icon. His feminization—through transvestism, fetishism, and literary synecdoche—places him firmly beyond the pale of what is comfortably *svoi* in the Russian worldview.

Misogynist Satire

Regendering Stalin relies on the rich traditions of misogynist satire, which is ubiquitous in the West and Russia. As Matthew Hodgart has noted, "The fact that, unlike racial minorities or political regimes, women cannot be banished or abolished but are here for ever [*sic*] is . . . a deeper source of irritation to the male satirist as well as a more persistent stimulus to writing than those produced by any other subject."[3] Satire targeting women conventionally relies on the gap perceived by the satirist between real women and feminine ideals of modesty, purity, and docility. A sixth or seventh century B.C. model of misogynist satire is a poem written by Semonides of Ceos in which bad wives are compared to animals (the yapping bitch, the lazy sow, the vixen, and so on). Lucretius, writing in the first century B.C., devoted the fourth and longest book of his monumental *De Rerum Natura* to a diatribe against women. Juvenal's "Satire 6" dating from the second century A.D., has become the prototype for misogynist satire; in order to illustrate the gross sensual appetites of women, Juvenal provides portraits of their perfidy and immorality. Boccaccio's *Il Corbaccio,* or *The Labyrinth of Love* (1355) owes much to Juvenal. In this prose satire a series of extremely negative portraits of women are woven into a composite caricature. It is foolish to love any woman, Boccaccio insists, because they are all cruel, petty, dirty, and corrupt. Shakespeare's plays include bitterly satirical attacks on women, the most vituperative of which is probably Hamlet's harangue against Ophelia: "God hath given you one face, and you make yourselves another. You jig, you amble, and you lisp, and nickname God's creatures, and make your wantonness your ignorance."[4] Shakespeare's misogynist satire, however, is fleeting; for all its force, it never constitutes the core of a work as it does in Juvenal's or Boccaccio's texts. Boileau's "Satire X" (1692–93) portrays women in a most unflattering light. He gives us a verbal gallery of negative types, some meant to be universal, others specific to late-seventeenth-century France (e.g., the dishonorable woman, the flirt, the nag, the jealous wife, the hypochondriac). A special place in the pantheon of misogynist satire must be reserved for Jonathan Swift's eighteenth-century poems on women. Like Juvenal, Shakespeare, and Boileau, Swift is horrified by what he perceives as woman's penchant for deception and concealment. Pope's satires on women (also dating from the eighteenth century) seem gentle by comparison, but they also express hostility and disdain. Beginning with the Enlightenment, pro-feminist sentiment became rather fashionable and blatantly malicious works declined in number. The Romantics as a whole were also not inclined toward misogynist satire. In modern literature misogyny tends to be more subtly expressed in works that are not primarily satirical.[5]

Anti-feminine stereotypes have been a staple of Russian satire from its beginnings in the seventeenth century to the present day. "The Comely Cook," one of the earliest secular tales, relies on a popular perception of women as naïve, weak, and capricious for much of its satirical effect. Fonvizin's play *The Minor* is exemplary of eighteenth-century satire in its portrayal of women as petty and manipulative. Although completely deprived of power in the political and economic realms, women are tyrannical in the domestic sphere; such is the picture presented by eighteenth-century Russian satirical literature. The classics of nineteenth-century satire— Griboedov's *Woe from Wit* (*Gore ot uma*), Gogol's *Dead Souls* (*Mertvye dushi*), Saltykov-Shchedrin's *Golovlev Family* (*Gospoda Golovlevy*)—all depend at least in part on misogynist stereotypes; young women are temperamental and irrational, whereas older women are harsh and domineering. One can discern echoes of these stock attributes in the female characters of twentieth-century Russian satire as well. In Mayakovsky's *Bedbug* (*Klop*), Zamiatin's "X" ("Iks"), Ilf and Petrov's *Twelve Chairs* (*Dvenadtsat' stul'ev*), and other works we find female characters who are either foolish and gullible or deceptive and exploitative.

Feminine images function particularly effectively as object or other in Russian satire because of the strongly patriarchal nature of Russian culture. As Francine du Plessix Gray asserts, "The female may still experience a greater alienation and otherness in the Soviet Union than in any other advanced nation that comes to mind."[6] Indeed, the perception of woman as object—characterized by immanence and passivity—is pervasive in Russian life and art. This tradition has been shaped and strengthened by history. The Orthodox Church tended to demonize women, associating them with sin and depravity.[7] Russian folk sayings reflect deep-seated misogyny: "Long in hair, short in brains"; "A girl seen is copper, a girl unseen is gold"; "I thought I saw two people, but it was only a man and his wife." In nonsatirical literature the tradition of denigrating women has been manifested in the widespread image of the "demonic woman" (e.g., Turgenev's Zinaida in "First Love" ["Pervaia liubov'"], Dostoevsky's Natas'ia Filippovna in *The Idiot* [*Idiot*], Tolstoy's Anna Karenina), an intensified variation of the "strong woman."[8]

Because of these strong currents of misogyny in Russian culture and Russian art, rendering Stalin as a feminine or androgynous entity is an effective satiric procedure. On the basic level of stereotype, portraying him as a woman or a feminized man is a gesture of diminution and mockery. As Tzvetan Todorov has demonstrated, the "worst insult . . . that can be addressed to a man is to treat him as a woman."[9] On a deeper level, feminizing Stalin is a powerful satirical strategy because of the connotations of feminine otherness. For Emmanuel Levinas feminine alterity is the most radical case, "the absolutely contrary contrary, whose contrariety is in no way affected by the relationship that can be established between it and its correlative."[10] In much psychoanalytic discourse woman is defined in terms of absence; she is a negative construct. Not having identity or autonomy of her own, she is not-man, differentiated only in regard to man. Elaborating on this question, Simone de Beauvoir writes: "She is the incidental, the inessential as opposed to the essential. He is the Subject, he is the Absolute—she is the Other."[11] In satire feminine images are productively projected onto the foreigner, or onto one whom the satirist would cast as a foreigner.[12] Julia Kristeva has shown that the prototypical foreigners, the Danaïdes, are indeed women. These mythical foreigners are descended from Io, a woman condemned to exile for her passion, to permanent foreignness. Moreover, in Io's likeness, the Danaïdes are bestial (another aspect of otherness).[13] In various texts and illustrations treating "savages," one sees that the most savage individuals are females; they are often the most enthusiastic cannibals.[14] Although studies on cannibalism indicate that this situation bears little resemblance to reality, imagining women's extreme cruelty and brutality nevertheless reinforces their otherness.

The feminine other is often demonized in Russian culture. Mikhail Vrubel's depiction of the Demon in several works (*The Seated Demon, Head of the Demon, The Flying Demon*) establishes the prototype of the androgynous, feminized devil. In a marked departure from Lermontov's conception of the Demon, Vrubel's rendition reflects Solovev's philosophy of androgyny as the fusion of the earthly and the divine (or the demonic). In literature Tsvetaeva's devil in the autobiographical story "The Devil" ("Chert") is endowed with feminine characteristics. It is described as both Great Dane and lioness, likened to both a Ryazan peasant woman and the serpent of Eden, bisexual if not androgynous. As Pamela Chester has noted in her analysis of Tsvetaeva's devil, diabolic power need not be phallic.[15] Of course, Vrubel and Tsvetaeva have individual aesthetic and philosophical bases for depicting the devil as an androgyne. Yet it seems to be the case in other, non-Russian works as well that a feminized devil is more threatening than an unambiguously male demon: "The devil stands as an accepted, almost respected, member of the society. He operates from a position within the psychological and religious structure of the culture. The demon woman, in contrast, is the outsider, more dangerous by far because she questions the validity of all aspects of a patriarchal society's assumptions."[16]

Feminizing Stalin, then, is a satirical device that carries a heavy connotative charge. To imagine Stalin as a woman or androgyne is to confine and define him, to make him the object of regard; the procedure enhances his otherness. The dynamic of positioning the feminine as definitively alterior has been convincingly challenged on philosophical grounds.[17] Recent criticism has also shown that the otherness of the feminine is more complicated than mere opposition. However, in the context of Russian satire—particularly anti-Stalinist satire—casting the target as feminine or androgynous is remarkably powerful.

Voinovich's *Ivan Chonkin*

Probably the most explicit example of the satirical feminization of Stalin is found in Vladimir Voinovich's *Life and Extraordinary Adventures of Private Ivan Chonkin.* Voinovich's own biography—like that of many of his contemporaries—was shaped by Stalinism, and his anti-Stalinist stance is clear. It is certainly relevant that when he was a young boy his father was arrested on what Voinovich calls "an absurd political charge"[18] and spent about five years in the camps. Apparently his becoming a dissident was a gradual process and began in earnest only after Stalin's death (which, given the fact that Voinovich was twenty-one in 1953, is hardly surprising). Nevertheless, Robert Porter's assertion that the moral imperative underlying Voinovich's writing is just as strong as that which drove Solzhenitsyn is well taken;[19] for all the humor of his work, it is firmly centered on humanist ethics.

Voinovich's publicistic writings confirm that he feels tremendous personal antipathy toward Stalin. In a feuilletonistic piece entitled "Nostalgia" ("Nostal'giia") included in *The Anti-Soviet Soviet Union* (*Anti-sovetskii Sovetskii Soiuz*), he refers to Stalin as a criminal and compares him with Hitler, Mussolini, Mao Zedong, and Enver Xoxha. Musing on Svetlana Alliluyeva's motives in returning to the Soviet Union, he expresses his own desire that Stalin's legacy might be eradicated: "I personally would have hoped the grave had been overgrown with tall weeds and its sinister spirit had ceased hanging over Russia."[20] In a 1983 article he ironically credits Stalin with introducing collectivization, industrialization, and "gulagization," but notes that his efforts to undermine belief in communist ideology were only partially successful.[21] This quite serious enmity has not prevented Voinovich from treating Stalin humorously in his literary works. In "A Circle of Friends" ("V krugu druzei"), for example, Stalin is portrayed as a buffoon; this story depicts Stalin's inner circle of henchmen crudely carousing on the night of Hitler's attack on the Soviet Union.[22] In *Pretender to the Throne* (*Pretendent na prestol*), the sequel to *The Life and Extraordinary Adventures of Private Ivan Chonkin*,[23] Stalin appears as a more developed character and takes on diabolical features.

Although he does not have the status of an independent character in *Ivan Chonkin*, Stalin is a major target of satire in this novel, being mentioned about twenty times in the text. In the following illustrative examples Voinovich suggests the pervasive nature of the cult of the dictator that forms the cultural backdrop for his story: children are taught to love Stalin more than their parents; toasts to Stalin are obligatory in all cases; his name and images of him are virtually sacred. The paranoia that permeates Soviet society is brilliantly satirized in a scene in which Borisov, the secretary of the District Commission Machine and Tractor Station, inadvertently strikes a bust of Stalin in a gesture of emphasis. Both Borisov and Golubev, the kolkhoz chairman, are terrified of the implications of this act: "His mouth suddenly went dry. He opened his mouth and stared at Golubev as if hypnotized. Golubev, meanwhile, was scared to death himself. He hadn't wanted to see it, but he had seen it, he had! And now what was there to do? Pretend he hadn't noticed? But what if Borisov ran and confessed, then he would be out of trouble, but he, Golubev, would catch it for not reporting it in the first place. And if he did report it, they'd be glad to lock him up just for what he'd seen."[24] Much of the humor of this passage derives from incongruity. Although Stalin is merely a bust, even in this guise he acts forcefully on the other characters and inspires terror in them. The episode of Moisei Solomonovich Stalin's encounter with the security organs emphasizes the degree of fear connected with Stalin's name. Sensing the likelihood of severe retribution for abusing the shoemaker Stalin, Svintsov becomes obsequious. A slight mistake in proofreading, whereby Stalin becomes a "gelding" (*merin*) rather than the "measure" (*merilo*) of greatness indirectly causes the editor's death. All of these consequences of Stalin's presence—only as a name or image—are exaggerated ad absurdum. The fact that Stalin does not appear is indeed the point; his disembodied but omnipresent spirit is sufficient to inspire dread.[25]

In satirizing Stalin in *Ivan Chonkin*, Voinovich generally employs conventional descriptors. His voice emerges from the loudspeakers "with a distinct Georgian accent" (167) and Chonkin listens to "the words spoken with the noticeable Georgian accent" (167–68). While Voinovich does not actually render Stalin's accented speech (as, for example, Solzhenitsyn does in *The First Circle*), he emphasizes this peculiarity by way of humorously diminishing his stature. Even in Chonkin's dreams Stalin is described in largely conventional terms: he holds "his famous pipe" and "grinned slyly into his mustache" (99). One of Voinovich's dream sequences provides a most unusual depiction of Stalin, and it is this passage that accomplishes the work of feminizing Stalin. Since it is brief, it bears quoting at length:

> Just then Comrade Stalin descended slowly from the sky. He was wearing a woman's dress and had a mustache and a pipe between his teeth. There was a rifle in his hands.
>
> "Is this your rifle?" he asked sternly, with a slight Georgian accent.
>
> "Yes," mumbled Chonkin, tongue-tied, and he reached out for his rifle. But Comrade Stalin moved away and said: "And where is the sergeant?"
>
> The sergeant dashed over, riding Trofimovich. Trofimovich pawed impatiently at the ground with his hooves, trying to buck the sergeant off, but the sergeant held him firmly by the ears.
>
> "Comrade Sergeant," said Stalin. "Private Chonkin has abandoned his post and lost his combat weapon as well. Our Red Army has no need for soldiers like this. I advise you to shoot Comrade Chonkin."
>
> The sergeant slid slowly off Trofimovich, took the rifle from Comrade Stalin, and ordered Chonkin: "Lie down!"
>
> Chonkin lay down. There was dust beneath him, marshy dust that sucked at him and got into his mouth, his ears, his eyes. He tried to rake the dust away with his hands and he waited for the command "As you were!" But there was no command, and he was sinking in deeper and deeper. Just then something cold touched the back of his neck. He knew it was the barrel of a rifle and that any second a shot would ring out . . .
>
> . . . He woke up in a cold sweat. (51–52)

Chonkin's vision of Stalin descending from the sky in a dress is amply motivated by the text. Political Instructor Yartsev, having metamorphized into a beetle at the outset of the dream, has told Chonkin that Stalin is a woman; on one level, the dream realizes this assertion. In considering the significance of his regendering, it is worth noting that this notion is extended beyond the limits of Chonkin's dream. Listening to Stalin's "Brothers and Sisters" speech on the radio, Chonkin is confused by Lidiia Ruslanova's singing. He presumes that it is still Stalin's voice he hears: "He sings good too. 'Valenki, valenki.' Only why in a woman's voice?" (168). Of course, Chonkin's musings are humorous, and the reader understands that his perception of the situation stems from his dim-wittedness. Yet this passage subtly underscores the idea of Stalin as feminine that is established in the dream sequence. Furthermore, there may be a historical basis for Voino-vich's portrayal of Stalin in a dress. In his memoiristic account of Stalin, Trotsky recalls the latter's attempt to elude the tsarist police by slipping out of a concert "dressed up in a woman's mantle."[26] While this story may be apocryphal, it seems to have influenced Voinovich's satirical procedure and—since it is part of popular lore about Stalin—reinforces the image of Stalin as a transvestite that Voinovich overtly presents in his text. This vi-gnette may also echo (as does Trotsky's account) the Soviet myth that in October 1917 Kerensky escaped from the Winter Palace dressed as a woman. Voinovich thus makes use of a means of ridicule previously employed by both Stalinist and anti-Stalinist propaganda.[27]

Chonkin's dream of Stalin has intrigued commentators. Peter Petro suggests that the dream functions primarily to characterize Chonkin and that Stalin's descent from the sky indicates that Chonkin views him as lord. Sally Anne Perryman compares the dream to those found in Gogol's works and views Voinovich's Stalin as a mythical figure. Evgenii Gollerbakh spec-ulates that the passage reveals a conflict in Chonkin's psyche between his loyalty toward Stalin and his love for Niura. Certainly Grigori Svirski's point that the dream serves to express the paranoia and anxiety endemic to Sta-linism is well taken. Porter detects relatively uncomplicated ridicule of Sta-lin in this passage. Rancour-Laferriere posits symbolic castration of Stalin as the underlying meaning of the dream.[28]

Stalin's appearance in a dress depends in part on the conventions of misogynist satire. The dress reminds us of the deceptive nature of women, for according to this tradition the feminine arts (including feminine cloth-ing) are a means of concealing carnal impurities and corruption. Stalin's clothing thus suggests his own duplicitous nature; by wearing a dress, he signals to the reader that he is concealing his true essence. Moreover, trans-vestism brings the cross-dresser's attempt at deception into sharper focus; Stalin's overt donning of women's clothing paradoxically emphasizes the duplicity of his attempt to disguise himself. This effect is heightened by the selectivity of Voinovich's account. Stalin's mustache and pipe are markedly male accoutrements, and they easily belie his costume. The rifle that he carries is also traditionally (and symbolically) associated with maleness, and its presence emphatically contradicts the deception of the dress.

The force of Voinovich's satirical exposé of Stalin is enhanced by the fact that the transvestite is even more alien than is woman vis-à-vis the male cultural self. Transvestism carries connotations that are related but not identical to those of the feminine. For example, cross-dressing is explicitly forbidden in the Old Testament. Deuteronomy 22:5 counsels: "A woman shall not wear an article proper to a man, nor shall a man put on a woman's dress; for anyone who does such things is an abomination to the Lord, your God." Religious decrees have sometimes advocated excommunication as the penalty for breaking this law.[29] The basis for this taboo seems to be the danger of gender confusion, with the potential result of sexual deviance. It is noteworthy that in some religious and folkloric rituals cross-dressing simulates androgyny, which in turn implies the reintegration of opposites and a return to chaos.[30] Most importantly, transvestism is perceived as liminal and dangerous because it is located in the same "tension field" as homosexuality. In fact, transvestism has no particular association with homosexuality. Recent research in this area suggests that a desire to dress in the clothes of the opposite sex does not imply a lasting wish to be a member of that sex.[31] However, satire is not so much concerned with fact as it is with popular or readerly perception. The implications of Stalin's female attire in this passage are sufficiently explicit (especially in the homophobic context of Russian culture) to cast him beyond the pale.

Chonkin, too, may be regarded as a transvestite, for he begins to wear Niura's apron after he moves in with her and takes up domestic duties in her house. (This interpretation necessitates adopting the broadest possible definition of transvestism to include the behavior of characters not consciously attempting to cross-dress; rather "the authors . . . represent the subject garb in terms that gender it as masculine or feminine—i.e., as cross-gendering the wearer.")[32] This detail creates a parallel between Chonkin and Stalin that is potentially problematic since Chonkin clearly represents the moral antithesis of Stalin's evil. Laura Beraha suggests that this shared proclivity is one aspect of what she calls a "symmetry of inversions." In her reading Stalin is an imposter, a corrupt mirror image of Chonkin's rogue character.[33] The distinction between Chonkin's and Stalin's versions of cross-dressing is also pertinent. That is, Chonkin's donning an apron to do housework is a comedic gesture; it feminizes him, but the effect is incongruous and humorous. Indeed, his masculinity seems to be enhanced by his wearing an apron, for he pursues Niura tirelessly. Stalin's dress, by contrast, contributes to the surreal quality of Chonkin's nightmare. Not particularly funny, it is instead associated with terror, for it is Stalin, clad in a dress, who orders Chonkin to lie down to be shot. Thus, the nature of Stalin's transvestism is quite different than Chonkin's, and the connection established between them through this detail primarily serves to emphasize their dissimilarity.

Although transvestism bears only a tangential relationship to androgyny,[34] Stalin's dress implies the possibility that he is androgynous. This implication appears to be underscored by an association made in Chonkin's dream between Stalin and Baba Iaga. Halimur Khan has astutely pointed out the passage's folkloric subtext: Stalin "flies" down to confront Chonkin, and his pipe and rifle are analogues of Baba Iaga's mortar and pestle. The mortar and pestle—respective symbols of the womb and the phallus—coexist in the image of the witch, resulting in an androgynous whole.[35] One can see a similar dynamic at work in the combination of Stalin's pipe and rifle, overlaying as it does the suggestion of androgyny established by his clothing. Buttressed by the implication of androgyny, the parallel Voinovich draws between Stalin and Baba Iaga suggests that Stalin, too, is a sinister, predatory being. In addition, this linkage hints at Stalin's relationship to the demonic or the unclean force, which is more fully developed in other works (see chapter 5).

Although the androgyne is often credited with magical powers in other cultures, in the Russian cultural context he is placed in a liminal position that is decidedly negative.[36] Like the homosexual, the androgyne is widely despised as a symbol of the undesirable and disturbing blurring of gender categories. To insinuate that Stalin is an androgynous figure is a particularly powerful device, given that his image (the created product of the cult of personality) is a markedly masculine one. In socialist realist art, for example, he is often portrayed as larger than life;[37] in portraits and in films he stands physically taller; and in literature he is figuratively greater—wiser, more insightful, more prophetic, more humane—than his comrades. Furthermore, he is usually pictured visually and verbally with his masculine accoutrements of mustache and pipe. The appellation frequently applied to him in official propaganda—the Father of Nations (*Otets narodov*)—is markedly masculine. Sots art has parodied precisely this aspect of Stalin's persona in its irreverent depictions of the dictator, most notably in Komar and Melamid's "Nostalgic Socialist Realism" series.

Finally, rendering Stalin androgynous, or potentially androgynous, as Voinovich does may link him with Christ, who is sometimes regarded as an androgynous figure.[38] This association is probably strengthened by the association made in socialist realist art between Stalin and Christ. Socialist symbols are frequently used to produce "pseudo-religious allegory,"[39] where the figure (the portrait-icon) of Stalin takes the place of Christ blessing, sanctifying, and protecting. By linking Stalin with Christ Voinovich does not, of course, imply similarity. Rather, he underscores Stalin's diametric opposition to Christ, his position as antipode.

Aleshkovsky's *Kangaroo*

While Voinovich casts Stalin as other by dressing him in feminine attire, Aleshkovsky establishes Stalin's alterity by deconstructing the body and gendering its parts. Aleshkovsky has been one of the most vociferous opponents of Stalinism; his entire career has been devoted to debunking and deriding the Soviet state in general and Stalinism in particular. He spent several years in the early fifties in prison camps, ostensibly for breach of military discipline during his service in the navy. Following his release, he worked as a truck driver and a laborer on construction sites, while also developing a literary career. His was one of the first "free voices" of the Thaw. Officially Aleshkovsky was a member of the Soviet Writers' Union, authoring children's books and screenplays, but he had a second life performing his own songs. His "Song about Stalin" ("Pesnia o Staline") (also called "Comrade Stalin" ["Tovarishch Stalin"]) is one of the best known underground works of the Thaw period.[40] Although his prose works only began to appear in the West in 1980, they circulated widely in samizdat much earlier. In particular, the tale *Nikolai Nikolaevich* (published in 1980) enjoyed great popularity as a samizdat text. The *Metropole* anthology of 1979 included three of Aleshkovsky's songs, one of which treated lesbian sex (a subject strictly taboo at the time). Aleshkovsky emigrated the same year and continued to voice strident opposition to the Soviet regime in exile. According to one reviewer, he should be regarded as a major figure of the older (*zastoi*) generation and the single most influential writer of "non-normative" prose.[41] In the post-Soviet era his works have been published in a three-volume collection with an introduction by Brodsky.

Aleshkovsky's prose works—both novels and stories—are explicit diatribes against Soviet communism. *Masquerade* (*Maskirovka*, 1980), *The Modest Blue Handkerchief* (*Sinen'kii skromnyi platochek*, 1982) and *Carousel* (*Karusel'*, 1983) all satirize Soviet ideology. *The Hand* (*Ruka*, 1981) is an extended monologic expression of rage against the crimes of Stalinism. *Kangaroo* includes a lengthy satirical portrait of Stalin. Aleshkovsky was overt in his condemnation of the Soviet system in his public statements and interviews. The following excerpt from an address he delivered at a 1982 conference of Soviet and East European dissidents illustrates his outspoken style:

> But why then the Soviet regime? Please don't think that up until that [first] morning in Vienna I had never pondered the nature of Marxism-Leninism and the bloody Stalinism it engendered. Possibly I was too intent on finding a metaphysical solution to the problem; or perhaps the search for a convenient sociological system of explanation interfered with the posing of that extremely simple and even seemingly idiotic question: But why then the Soviet regime? Why does it exist, Lord, if three hundred million people have been deprived of the possibility of eating normally for decades[?] Why if in something over half a century's time a centuries-old natural culture has been almost completely razed? Why does it exist, if, in the place of a futile striving toward social equality, toward brotherhood, toward freedom, the masses have lived in that which at times is shamefully called in the West a "closed society" and, to put it more precisely, a prison of entire peoples unprecedented in the history of mankind?[42]

Aleshkovsky's anti-Soviet stance, while extremely firm, is expressed in an idiosyncratic manner. His extensive use of *mat* (obscene language) and camp jargon is—or, rather, was—controversial. However, his profane diatribes effectively convey the rage and frustration of his narrators. (He almost always uses extended first-person narration in his texts.)[43] Just as he has flouted linguistic taboos, so he has challenged thematic conventions, most notably the treatment of sexuality. Priscilla Meyer suggests that for Aleshkovsky delicacy with respect to sex was a lie perpetuated by the Russian literary tradition.[44] He writes what might be considered pornographic texts; sexuality is debased, perverse, violent. However, what appear to be blatantly misogynist works are on some level allegories about the abuse of power, the ruling theme of Aleshkovsky's prose. Because women are often the object of brutalization and coercion in his work, his feminization of Stalin in *Kangaroo* is especially significant. Positioning Stalin as feminine other is, in the larger context of Aleshkovsky's oeuvre, a decisively reductive, diminishing gesture.

The consistent narrative voice in *Kangaroo* is that of Fan Fanych, a recidivist thief who has fallen into the hands of the KGB. Throughout most of the book Stalin is a peripheral figure; although Fan Fanych's references to him are scathing and vituperative, he stands outside the narrative proper. He is indicted for his role in the Second World War; Fan Fanych tells his interlocutors in prison "about the greatest commander of all times and all peoples, who should have been hauled up before the law for killing and dismembering millions of soldiers."[45] Aleshkovsky draws numerous parallels between Stalin and Hitler (a notion that was still very shocking in the seventies). He has Hitler himself ask Fan Fanych: "Did you ever see their Führer, Stalin?" (*A fiurera ikhnego videl, Stalina?*) (117). Fan Fanych alludes to Stalin's role in violent revolutionary "expropriations" (attested by numerous biographical sources) in his summary of Stalin's career change: "He wasn't a bad crook, but he got out of the business. Became General Secretary" (*Neplokhoi byl urka, no ssuchilsia. Gensekom stal*) (118). Stalin is deprecated as old and weak. When Fan Fanych speculates that security measures are being taken in preparation for Stalin's arrival, he muses: "Maybe that's Suliko with the mustache. And he's decided to warm up his hands, cramped from hanging on to the wheel of state and party" (127). When he does actually appear in the narrative, he is described by Aleshkovsky in quite conventional terms: he is mustached, his face is pock-marked, and he smokes a pipe. He leers "like a murderer who's got away" (130) and he is compared to a wolf that kills for pleasure: "A normal wolf just kills one sheep, eats till its belly's full, and wanders around the Bryansk forest until it's hungry again. But this one, the worst of the lot, it snaps its jaws and kills the sheep that it can't eat, that weren't meant to die that day. It kills indiscriminately, nibbles a mouthful, letting the blood gush out . . . Silence . . . He knocked his pipe against his right heel. His 'Herzegovina Flor' tobacco fell on the ground" (131). Aleshkovsky charges that Stalin is soulless: "The shit was boiling up inside the leader just in the place where an ordinary guy has a soul" (131).

Most interesting in considering Stalin as feminized other is the long chapter in *Kangaroo* that recounts the dictator's participation in the Yalta Conference of 1945. This chapter is actually an embedded narrative and constitutes an independent story. The premise of this episode is that Stalin's right foot stages a rebellion and turns on him, excoriating, cursing, and taunting him with predictions of ignominious death. There is some slight historical basis for this fantastical narrative. In his memoirs R. Arsenidze recalls that Stalin was nicknamed for his extreme devotion to Lenin: "He worshiped Lenin. He lived by his arguments, his thoughts; he copied him splendidly, so much so that we mockingly called him 'Lenin's left foot.'"[46] There is, then, wicked irony in his right foot's derision: "I told you not to write *Marxism and the Nationality Question*, asshole. I told you not to go running to that bald devil Lenin with it" (147).

Stalin makes repeated attempts to silence his foot by stepping on it and rubbing it; he even briefly considers the possibility of amputation. However, it persists in blaring out the truth in the most vulgar terms. Rosalind Marsh has noted that the foot's curses parody the inflated praises characteristic of the cult of personality: "Asshole of all time! Shit of all peoples!" (*Zhopa vsekh vremen! Govno vsekh narodov!*) (133).[47] M. Keith Booker sees a parallel between Stalin's attempted suppression of his foot and his political tyranny: "Stalin's physical body becomes a locus of truth and a source of opposition to his duplicitous policies. He responds by suppressing that truth and attempting to efface the physical reality of his own body."[48] Following Booker's reading, amputation may be analogous to the national self-mutilation effected by the purges. That Stalin's own limb would rebel suggests that dissidence is a spontaneous, instinctive reaction to evil. For Aleshkovsky the physical body irrationally resists oppression even when the mind rationally complies. It is significant that it is the right foot (*pravaia noga*) that opposes him, for embedded in the adjective are connotations of "right," "true," and "just."

Somewhat surprisingly, Aleshkovsky evokes a degree of sympathy for Stalin in this text. In relating Stalin's reaction to his leg's curses, Fan Fanych tells his silent interlocutor: "You should have heard how forlornly he asked this, Kolya, how his steel voice trembled" (147). He senses the great burden of Stalin's evil and links him with Satan through this detail: "Truly, Kolya, God had it in for the bastard [*Voistinu, Kolia, Bog shel'mu metit*]. I was beginning to realize just how monstrous and unbearable Joseph Vissarionovich Stalin's grief and evil were" (133). Aleshkovsky's mixing of elevated stylistic elements with a colloquial—even vulgar—lexicon is particularly felicitous. The divorce of Stalin's limb from his body underscores his spiritual sickness, what Jacques Sarano terms *dis-grace*. According to Sarano, the perception of the body (or part of the body) as an object distinct from oneself is a pathological condition arising from sin or the Fall.[49] Continuing this line of interpretation, Aleshkovsky may be alluding to the well-known passage in the Gospel of Mark (9:45) that cites Christ's directive to reject sin in physical terms: "And if thy foot offend thee, cut it off: it is better for thee to enter halt into life, than having two feet to be cast into hell, into the fire that never shall be quenched." Paradoxically—and the biblical reference underscores the paradox—it is Stalin's right foot that can claim to be part of the cultural self; it speaks the truth, its voice is earthy and honest, it expresses the sentiments of Fan Fanych—and presumably the author.

The rebellion of Stalin's foot in Aleshkovsky's text also serves to feminize him, although the mechanism is less straightforward than in Voinovich's dream episode. According to Freud, the foot is a primitive sexual symbol found in many myths and is traditionally a male symbol, whereas shoes, slippers, and boots are considered female sexual symbols.[50] Rancour-Laferriere has demonstrated that boots had special significance for Stalin, serving as they do as reminders of physical violence.[51] Kicking, with all its connotations of humiliation and degradation, is implied in Aleshkovsky's emphatic focus on Stalin's boots. Indeed, Stalin is first described through synecdoche as a pair of boots. Locked in a cellar, Fan Fanych peers out of a window at ground level and recounts Stalin's arrival: "The door of the Lincoln opens, four kid boots get out on each side. First one foot in a laced boot, breeches striped down the seam, comes poking out the door and then another. The left. The expression of its black mug seemed to me more important than the right's" (128). On one level the amalgamation of the foot and the boot into a single entity suggests the confusion of Stalin's gender identity. A noteworthy literary precedent for this procedure may be found in Isaac Babel's short story "My First Goose" ("Moi pervyi gus'"). Savitsky's legs, famously described as girls "clad to the shoulders in shining jackboots,"[52] bespeak the narrator's sexual ambivalence, his attraction to and/or repulsion by the Cossacks.

The right foot that separates itself from Stalin also seems to represent his inner voice.[53] Certainly the foot's relationship with Stalin is intimate; the dialogues it initiates are uninhibited. It addresses Stalin familiarly as "Katso" and "Soso," and pours out remonstrations and advice saturated with *mat*. The foot's language, which is natural and spontaneous, provides an antidote to official, bureaucratic Russian. Its heavy use of *mat* may, in fact, serve a purifying purpose. Boris Uspenskii has shown that in some cases the use of taboo words is functionally related to prayer. In folk belief it is sometimes precisely what is needed to protect oneself against the devil or unclean spirits.[54] Stalin's foot, then, may be protecting itself by using *mat*, exorcising the demon that is Stalin's essential evil. Significantly, the foot exhorts Stalin to reject his perverse, distorted existence and embrace a more human life: "Have Beria expose the false theory of bases and superstructures . . . have him give the land back to the peasants, loosen the knot around the economy's throat, live like a Man a little for the rest of your days, you shitass" (144). The foot that expresses these sentiments is endowed by Aleshkovsky with feminine characteristics, such as "nature" and immanence. Its feminine identity is linguistically emphasized by numerous references to it as *ona* (since the noun *noga* is feminine); other pronominal forms and past-tense verbs follow suit: *opiat' zadoldonila* (133); *Esli ona . . . nachnet bespokoit' menia* (141); *Levaia noga, bylo, poprobovala zabrat'sia na pravuiu, no ta ee skinula* (141). Even the nouns Aleshkovsky uses to refer to the rebellious right foot are of feminine gender; it is variously *liubimitsa, svoloch'* and *predatel'nitsa.*

Aside from the issue of grammatical gender, the traditionally male symbol of the foot may become a female symbol through the mechanism of fetishism.[55] Aleshkovsky's choice of Stalin's foot as the rebellious member of his body quite clearly suggests fetishism, for the foot is a common fetish object. However, psychologists postulate that a fetishist prefers a fetish object because it is silent, safe, and cooperative. This hardly applies to Stalin's right foot, which is loud, defiant, and mutinous. There is considerable irony in the notion of a potential fetish object shrieking: "Stalin's an asshole and a fool and a miserable piece of shit! Soon you'll breathe your last and die! You've blown your life completely" (150). Aleshkovsky enhances the satirical effect of the situation by adding a second layer of incongruity: the foot's insurrection is amplified because it refuses to comply *both* as a physical appendage *and* as a fetish object. The rebellion of Stalin's foot is an echo of Fan Fanych's misadventures with his suit, which he has had turned; resenting this ignominious treatment, the suit behaves atrociously, causing Fan Fanych much embarrassment and discomfort. One could also read the suit as a fetish object (items of clothing frequently serve this function) since the humor of this episode likewise depends on the active noncompliance of an inanimate object.

Returning to Stalin's foot, it is significant that fetish objects are typically favored by fetishists because they can be harmed or destroyed without consequence. The twist in Aleshkovsky's text is that the foot is the fetishist's own and can be muffled or destroyed only to the detriment of the owner. In an effort to silence the right foot's curses, Stalin paces, rubs it, and stamps on it with his left foot. He even considers amputating it, allowing the narrator to engage in an extended reductio ad absurdum:

> The really terrible part of it was, you can't close its mouth with a blow. You couldn't *make* it shut up. You can make your conscience shut up—that's what millions of people do. But a foot isn't a conscience. So how do you get around her, the bitch? Have the presidium of the Supreme Soviet issue an *ukaz*? Well, okay, that's settled; let's amputate it. We'll attach a prosthesis. What then? Can you rely on the left foot? No! Enemies and traitors are everywhere. Consequently you have to liquidate the left foot, too, and ride around in a wheelchair like Roosevelt. . . . Anyway, to be a successful statesman you need your head more than your feet. But what if my head starts going back on the basic postulates of historical materialism? Say, what if my

head says it isn't matter that's primary, that the most important thing is—freedom of the spirit? An interesting situation. (134)

This predicament is, of course, satirically satisfying. The reader senses justice in Stalin's impasse. The feminized fetish object—his own right foot—is part of him, which suggests Stalin's androgyny or the blurring of his gender identity.

Conclusion

The dynamic of regendering Stalin's character in satire problematizes the issue of responsibility or culpability in very interesting ways. On the one hand, the dictator is cast as feminine or androgynous and his persona is thus separated from the Russian cultural self, which is strongly male. By feminizing him, these satirists effect a partial absolution; the disturbingly androgynous Stalin is an alien, a stranger, even a pretender vis-à-vis the healthily male center. On the other hand, Stalin's androgyny in these texts calls into question the very essence of the self, leaving the question of responsibility for the crimes of Stalinism open-ended. Voinovich dresses Stalin in women's clothing in a dream episode, casting him as a transvestite or androgyne. The intentional blurring of categories that occurs in this text places Stalin in a particularly problematic position, removed from the male realm but not fully female. There is no rationale other than dream logic for his wearing a dress, and this obscuring of binary categories (particularly in a society where men dressing up in women's clothing was banned)[56] calls attention to his marginality. As Marjorie Garber writes, "The apparently spontaneous or unexpected or supplementary presence of a transvestite figure in a text (whether fiction or history, verbal or visual, imagistic or 'real') that does not seem, thematically, to be primarily concerned with gender difference or blurred gender indicates a *category crisis elsewhere,* and an irresolvable conflict or epistemological crux that destabilizes comfortable binarity, and displaces the resulting discomfort onto a figure that already inhabits, indeed incarnates, the margin."[57] Aleshkovsky makes parodic use of psychological theories to carry out the process of alienation through feminization. The foot, a strong male symbol, establishes its independence and difference from its "owner." However, the foot also takes on feminine characteristics through its connection with the boot (a female symbol). It is also consistently feminized by its grammatical gender; when it takes on an autonomous existence, it becomes *ona.* Furthermore, the foot is rendered feminine through the mechanism of fetishism implicit in Aleshkovsky's objectification of Stalin's limb. It is significant that the foot is inseparable from the body as a whole, for the body (or persona) is rendered androgynous through its contiguity. Stalin's feminine otherness in these texts is best understood in the context of the broad cultural effort at lustration. Regendering him satirically in a strongly male cultural context is deeply unsettling. It is a gesture that interrogates the categories of self and other and defies any clear separation of Stalin—as anima—from the integrated self.

4

The Monster Lurks Within

A guise that Stalin assumes in some satirical texts is that of a monster, a fantastic, unnatural creature. The monstrous, laden as it is with ambiguity and hybridity, is a particularly apt metaphor for Stalin's alterity. On the one hand, Stalin as a monster originates outside the realm of Russian culture and seizes power, oppressing and distorting an essentially healthy society. On the other hand, his monstrous nature and behavior suggest the complicity or at least the passivity of those in his thrall. In order to explore the mechanism and significance of casting Stalin as a monster, I will examine two seminal texts in this chapter: Evgenii Shvarts's 1944 play *The Dragon* (*Drakon*) and Vasilii Aksenov's tale *The Steel Bird* (*Stal'naia ptitsa*), written in 1965 and published in 1977. Stalin is portrayed in these works as a poisonous dragon and a tyrannical steel bird, respectively. As we shall see, both portraits are based on rich and diverse sources; they contribute to the debate about Stalin's otherness and problematize the issues of guilt and complicity in the crimes of Stalinism.

Monsters and Satire

Aristotle, who treated monsters as part of the natural world in *Generation of Animals,* regards difference as their defining characteristic. The monster is "unlike its parents" and monstrosity is "a sort of deformity."[1] Aristotle's ideas about monstrosity, though intended to contribute to biological discourse, have been influential in other spheres (e.g., anthropology, geography, theology) as well.[2] For the Greeks and for the Plinius the Elder monstrosity was marked by deviation from physical, geographical, and linguistic norms. Monsters exhibited gigantism, dwarfism, and many other physical deformities; they engaged in bestiality and cannibalism; they inhabited liminal spaces beyond the boundaries of the known world; and they communicated in an incomprehensible, alien language. Monstrosity, then, is behavioral as well as physiological in the classical tradition, and this moral aspect is perceptible in contemporary satirical usage as well.

Monsters resist classification within the natural order. They defy our urge to categorize and are thus disturbing to our minds. They imply disorder and chaos: "The monster is dangerous, a form suspended between forms that threatens to smash distinctions."[3] For the medieval mind transgression of the boundaries of nature was the source of monstrosity. Mixing the natural elements resulted in disease, insanity, and deformity. Preoccupation with the external, natural order reflects a concern with internal balance and projects radical otherness onto phenomena or ideas that defy these systems. According to David Williams, "The negation of the structural order of physical nature is another means of transgressing the affirmative limitations placed upon reality. Like the human body, nature's 'body' provides a kind of text of the mind and its rational workings that, through rearrangement and deformation, can be expanded and rewritten to include its own negation."[4] Bodies that are incoherent compel us to question what is self and what is other and create productive discomfort about identity.

In considering monstrosity as a satirical device of characterization, both similarity to and difference from human norms are important. Indeed, the monster's human essence is a crucial element in the portraits to be examined here. Like the Plinian races, contemporary satirical monsters are neither divine/demonic nor animal but essentially *human*. Classical accounts of monstrous races always endow them with recognizably human features,[5] and this tradition is supported in modern usage. Elements of the human body are deformed, disfigured, and recombined to produce fantastic and grotesque hybrids. Descriptions of monsters are reflections on the limitations and boundaries of the self (physical or cultural) insofar as they challenge and transgress those boundaries.

As Jeffrey Jerome Cohen notes, there is ample historical precedent for casting an ideological adversary as a monster: "A political figure suddenly out of favor is transformed into an unwilling participant in a science experiment by the appointed historians of the replacement regime: 'monstrous history' is rife with sudden, Ovidian metamorphoses, from Vlad Tepes to Ronald Reagan."[6] Representing Stalin as a monster in satire may function to expel him from Russian culture. By characterizing him as a dragon or a steel bird, satirists are distancing him from the healthy norms

of the Russian cultural self, of what is *svoi*. Furthermore, such characterization serves to delineate these very norms. The reader of these texts may
(consciously or unconsciously) question precisely which boundaries the
monster transgresses in his deformity. Thus, the identity of the cultural self
is strengthened and its limitations affirmed. It may well be that the demar-
cation of the norms of culture is the most significant function of what spe-
cialists call "teratalogical discourse." In constructing a deviant other, these
authors contribute to identity definition and validation. This process has
been of paramount importance in the process of reevaluation and reconciliation vis-à-vis Stalinism. Monstrosity, however, is also internalized and
assimilated by those oppressed, and this complicates the function of the
monstrous in interesting ways. The monster (Stalin) is tolerated and even
actively supported by some segment of the citizenry. Moreover, complicity
is not simply evil or foolish but is rooted in complex human motivations
with which these satirists sympathize. Exculpation, therefore, is qualified:
Stalin as a monster is both outsider and part of the self.

In considering the function of the monstrous in satirical portraits of
Stalin, it is crucial to note the open-endedness of these texts. Not only are
the descriptions of the Stalin-monsters in these works somewhat ambiguous, but the fates of the creatures are also rather uncertain. In other words,
it is not entirely clear that the monster is vanquished or cast out. This is in
keeping with teratalogical literary tradition, for the monster (liminalized
and marginalized) can only be repressed. Because it represents transgression of cultural boundaries, it is "always coming back, always at the verge of
irruption."[7] Therefore, casting Stalin as a monster in satirical texts warns of
the possible return of Stalinism, suggesting that it lurks within the culture
itself. This implication gives these texts richness and profundity that
transcends an ideological settling of scores.

Shvarts's *The Dragon*

Evgenii Shvarts's life (1896–1958) encompassed Stalinism and the period of
his adulthood was nearly contemporaneous with Stalin's rule. Reminis-
cences of Shvarts and accounts of his work in the Soviet theater are nearly
unanimous in recalling that he was an ethical, highly principled man.[8] All
evidence supports the conclusion that he was also a patriotic Soviet citizen.
By 1937, however, he was aware of and horrified by what was happening in
the Soviet Union. Following the arrest and execution of the children's author Nikolai Oleinikov, a friend of Shvarts recalls his asking: "How could

this happen?" The same friend comments wryly: "The question was posed as though I could answer it."⁹ However, Shvarts did not openly confront the dragon (as does Lancelot, his fictional hero); he confided his doubts only to his closest friends and cultivated the public persona of an apolitical writer of fairy tales.

Nevertheless, the finest of these fairy tales—the plays *The Naked King* (*Golyi korol'*), *The Shadow* (*Ten'*), *The Dragon*—are all on some level exposés of totalitarianism. Shvarts's fairy tales are not straightforwardly or simply allegorical. His opinion concerning the function of the fairy tale is often quoted. It is not necessary, he writes, "to look for hidden meaning. A fairy tale is told not to conceal but to reveal, to say with all your strength and at the top of your voice what you think." Concerning the use of fantasy in literature, he asserts: "A miracle that focuses attention is wonderful. A miracle that distracts [the reader] is harmful."¹⁰ Shvarts believed that Aesopian writing appealed to a limited readership, whereas his fairy tales were intended to be accessible to all. Perhaps the most useful generic description of Shvarts's tales is the "Faërie story." According to Irina Corten, these are works, like Tolkien's, that "deal essentially with atmosphere, with creating a new world, tangible yet distinct from that which we call 'real' and subject to its own laws."¹¹ This understanding of Shvarts's works allows us to approach them as marvelous stories with a satirical subtext.

The Dragon is the richest and most profound of Shvarts's plays in terms of its treatment of Stalinism. Written between 1941 and 1943 while Shvarts was living in evacuation in Central Asia, the play was only performed once in 1944 by Nikolai Akimov's Leningrad Comedy Theater in Moscow. The reason for its being shut down was ostensibly its lack of *ideinost'*, its treatment of fascism in an unduly trivial manner. S. Borodin savaged the play in a 1944 review: "Shvarts has written a pasquille on the people's heroic struggle with Hitler for liberation. His fairy tale is a slander on the people suffering under the power of the dragon, under the yoke of Hitler's occupation, on the people struggling with Hitler's tyranny."¹² Yet it is clear from memoir accounts that the play was felt to be potentially subversive closer to home. The parallels suggested by Shvarts's fairy tale with Stalin's Soviet Union were uncomfortably obvious to the audience. It seems likely that the possibility of an anti-Stalinist interpretation was the real reason for its removal from the stage in 1944.¹³

The Dragon was published in 1944 in a modest printing of four hundred copies and was included in a 1960 collection of Shvarts's plays. It was revived in the sixties both in the Soviet Union and in Poland, Germany, and the United States.[14] Akimov finally staged the play successfully at the Comedy Theater in 1962, and it was slated to be performed at the Sovremennik Theater the following year. However, this run of *The Dragon* ended prematurely as well; the reference in the play to the sudden disappearance of butter and sugar from shops during Lancelot's battle with the Dragon was all too topical in 1962, when butter prices were raised in the Soviet Union.[15] The play was scheduled to be restaged in 1968, but the political climate turned extremely chilly that year and the project was never realized. Mark Zakharov's 1988 film *To Kill a Dragon*, based on Shvarts's play, was an important work of the glasnost period. Although he took considerable liberties with the content,[16] Zakharov retained much of the tone and atmosphere of Shvarts's work, updating it to give it relevance to Gorbachev's reforms.

The identity of Shvarts's Dragon (and hence the target of his satire) has been the crux of most of the criticism devoted to the play. Of course, much depends on how the work is staged; the text is sufficiently ambiguous to permit differing interpretations. Soviet as well as some Western criticism has held that *The Dragon* is an allegorical satire on German fascism, and there is ample evidence to support this reading. Shvarts had begun writing the play—indeed, had completed a draft of the first act—before the Nazi invasion in June 1941.[17] It may be that he perceived the growing threat of fascism (which was certainly in the air). In any case, the play deals more with the psychology of totalitarianism than with military action. In his stage directions Shvarts specifies Gothic lettering on the town hall, which enhances the Germanic atmosphere. Many of the characters' names sound distinctly German to the Russian ear: Genrickh, El'za, Burgomistr, Sharleman'. The reference in the play to the Dragon ridding the kingdom of Gypsies certainly suggests Hitler's "final solution." Veniamin Kaverin notes that the propagandistic jargon mouthed by Charlemagne with respect to the Gypsies echoes the racist rhetoric popularized by Goebbels.[18] Charlemagne assures Lancelot that the Gypsies are "vagrants by nature and by blood. They're enemies of any government system, otherwise they would settle down somewhere and not wander all over the place."[19] The Dragon's assertion that he arose from the carnage of a battlefield would also seem to be an allusion to nazism. He tells Lancelot: "The blood of dead Huns flows in my veins. It's cold blood" (280). A reading of the Dragon as Hitler leads to an interpretation of the Mayor as a representative of the Allies; they aggressively move in to seize power when the dragon of fascism is mortally wounded. It is interesting that even Borodin's 1944 attack on Shvarts's work proceeds from the assumption that the play is about Nazi Germany.[20]

Perhaps Shvarts's "screens" functioned effectively enough to deflect another reading (i.e., he was eluding the censor by creating a vaguely Germanic setting); or perhaps, as Kaverin has suggested, it was awkward for censors and other literary bureaucrats to identify themselves as targets of Shvarts's satire.[21]

Another school of thought regards *The Dragon* as a generalized allegory attacking corruption, pernicious ideology, and institutionalized evil of any stripe. The Dragon's tyranny is generic, unconnected to a specific time or place. This point of view was argued forcefully by J. Douglas Clayton:

> It should be further said that to read the play as a close representation of either Fascist Germany or of Stalin's "socialism in one country" seems patently absurd. Shvarts could not foresee, in 1943, the rise of West Germany (the correlative of the Burgomaster, if we accept the Dragon as Hitler), any more than he knew that some twelve years later Khrushchev would manoeuvre himself into some of the power that Stalin had wielded. This play is primarily a comedy of human manners, an idealized representation of the struggle for social good against eternal human misery and venality.[22]

Akimov also insisted that the play resists reading as a direct allegory (though his motivation was probably very different from Clayton's).[23] *The Dragon* can, of course, be interpreted broadly as a moral tale, an account of the eternal struggle between good and evil. Precedents for ambiguity had already been established by Shvarts in *The Naked King* (1934) and *The Shadow* (1940), and a reading of *The Dragon* as nonspecific allegory is justifiable. The Dragon itself has three heads and three human manifestations, which suggests the coexistence of alternate personalities and the possibility of diverse interpretations.

Western criticism has tended to regard the play as anti-Stalinist. The resemblance of the Dragon to Stalin, which Clayton dismisses as an "unhappy coincidence,"[24] is emphasized in this interpretation. Norris Houghton asserts: "A reading of the text of *The Dragon* . . . makes it unavoidably clear that in this play Schwarz had the Stalinist Terror in mind, when he wrote of a fear-ridden city which cowered under the bloody talons of a dragon."[25] Shvarts and his contemporaries were aware that his play permitted this interpretation. In 1944 Leonid Maliugin implicitly acknowledged the possibility of an anti-Stalinist reading when he suggested to Shvarts: "Let's agree that this city is located in German territory and then it becomes easier."[26] Recent Russian criticism has tended to endorse this interpretation of *The Dragon* as an allegorical evocation of Stalinism. Those readers who lived under Stalin, suggests Kaverin, immediately recognize the psychology supporting the Dragon's tyrannical hold on the people.[27] Lev Loseff has convincingly demonstrated that the play may be—and probably was—read on an Aesopian level. The markers apparent to a sensitive reader are verbal formulae characteristic of sovietized Russian speech and plot situations that echo typical Soviet practices and rituals. Moreover, the density of these markers in the text gradually intensifies in the course of the play, strengthening an Aesopian reading.[28]

When the Dragon first presents himself as a man, his appearance is quite unremarkable; he is described as middle-aged but strong, with a crew cut and a soldier's bearing. Although he is not visually identifiable as either German or Russian, his slangy, colloquial greetings—"Hey, guys!" (*Zdorovo, rebiata!*) (277)—underscores his Russianness. The communiqués issued during Lancelot's battle with the Dragon suggest the misinformation disseminated by the Soviet Union as much as they parody Nazi propaganda.[29] Moreover, the appellations bestowed on the Dragon, such as "brilliant strategist and great tactician" (275), echo the hyperbolic praise lavished upon Stalin during the war. The Dragon's attack strategy may refer to Hitler's treachery, but it also sounds remarkably like Stalin's political maneuvering: "He always attacks suddenly; he bombards his opponent with rocks from above, then he swoops down straight at the head of his opponent's horse and breathes fire on it, so that the poor beast is completely demoralized. Then he tears the rider to bits with his claws" (275). While the Dragon's rhetoric about the Gypsies does indeed resemble fascist propaganda, it is worth noting that Stalin also made quotable negative pronouncements concerning minorities, especially as People's Commissar for Nationalities, a post he held prior to the Revolution.[30] Yet another reference to Stalinism in the play is the Gardener's experimentation with roses; his ideas about botany are quite fantastic and probably allude to Michurinist genetic theory. Finally, the Mayor's exchange with the busy Jailor in the third act suggests the prevalence of denunciations and mass arrests under Stalin. Both textual and extratextual evidence supports a dual reading, namely, that Shvarts was expressing opposition to Stalinism even as he targeted fascism in his play.

In casting Stalin as a dragon, Shvarts characterizes him as distinctly nonhuman. The talking cat calls him both "damned lizard" (*prokliataia iashcheritsa*) (272) and "old lizard" (*staryi iashcher*) (282). He emphasizes his cold-bloodedness, a feature that is not merely metaphorical in the context of Shvarts's play. The Dragon is, in fact, reptilian; he is related to snakes and gives off a smell of fish when he is preoccupied or nervous. According to the cat, he has three heads, four paws with razor-sharp claws, scales, wings, and a tail; he is as tall as a church and breathes fire. The building in which he lives has a sign affixed to it: "People strictly forbidden" (287). He is associated with a lake near the city, for as Jung notes in one of his lectures on Nietzsche, "The dragon is a water worm, and dragons are always supposed to live near the water."[31] The maidens who are sacrificed yearly to him die of loathing, and Lancelot notes that strangling him will be disgusting (300).

In spite of all of these nonhuman attributes, the Dragon appears in the play as a man or, rather, as three different men. With each metamorphosis, he grows older, but all of the descriptions of the Dragon in human form are quite ordinary. In his first embodiment he is distinguished only by his slight deafness: "Altogether his manner, though somewhat bluff, is not without a certain charm" (277). In his second guise he is serious and restrained and speaks dryly. His last transformation leaves him old, pale, and speaking in a cracked falsetto. The Dragon's alterity is qualified and complicated by his taking on human form at will. As Charlemagne explains, "Sir Dragon has been living among people so long that he sometimes turns into a man himself and drops by like a friend" (278). On one level the Dragon's appearance as a human solves the technical problem of how to present a reptilian monster onstage. However, Shvarts's dual characterization of the Dragon is not mere dramatic convention. His ability to transform himself qualifies his otherness; his taking on human form while remaining a dragon problematizes his dissimilarity to the self.

Details that Shvarts provides about the Dragon's origin affirm his otherness. He appeared in the world, he tells Lancelot, on the day when Attila was defeated, crawling out of the blood-soaked battlefield with the enormous black mushrooms called *grobovniki*.[32] In relating the history of the Dragon's reign to Lancelot, the cat reiterates that he came to the city from elsewhere: "a dragon settled in *our town*" (*nad* nashim gorodom *poselilsia drakon*) (272); "[h]e exacted tribute from *our town*" ([o]n nalozhil na nash gorod dan') (272); "he has lived *with us* for four hundred years" (*on uzhe chetyresta let zhivet* u nas) (274).

Shvarts consistently characterizes the Dragon as other through his inhuman, "cold-blooded" behavior. To persuade Lancelot that challenging him is pointless, the Dragon lists the individuals and groups he has annihilated and incongruously concludes by politely inviting Lancelot to sit down. When Charlemagne realizes that Lancelot might, in fact, save his daughter, he makes an impassioned speech defending his right to support Lancelot.

The Dragon is utterly unmoved by Charlemagne's plea, which is based on the universal human values of love for one's child and hospitality, and replies: "Okay. Now I'll destroy the whole nest" (282).

Several features mark the Dragon's speech as foreign, but in this respect his otherness is again qualified. As was noted previously, his speech initially emphasizes his Russianness; his language is markedly colloquial. However, the affectionate phrases he uses to address Elsa resemble the patter one might use with an animal: "Give me your paw . . . you scamp. Naughty thing. What a warm paw. Chin up! Smile. That's the way" (*Dai lapku . . . Plutovka. Shalun'ia. Kakaia teplaia lapka. Mordochku vyshe! Ulybaisia. Tak*) (278). Moreover, this is a demonstration of power for Lancelot's benefit, with no verbal response expected from Elsa. When he attempts to express his deep attachment to the townspeople, his emotional outburst is weirdly interlarded with mild but inappropriate obscenities: "I remember your great-great-grandfather in short pants. Damn! An unbidden tear. Ha ha! The visitor's eyes are popping out. You didn't expect such sentiments from me? Well? Answer! He's all upset, the son of a bitch. Well, well. Never mind" (*Ia pomniu vashego prapradeda v koroten'kikh shtanishkakh. Chert! Neproshennaia sleza. Kha-kha! Priezzhii tarashchit glaza. Ty ne ozhidal ot menia takikh chuvst? Nu? Otvechai! Rasterialsia, sukin syn. Nu, nu. Nichego*) (278). The Dragon has an alternate voice that is completely inhuman. His first roar (produced offstage) is supposed to be "deafening, terrible, triple" (279), with Shvarts emphasizing in his stage directions that "there is nothing human in this roar" (279). When the Dragon's roar is heard next, it has elements of wheezing and moaning in it. Shvarts is even more explicit in his stage directions: "This is a huge, ancient, evil monster roaring" (282). The Dragon's speech, then, ranges from primitive and monstrous to familiar and comprehensible, but even in this latter manifestation it is oddly skewed.

Shvarts's characterization of Stalin as a dragon draws on a number of mythological and literary sources.[33] The basic plot on which the play turns is a common fairy-tale *fabula* in which a brave youth saves a beautiful virgin from being killed by a dragon. The hero is then nearly robbed of his just reward (the maiden's hand) by an evil enemy.[34] This is essentially a variation of the Greek myth of Perseus, who rescued Andromeda from the sea serpent. Indeed, Lancelot lists Perseus among his ancestors. That a fairy-tale plot motivates Shvarts's work is significant, for it implies that the Dragon's (i.e., Stalin's) power is supernatural and can only be overcome through a miracle or magic.

Our popular conception of the dragon is derived from classical mythology. In addition to Perseus, Apollo battles with a dragon in Greek myth. Hercules has to combat dragonlike monsters in two of his twelve labors (he must defeat the Hydra and the serpent Ladon). *Drako* in Latin and *drakon* in Greek mean "large serpent" as well as "dragon," and classical iconography also consistently conflates these images as "evil obstacles to the forces of good."[35] The dragon is a creature of all four phenomenological realms (water, earth, air, and fire), which makes it a powerful negative symbol. It denies and transgresses the boundaries between these realms and so effectively expresses disorder and ambiguity.[36]

Western—especially Christian—tradition uses the dragon allegorically as a symbol of evil and foreignness.[37] The Bible includes numerous references to dragons, and these usually represent the devil (see chapter 5). Like the serpent of Eden (which is sometimes depicted as a dragon), other biblical dragons embody the power that God will ultimately destroy. Old Testament dragons (e.g., in Psalms, Isaiah, and Job) are not described in detail, but they generally inhabit the sea.[38] The dragon of Revelation (12:9), by contrast, is vividly characterized and is equated by John with Satan: "And the great dragon was cast out, that old serpent, called the Devil, and Satan, which deceiveth the whole world: he was cast out into the earth, and his angels were cast out with him." Several of the discredited saints who were reinstituted during the Crusades were dragon slayers. The dragon in the Middle Ages thus came to symbolize paganism and the rescued maiden became the church. Dragons are described "scientifically" in medieval bestiaries and are understood to embody sinfulness.[39] As symbols of evil, dragons have been employed allegorically to satirize or expose local tyranny.

Of the various saints associated with dragons, Saint George is the most well known. The Mayor in *The Dragon* at first confuses Lancelot with Saint George, and we learn that they are indeed related:

MAYOR (*hysterically*): Glory to you, glory, hosanna, George the Dragon Slayer! Oh, excuse me, I took you for someone else in my delirium. It suddenly seemed to me that you so resemble him.
LANCELOT: That could very well be. He's my distant relative. (290–91)

The story of Saint George exists in many different versions, and the popularity of the legend is such that he is the only martyr, aside from Saint Stephen, who is venerated by the entire Western Church.[40] He is the patron saint of Moscow as well as of England. Both the ecclesiastical and the popular versions of the Saint George legend closely resemble the Perseus and

Andromeda myth. As Edwin Sidney Hartland concludes, "The Church may be congratulated on having converted and baptized the pagan hero, Perseus."[41] Given this amalgam of popular and ecclesiastical roots, it is significant that Shvarts's hero, Lancelot, does not fulfill the crucial medieval ambition of standing atop the Dragon following his victory. His failure to meet this expectation, set up by Shvarts's references to classical and medieval models, is important in understanding the satirical import of the play.

Assuming the Dragon represents Stalin—and in light of the multiple sources of Shvarts's dramatic portrait—one can consider the ramifications of his characterization. Certainly casting Stalin as an inhuman, fire-breathing monster removes him from Russian culture and suggests that he is a pernicious force intruding from outside. However, it turns out that the Dragon has been internalized to some degree by Shvarts's townspeople, and he is not simply other. In particular, the Mayor and his son, Henrikh, have adopted the psychology of the Dragon and have become dragons themselves. They initially serve as comic foils for the more obvious evil of the Dragon, but once the Dragon has been slain, their tyrannical qualities become more apparent. Compelled to marry Henrikh against her will, Elsa articulates the dehumanization of the townspeople in a monologue delivered in the last act. Previously she had thought the Dragon's subjects obeyed him "as a knife is obedient to a robber" (332), but now she sees that they act willfully and independently, having internalized his evil: "Has the Dragon really not died, but, as often happened with him, turned into a man? Only this time he's turned into a multitude of people, and they're killing me. Don't kill me! Come to your senses! My god, what anguish. . . . Tear away the spider web in which you've all gotten tangled" (332–33). It was Shvarts's intention (expressed in a 1944 letter to Akimov) that Henrikh should not even know that he is lying and that it should be unclear to the audience whether the Mayor's mental illness is genuine or feigned.[42] Their cynicism and soullessness is perhaps more frightening than the Dragon's overt malice.

The Dragon claims an intimate relationship with the townspeople that suggests he has become at least partly *svoi*. He assures Charlemagne, "Yes. We're truly friends, my dear Charlemagne. I'm more than just a friend to each one of you" (278). Thanks to his longevity and, more important, his dual monstrous/human nature, the Dragon has become part of the fabric of society. The townspeople have become used to him. The Dragon's contention that "we came to understand each other a long time ago" (280) seems true enough. The Dragon has become the town's "very own dragon" (*svoi sobstvennyi drakon*) (276), an agent of defense against other dragons. His assimilation implies that he may now be an integral part of the culture he inhabits, that the relationship has become symbiotic rather than parasitic. Perhaps the most vivid and cynical indictment of the townspeople's complicity is the Dragon's own account of his achievement in destroying their souls. He tells Lancelot: "I personally crippled them, my dear fellow. I crippled them properly. Human souls, my dear fellow, are very hardy. You cut a body in two and the person dies. But you destroy his soul, and he'll just become more obedient. No, no, you won't find such souls anywhere else. Only in my town" (298).

The alterity of the Dragon is thus significantly qualified. Because Shvarts allows him to appear onstage as three different men while maintaining his alternate status as a reptilian monster, his otherness loses its absoluteness and he becomes "other than." Keeping in mind that encountering the other is a means of coming to terms with the self, one sees that Shvarts insists on more than simple exorcism or expulsion of the other. Following Freud, Otto Rank suggests that the concept of a dragon slayer is derived from the Oedipal situation, that is, killing the dragon in myths and fairy tales represents patricide.[43] Stalin, of course, was a paternal figure for Shvarts's generation; his symbolic slaying might well have aroused ambivalence on the part of both playwright and reader/viewer.

Nietzsche's dragon imagery is an important model useful in the interpretation of Shvarts's play. Jung asserts that the dragon of *Thus Spake Zarathustra* is the devil, but the devil is "the authoritative principle of the church, or the principle of any traditional morality or ethics or conviction."[44] Thus, God (or, in the case of Shvarts's work, Stalin) has been transformed into the devil and is represented as a dragon. Jung adds that the dragon of mythology often guards treasure and that the hero must overcome the dragon to liberate and take possession of the treasure. If the treasure takes the form of a maiden, then she may be a symbol of the anima, "the innermost value of man, individuality or the self."[45] This appears to be a plausible reading of Shvarts's adaptation of the myth, for individuality—creative, artistic freedom—was certainly held in thrall by the dragon of Stalinism, and this situation would have been of paramount interest to Shvarts.

There is, then, tension in *The Dragon* between exculpating the Russian people for the evils of Stalinism and indicting them for apathy and inertia. One reviewer of a 1968 American production of the play concluded that the townspeople have chosen security over freedom and do not really want to be released from the tyranny of the Dragon.[46] Commenting on the play in

1964, Stanislav Rassadin charged that the townspeople value peace so much that they fear liberation from slavery.[47] As Lancelot prepares to do battle with the Dragon, he learns that the town's single lance is under repair and cannot be loaned to him; the townspeople are afraid to help the challenger and may even be complicit with their oppressor. However, it is worth noting that there are various kinds of people in Shvarts's fairy-tale city. Some are true scoundrels and work on the side of the Dragon (the Mayor and Henrikh), others actively help Lancelot in his quest to slay the Dragon (the artisans), but most simply prefer to live quietly. The majority do not rebel or express opposition to the Dragon until it is certain that he will lose the battle with Lancelot. Their subversive tendencies, it seems, are tempered by caution and a strong sense of self-preservation.

If, as he claims, the Dragon has successfully warped their souls and crippled them, then what was *chuzhoi* has become *svoi*. Shvarts explores this process of spiritual repression and distortion in the play. As Lancelot discovers, the townspeople need saving twice: first from the Dragon that threatens physical destruction, then from the dragon of totalitarianism—specifically Stalinism—that has come to reside within them. The Gardener would seem to speak for Shvarts when, at the end of the play, he urges Lancelot to proceed with compassion: "But be patient, Sir Lancelot. I beg you, be patient. Tend us gently. Light the fires, and the warmth will help us grow. Tear up the weeds carefully, so you don't hurt the healthy roots. Really, when you think about it, people also, you know, when all is said and done, deserve careful treatment" (338–39). The issue of the Dragon's otherness is complicated by the fact that Lancelot is marked as an alien. Various other characters call him *prokhozhii, chuzhoi, chuzhak,* and *strannik*—all terms meaning "wanderer" or "outsider." The last appellation is particularly significant, for the *strannik* is related to the Holy Fool (*iurodivyi*) in Russian cultural tradition.[48] Shvarts has cast Lancelot as a foreigner because his role—like that of the Holy Fool—is to tell the truth, to show the townspeople that the Dragon's (Stalin's) evil has been partially internalized, that the other is encroaching dangerously upon the self.

Aksenov's *The Steel Bird*

Vasilii Aksenov's childhood and youth were shaped—or, rather, distorted—by Stalinism. Born in 1932 in Kazan, he was only five when his parents were arrested and sent to the camps. His mother was Evgeniia Ginzburg, a Communist intellectual, who described the purges and the camps in her autobiography *Into the Whirlwind* (*Krutoi marshrut*). In 1948 –50, when she was still living in exile in Magadan, Aksenov was allowed to join her and attend high school there. He recalls that this experience made him a firm anti-communist: "When I went to my mother in Magadan and saw what was happening there, I somehow reached the conclusion in my own mind that this is a completely criminal society. Criminal from beginning to end and one hundred percent."[49] Persuaded by his mother and stepfather that becoming a doctor would ensure him an easier existence in the camps if he should be arrested, Aksenov resolved to study medicine. Although he was expelled from the University of Kazan in 1953 as a son of enemies of the people,[50] he was able to complete his medical degree in Leningrad.

Even while he embarked on a medical career, Aksenov was experimenting with fiction writing. His first major success as a writer was the publication of *Colleagues* (*Kollegi*) in *Iunost'* in 1960, after which he decided to devote his full energies to literature. He was very much in the forefront of the "Youth Prose" movement centered around *Iunost'* and became editor of the journal in 1962. With the end of the Thaw, Aksenov's star began to wane. Priscilla Meyer dates the end of his first, "happy" period to the political refreeze of the mid-sixties—specifically to his forced recantation at a writers' meeting in 1963.[51] After this juncture, Aksenov's most daring works— formally experimental and ideologically outspoken—were circulated only in samizdat or *tamizdat*. His public displays of dissidence increased and included protesting the placement of a bust of Stalin near the Lenin Mausoleum in 1966. The events of 1968 apparently solidified his oppositionist stance and erased any lingering traces of communist idealism.[52] The *Metropole* affair of 1979 marked the de facto end of Aksenov's career as a Soviet writer. As a result of the scandal surrounding the unauthorized publication of this literary almanac (representing the collective effort of twenty-three authors), Aksenov was banned from publishing and the projects he had under way were halted.[53] While travelling abroad in 1981, he was stripped of his Soviet citizenship.

After a series of brief institutional affiliations, he settled into a permanent teaching position at George Mason University. He was relatively prolific and successful in emigration. His works were translated and reviewed widely, and he was a frequent commentator on Russian culture in the American media. While he stressed the professional obligations keeping him in the United States, he compared the émigré writer to an amphibian that "always risks ending up in a garden where the air is sparse and there is no water. That's precisely the reason—not nostalgia for birches—that I constantly think about returning to my homeland."[54] His Russian passport was returned to him in 1993 and he began to travel more frequently to Russia on visits. Since 2004 he has lived in Moscow and maintained a second home in France.

Stalinism has been a central theme of Aksenov's prose since the mid-sixties. Even in his very early works it is clear that he admires the West, its jazz, its technology, its comparatively liberal sexual mores—values that are implicitly anti-Stalinist. His use of colloquial Russian interlarded with English and French borrowings also suggests an outlook at odds with socialist realism. When his avenues for publication in the Soviet Union were closed, Aksenov became more outspoken in his condemnation of Stalinism. The journalist-protagonist of *The Island of Crimea (Ostrov Krym)*, published in 1981, composes a virulently anti-Stalinist tract called "The Nonentity: On the Hundreth Anniversary of Stalin's Birth," in which he excoriates Stalin as megalomaniacal, incompetent, and sadistic:

> No, Stalin did not die in 1953. He is alive today. His presence is felt in a propaganda machine of unprecedented scope, in the sessions of the so-called Supreme Soviet, in the sham elections, in the rigidity of the contemporary Soviet leadership (or at least the group carrying on the legacy of Kalinin and Zhdanov and its aversion to reform), in the breakdown of human economy (food, clothing, services—all areas of *human* existence are stymied by Stalinist dementia) and the growth of inhuman economy (tanks, rockets, bombs—all means of destruction loom like a phantom of syphilitic delirium), in the rejection of all iconoclasm and the imposition of a stale, dated ideological boiler plate [*sic*] on a nationwide scale, in the spread of what is known as "mature socialism" (and is in fact social and spiritual stagnation of the worst kind) beyond Soviet borders.[55]

Aksenov's most extensive treatment of Stalinism is *The Burn (Ozhog)*, written in 1969–75 and published in 1980. The novel examines his generation's efforts to come to terms with Stalinism in the late Thaw period even as the intelligentsia's hopes of liberalization were fading. Although the work is not centrally about Stalin, he is a constant presence. As Samsik Sabler, Aksenov's jazz saxophonist, bluntly puts it: "Everyone was sick to death of living in our stinking shack, alongside the rotting corpse of Big Daddy. Everyone— Party members, People's Artists, KGB men, record-breaking coal miners— everyone, except the bats hanging upside down in dark corners."[56]

The Steel Bird is a "threshold work," written in 1965 on the temporal border between Aksenov's "happy" and "angry" periods.[57] Predating both *The Burn* and *The Island of Crimea*, this tale is the most overtly political of

Aksenov's early works. It may be that Khrushchev's attack on the Youth Prose writers in 1963 motivated Aksenov to write *The Steel Bird*; it is imbued with the threat of the reimposition of Stalinism. Aksenov read the work in the Prose Section of the Soviet Writers' Union in 1966 (setting the unofficial record for a reading, since the audience wanted to hear the entire tale). However, the manuscript was rejected for publication by Soviet editors for over ten years, with the minor exception of an excerpt called "The Courtyard on Lamplight Alley" ("Dvor v Fonarnom pereulke"), which appeared in *Literaturnaia gazeta* in 1966. It was finally published in the United States in 1977, where it also came out in an English translation. In 1991 the work was included in a collection of stories by Aksenov that appeared in Russia. *The Steel Bird* is one of the finest of Aksenov's early works and marks an important step in his coming to terms with Stalinism. It is significant in the context of the author's oeuvre as "a distillation of [his] mature style and themes."[58]

The key to any reading of the tale as satire is an assessment of the nature of Popenkov, Aksenov's protagonist. One approach has been to regard the tale as a pro-Soviet satire in which Popenkov represents an aberration, a tyrant who instigates a cult of personality and attempts to lead Soviet citizens down a false path. Aksenov himself endorsed this reading, arguing that to see the work as anti-Soviet was to suggest that Soviet society is inherently totalitarian.[59] In his review of *The Steel Bird* Anatolii Gladilin interpreted it as a satire on petty bourgeois vestiges in Soviet society. However, his assertion that the tale is pro-Soviet seems disingenuous, especially in light of the last paragraph of his review: "I already noted that for the Soviet leadership it is possible to explain the tale as completely 'pro-Soviet.' But it is possible to understand 'The Steel Bird' differently and find in it . . . no, keep away! I am not going to help the comrades from a certain department fabricate a case against Aksenov."[60] However, the text itself makes a simple allegorical equation of Popenkov with Stalin impossible. Popenkov attends Stalin's funeral and the temporal frame of the tale extends well beyond the time of Stalin's death. Of course, these details may simply be a red herring to evade the censor. M. Keith Booker and Dubravka Juraga offer an interesting resolution of this paradox in their reading of the tale as a dialogic discourse. They see the anti-bourgeois strain in the story in dialogic confrontation with the anti-Soviet strain and conclude that the work "criticizes bourgeois tendencies yet undermines the Soviet claim to superiority over those tendencies."[61]

Alternatively, the Steel Bird may represent abstract tyranny or the totalitarian impulse. Nina Efimov strongly supports the case for this interpretation, insisting that Popenkov is a universal figure who transcends the historical particulars of Stalinism.[62] Several critics regard the Steel Bird as a dictator in the tradition of Stalin but do not see it as a direct satirical portrait of Stalin. According to Konstantin Kustanovich, Popenkov "embodies an evil force of a Stalinist kind, but one more powerful, he believes, than Stalin's."[63] The Steel Bird is thus larger than Stalin and his disappearance at the end may be read as an open-ended warning. The final "Chorus" is a celebration of freedom and happiness, for the wind (which represents political and social change) has dispersed the dark trails left behind by the Steel Bird. Yet he is still alive and the specter of totalitarianism continues to threaten the Soviet people.

Acknowledging the validity of these interpretations of *The Steel Bird*, it is nevertheless possible to make a compelling case for the specificity of the satirical portrait Aksenov draws. There are several markers that suggest that the Steel Bird represents Stalin, including the title of the work; *stal'naia*, or "steel," implies a link with Stalin, whose pseudonym means "man of steel." Popenkov refers to himself as *khoziain*, a term often applied to Stalin, after taking definitive control of the vestibule: "Is it clear now who's the boss?" (*Iasno teper', kto zdes' khoziain?*).[64] Zina calls him "mankind's genius" (92), an exaggerated title like those bestowed on Stalin. She also calls him "gigantic" (92), a possible reference to Stalin's monumental stature and to the cult that surrounded him. Popenkov smokes Herzegovina Flor cigarettes whenever he can obtain them; this was also Stalin's favorite brand.

Popenkov's origin is mysterious. He intentionally obscures his past; it is unclear where he has come from and how long he has been in Moscow. Aksenov suggests at the outset that "it is possible that he inhabited the capital even earlier [than 1948]—no one denies it—maybe even for a number of years; there are plenty of blank spots on the city map, after all" (25). He has ostensibly been living in the foundation of the Palace of Soviets, but he changes his account of his stay there from a year to a week to a month. Not only does this detail imply that the Palace of Soviets shelters a nest of Stalinist fledglings, but it also references Stalin's intentional obfuscation of his past. In a moment of ecstasy Popenkov breaks into a Georgian dance; his relatives have the Georgian names of Koka and Goga. His vaguely Georgian ethnicity is certainly another allusion to Stalin.

The time frame of *The Steel Bird* is 1948 to 1966, which spans the postwar years to the end of the Thaw (or the present for the author). Per Dalgård finds a distinction in the text between "then" and "now" established largely through adverbial phrases.[65] The "then" of the tale is the Stalin period, which is located in the past after the first chapter. A retired bodyguard longs for "the times of the violent Vissarion" (81). Zina prompts him to clarify that he means Vissarion Belinsky, but the name also echoes Stalin's patronymic, Vissarionovich. The change in Popenkov's physical appearance over two decades could easily describe Stalin's aging process: "Popenkov had changed little over the years; he had merely acquired a certain solidity, a heaviness, a categorical imperiousness in his gaze" (84).

Aksenov's descriptive details support Popenkov's association with Stalin. The foul odor that he initially exudes helps to characterize him as morally polluted and links him to the corruption of Stalinism. When he first appears on Fonarnyi Lane, he wears an old field shirt with two prewar buttons. Both the uniform and the buttons themselves—inscribed MOPR and "Voroshilov Gunner"—suggest that he belongs to the old Stalinist guard.[66] Popenkov's yellow eyes move the diver Fuchinian to exclaim "yellow fires, ugh!, his damned eyes" (*zheltye ogni, t'fu ty, prokliatye ego ochi*) (59). Margaret Ziolkowski has demonstrated that unsettling yellow eyes are frequently attributed to Stalin in negative biographical and literary portraits.[67] The color yellow signifies death in Russian folklore, and flaming eyes denote an unnatural mixing of the angelic/demonic and the human in the literary tradition of the monstrous.[68] It is significant that Fuchinian calls Popenkov's eyes "damned," perceiving his demonic nature at some (perhaps unconscious) level. The expletive *t'fu* that he instinctively uses echoes the phrase chanted to ward off the evil eye, part of the unclean force. Popenkov's avian qualities connect him to Stalin as well. Ziolkowski calls Stalin "the most prominent 'bird' in Soviet society in the 1930s and 1940s,"[69] variously represented as a falcon and an eagle in song and poetry. Popenkov is also part airplane. Airplanes, especially fighter interceptors, are also associated with Stalin. Soviet pilots were called "Stalin's falcons" and "Stalin's eagles" during the Second World War. Even earlier, in the thirties, the phrase "steel bird" was used in poetry to refer to Soviet aviation, one of Stalin's favorite spheres of influence.

Popenkov's psychological qualities are derived from Stalin's own pathological psychology. He is obsessed with power and stomps about in metal replicas of Peter the Great's boots to indicate that his victory over the nocturnal vestibule is complete. Before his successful coup, however, he waits patiently and carefully observes his surroundings; his takeover is accomplished gradually. He has, as Tolik Proglotilin concludes, "nerves like steel" (*nervy, kak stal'*) (59). His strange illness, which defies straightforward diagnosis, may be a manifestation of his lust for power.[70]

As in Okudzhava's poem "The Black Tomcat," the apartment house in Aksenov's story represents the Soviet Union. The inhabitants of 14 Fonarnyi Lane are a mixed lot, including members of the intelligentsia, workers, party functionaries, and even some remnants of the bourgeoisie. In short, they comprise a microcosm of the population of the USSR. Popenkov's pronouncement that "sacrifices, of course, will have to be made" (92) and the narrator's reference to his "great cause" (93) echo Stalin's euphemistic slogans. He plans to turn all the inhabitants of the apartment house into weavers of fake French tapestries, which suggests Stalin's predilection for kitsch in art and his rancor toward the intelligentsia.

Popenkov is strongly associated with consumption. He arrives carrying string bags of meat and fish. These seem unclean and perhaps suggest corpses,[71] for some dark substance continuously oozes from them. As Popenkov gains strength, he begins to "consume" people figuratively. This metaphor is realized in his night flight, where he gobbles up a series of monuments representing the past, the present, and the future. Aksenov uses a variety of expressions that intensify the theme of consumption: "If I want, I devour" (*Zakhochu i proglochu*); "I will eat up your horse" (*Ia loshad' vashu s"em*); "I've already eaten you" (*A vas ia uzhe s"el*); "I'll make kasha out of bronze" (*sdelaiu kashu iz bronzy*) (74–75). Moreover, Popenkov threatens to eat those who refuse to comply with his demands. All of these details imply that the Steel Bird is a cannibal; not coincidentally Stalin was called a cannibal (*liudoed*) among camp inmates and others.

Perhaps most interesting are the qualities of persuasion and manipulation Popenkov possesses. Although the doctor is repulsed by the Steel Bird, he feels bound to him by some "secret chains" (29). Nikolaev, the house manager, functions "as if under hypnosis" (38) in his dealings with Popenkov. The diver Fuchinian concludes that he has the power of "some kind of hypnosis" (57). The Steel Bird is brilliantly capable of exploiting people's weaknesses to inspire fear and dependency; he effectively renders the inhabitants of 14 Fonarnyi Lane compliant. For example, Nikolaev does not want anyone to know of his improvisations on the cornet, and Popenkov blackmails him with this secret. Stalin's penchant for manipulation through fear is well known, and many biographers and historians have speculated about his uncanny psychological insight. Finally, Popenkov shares Stalin's extreme, pathological distrust; once established as dictator, he is paranoid and constantly on guard against potential opposition or subversion of his authority.

Aksenov's portrayal of Stalin as a tyrannical steel bird draws on a number of sources for its satirical efficacy. Bird imagery is plentiful in fairy tales and folk songs, where avian characters (like animal characters in general) provide commentary on the psychology and behavior of humans. Some of the borrowings from folk sources in *The Steel Bird* are quite direct. For example, the arrival of an evil monster seemingly from nowhere (*otkuda ne vozmis'*) is a conventional motif of folktales.[72] However, Aksenov does not imitate the form of the *skazka* and is deliberately specific about time and place (in contrast to the conventional indefiniteness of the fairy tale). Metamorphosis of people into animals and birds is frequent in fairy tales. The basis for this transformation may be the folk belief that the soul is transformed into a bird at death.[73] That Popenkov is a *steel* bird suggests that he embodies Stalin's particular soul. His possession of supernatural power may also derive from the totemic beliefs reflected in folktales, where 'animals and birds are often magical. Furthermore, folktales allow for marriage between humans and animals (including birds); Popenkov's relationship with Zina makes sense in this context. Finally, Aksenov's treatment of consumption—particularly cannibalism—may draw on the fairy tale. The totemic belief that a transfer of attributes can take place between animals and man through consumption may motivate Aksenov's characterization of Popenkov as a cannibal. Popenkov increases his own strength and his power by figuratively "consuming" the inhabitants of 14 Fonarnyi Lane.

A specific possible source in folklore is the *skazka* called "Bird Language" ("Ptichii iazyk"). In this tale, as in Aksenov's work, the language spoken by the birds can only be understood by those with a special gift of comprehension. The important link in this case is ideational; in the *skazka* the birds pose a question about the relationship between generations. In particular, the mother and father crows pose the crucial question: To whom does their son belong? The little boy who understands their language provides the unequivocal answer: to the father. The tale's moral judgment finds an echo in *The Steel Bird*. Generational guilt is inevitable if the son "belongs to" the father and it is significant in this respect that Stalin was perceived as a paternal figure. In the fairy tale the boy's parents are told by a nightingale that they will become servants to their son, so they set him afloat in the open sea. At the end of the tale this prophecy is, of course, fulfilled; the son, now a rich nobleman, returns to his village and his parents unwittingly wait on him. He forgives them their past cruelty and the *skazka* ends with familial reconciliation. While *The Steel Bird* has no such clear moral appended, the issue of generational guilt remains central, and this link with the fairy tale suggests a possible resolution.

The Steel Bird's speech bears a remarkable resemblance to futurist *zaum*, and it is worth considering transrational language as a source of Aksenov's linguistic invention. The similarity is important in ascertaining the author's stance vis-à-vis the intelligentsia. Aksenov was certainly aware of Velimir Khlebnikov's and David Burliuk's work. In a 1991 interview he numbered the former among the three "poets of genius" who came out of Italian futurism.[74] Popenkov conflates the types of *zaum* described by Khlebnikov in his programmatic works. The dialect most relevant for Aksenov's text is *ptichii iazyk,* an onomatopoetic language created by Khlebnikov that imitated the sounds made by birds. Khlebnikov, an avid ornithologist, based *ptichii iazyk* on the associative power of birdsong,[75] and Aksenov similarly endows Popenkov's speech with allusive force. The first time the Steel Bird speaks in his own language, he chatters in a rhythm that suggests not only a birdsong but also a machine gun: "A-ta-ta-ta-ta-ta, A-ta-ta-ta-ta-ta" (38). One of his most frequent utterances closely resembles the cuckoo's voice; "kukubu," though never translated, is obviously associated with lust. The Steel Bird's language, then, draws on Khlebnikov's *ptichii iazyk* but distorts it to express Popenkov's monstrous nature.

Yet another probable source of intertextual discourse is Aristophanes' satirical play *The Birds.* Aksenov's rather extensive dialogue with Aristophanes (notably in *Aristophaniana with Frogs [Aristofaniana s liagushkami]*)[76] supports a comparison of *The Steel Bird* with *The Birds.* Aristophanes' play comments on the corruption of Athens. It targets the government's meddling in private life, the intolerable fines levied on the citizenry, the courts' incessant activity, and other topical problems.[77] In Aristophanes' text the bird-man Peisetaerus establishes a new city, wins a beautiful wife, and acquires the power of Zeus. In terms of plot, Popenkov's achievements seem to parallel those of Peisetaerus. Aksenov's characterization of his protagonist also echoes Aristophanes' model. Like Peisetaerus and his friend Euelpides, Popenkov is part bird, but he has retained his human nature as well. Peisetaerus's argument that birds once ruled the world and thus can reestablish their power finds resonance in Popenkov's plan to take over in stages. Furthermore, birds are prophetic and are used for divination. Popenkov has extraordinarily keen insight and both his night flight and his final flight are prophecies (or, more properly, warnings).

In Aristophanes' play Peisetaerus and Euelpides are searching for Tereus the hoopoe. This mythical subtext also has significance for a proper reading of *The Steel Bird*; in fact, it strengthens a specifically anti-Stalinist interpretation. Tereus, the king of Thrace, married Prokne, the daughter of the king of Athens. Prokne was lonely without her sister, Philomela, so Tereus went to fetch her but fell in love with her and raped her during the journey home. To prevent her from revealing his evil deed, he cut out her tongue. She nevertheless managed to convey the story to her sister by embroidering it on a cloth. To take revenge against Tereus, Prokne killed their son, Itys, and served his flesh to her husband for dinner. When Tereus discovered what he had eaten, he began to chase the sisters, but Zeus turned them all into birds: the nightingale (Prokne) mourns her son; the swallow (Philomela) chastises her oppressor; and the hoopoe (Tereus) searches for them.[78]

There are several important links between Aksenov's tale and this mythological source. Aksenov also utilizes the motifs of rape and suppression; Popenkov's rape of Tsvetkova in the elevator is an expression of his power and her vulnerability. Since she represents the idealism and innocence of the generation that came of age during the war, her symbolic destruction at Popenkov's hands suggests the violence of Stalinism: "A pause and silence, desire and lust, scuffling and profanation, loathing, rotting, rebirth and self-generation, quivering, swallowing, absorption, expulsion, smothering, annihilation of a live, light, good person with the gait of a calf, the eyes of a young deer, with apple-breasts, with emerald eyes, with a little orange of a heart and a mysterious soul, annihilation" (73 –74). The swallow Philomela, who in the myth protests against her tormentor, also presages the coming of spring. Given the centrality of weather imagery in the literature of the Thaw period, Popenkov's secret fear of swallows makes sense. Swallows both threaten to expose his tyranny and predict the arrival of spring (political liberalization, de-Stalinization). Aksenov's treatment of the theme of cannibalism may likewise be traced to the story of Tereus. There is in Greek myth a close connection between sexual crimes and cannibalism. (Tereus's terrible feast is thus a direct consequence of the rape of Philomela.)[79] Popenkov's appetites are similarly linked; his eating from the disgusting bags of meat and fish (which, as has been noted, suggests cannibalism) mirrors his insatiable lust.

The echoing of this classical bird story suggests another aspect of the *svoi/chuzhoi* contrast in Aksenov's tale. Bird stories of antiquity carry the semantic load of alterity: "The basic framework of a large number of the bird stories, and in particular those of the birds of the night, and birds of prey and their victims, depends on the opposition between the family order and the outside or animal world."[80] *The Birds* replicates this conflict between the self and the other in the skirmish between men and birds. It is adapted by Aksenov specifically in the rooftop struggle between the Soviet workers and Popenkov's relatives and generally in the citizens' opposition to Popenkov. This conflict typically occurs in transitional or liminal time periods in classical literature.[81] For Aksenov the Thaw is such a time.

The Steel Bird, then, is a pastiche, an aggregate of allusions to and echoes from numerous literary (and nonliterary) sources. These borrowings illuminate the meaning of the Steel Bird's monstrosity. His nature is ambiguous, but it is clear from the beginning that he is birdlike. He uses avian terminology in reference to himself ("I'll flit out" [*vyparkhivaiu*] [38]) and sometimes refers to others in this manner as well: "All the little birdies are already in their nests" (*Vse ptichki uzhe v gnezdyshkakh*) (38). The narrator uses the word "bird" in the figurative sense in considering his identity: "What kind of a bird is this" (*Chto, mol, za ptitsa*) (47). As the tale proceeds, however, Popenkov's aeronautical features become more pronounced. The inhabitants of 14 Fonarnyi Lane experience his steely, superhuman strength, and there are numerous textual clues that Popenkov is not human. He feels "tremendous malice toward the human race" (53); Tsvetkova expresses doubt that he is "really a person" (53); he is elated with "animal optimism" (67). Eventually a doctors' *consilium* concludes that Popenkov is, in fact, a steel bird.[82] Popenkov's mechanical qualities may suggest the "impersonal machine" that brought Stalin to power and enabled him to rule unopposed for so long. This was Trotsky's explanation for Stalinism,[83] and it may have influenced Aksenov's thinking about the question of culpability.

The Steel Bird is a monstrous hybrid, a grotesque combination of the animate and the mechanical. Descriptive details about the Steel Bird are symbolic rather than realistic,[84] reinforcing his unnatural quality. The narrator compares his eyes to railroad tunnels and adds that their yellow color is like the lights of oncoming trains (27, 29). Popenkov's blood type is stamped on his thigh. Aksenov stresses that Popenkov has ugly buttocks: "Buttocks of a very unpleasant appearance, they were like the edge of a forest where stumps had been grubbed out and then a forest fire had passed through" (28). While this extended simile may simply be a detail added to enhance the effect of the grotesque, it is worth noting that historic accounts of the monstrous races frequently include odd details about natives' buttocks.[85] The Steel Bird's gestures and his behavior are a strange mixture of the natural and the mechanical: "My patient began to tremble, at first gently, gently, then his whole body began vibrating violently; something popped and gurgled inside him, something whistled; sweat stains spread across the pillow, but this lasted no more than a minute" (28). His language is incomprehensible, a collection of sound combinations that are "hitherto unknown in the world" (64). As was noted previously, Popenkov's speech at times resembles the noise of a machine gun; in addition, a high rate of repetition of the sounds in his speech lends it a mechanical quality.

Popenkov-Stalin is rendered unnatural—indeed freakish—by Aksenov. His liminal nature is reinforced by the bags he carries. He assures Nikolaev that one holds meat, the other fish; this suggests the idiom *ni ryba ni miaso* ("neither fish nor meat"), which expresses indefiniteness and ambiguity. While staying in the vestibule of 14 Fonarnyi Lane, Popenkov spends his nights moving and reassembling the pieces of the frescoes but ends up with "monsters" (*chudovishcha*) (51). He, too, is a kind of monster, a combination of incongruous parts.

This characterization of Popenkov-Stalin as a monstrous hybrid is in keeping with Aksenov's departures from verisimilitude and his predilection for the fantastic. Moreover, the multiple shifts in narrative perspective provide varying views of the Steel Bird; the unreliability of the narrator enhances our uncertainty about Popenkov's nature.[86] In this tale Aksenov creates what Ludomír Dolozel terms a "hybrid world": "The hybrid world is a semantic structure where the modal opposition between the natural and the supernatural is neutralized, so that both natural and supernatural phenomena are integral constituents of one and the same world. In fact, the semantics of the hybrid world has to abandon the 'natural,' 'supernatural' terminology which was applicable to the mythological world; all phenomena of the hybrid world happen quite 'naturally' and as a matter-of-fact."[87] This fictional world mirrors and expresses the nature of its protagonist. The Steel Bird, like Stalin, is both weak and inhumanly strong. He is capable of manipulating and coaxing people and bullying or simply destroying them. Ruthless authoritarianism and petty bourgeois greed, which at first glance seem incompatible,[88] are combined in Popenkov's character and imply a similar admixture in Stalin's personality.

As we have seen, Aksenov is preoccupied with the causes and effects of Stalinism, and he probes the issues of complicity and guilt in this tale. By rendering Stalin as monstrous other, it would seem that he absolves the Russian people of responsibility for the crimes of Stalinism.[89] The Russian people are basically good; they are "not crocodiles" (34), in the words of Nikolaev's cornet. Indeed, except for the Steel Bird, none of the characters in Aksenov's tale are fully characterized psychologically. Although they do represent various types and social strata,[90] it is nevertheless possible to see them as a minimally individuated mass of Soviet citizens. It is noteworthy that workers and students band together spontaneously to defeat Popenkov. Aksenov's attitude toward the intelligentsia as a whole, however, is more ambiguous.[91] The doctor is the only member of the intelligentsia of the older generation who actively resists the Steel Bird's power. Yet the threatened consequences (viz. being eaten) are frightening, and Aksenov makes it obvious why one might capitulate. It is the doctor who most eloquently explains the Steel Bird's power to subjugate ordinary humans: "In the first place, it sometimes began to seem that there was something powerful and mysterious about him, in his organism, something of the sort that completely contradicts my outlook as a Soviet doctor. In the second place, I noticed each time that this secret force plunged me into a state of absolute abulia (i.e., the absence of all voluntary reactions), into the torpid condition of a domestic animal, merely waiting for orders, for the lash" (61). It is significant that the doctor is Jewish and fatalistically expects to be arrested at any moment. The house manager Nikolaev, conversely, admires and pities Stalin.[92] His cornet pleads with Samopalov not to bother Stalin, "the standard-bearer of peace, our own dear son and father" (34). Perhaps Nikolaev represents that segment of the intelligentsia that "played along" with Stalinism, acculturated to support authority and inclined toward peaceful coexistence. His liberation (symbolized by his playing his cornet publicly) at the end of the tale is therefore important since he actively celebrates freedom from the Steel Bird's rule. The old Stalinists (the deputy minister and his bodyguard), by contrast, continue to pine in retirement for a firm authoritarian hand.

The inconclusive nature of Aksenov's answer concerning culpability for Stalinism reflects the split (common to his generation) between the desire for retribution and the urge to forgive. Several "explanations" for Stalinism are embedded in *The Steel Bird*. The people are hypnotized and tyrannized by a monstrous, supernatural power in the person of Popenkov. More damning is the fact that the inhabitants of 14 Fonarnyi Lane simply get used to the Steel Bird and fail to notice his activity after he settles into their house. Ultimately this tale investigates and considers the causes of Stalinism without indicting the Russian people. In this respect the work is best seen as a step in the process of addressing the question of responsibility. In *The Burn*, undertaken shortly after this tale was completed, complicity and guilt become central themes. *The Steel Bird* can thus be read as a preliminary study for this larger, more explicit examination of Stalinism.

Conclusion

The two satirical texts examined in this chapter cast Stalin as a monster by way of assessing culpability for the evils of Stalinism. Shvarts and Aksenov both create allegorical portraits of Stalin as supernatural and monstrous. Shvarts's Dragon draws on rich mythological, religious, and literary traditions to express Stalin's role in twentieth-century Russian history. Deceitful, egomaniacal, foul-smelling, and cannibalistic, the Dragon is loathsome and threatening. Yet in the course of many years of ruling his kingdom, he has been internalized by his subjects; they are implicated in the Dragon's tyranny. Aksenov's Steel Bird is initially an alien in the culture he comes to control and oppress. Through hypnosis and manipulation, he takes over the entire apartment building and bends the will of the other inhabitants to his own. Characterized by Aksenov as a grotesque hybrid of the animate and the mechanical, the Steel Bird is a liminal figure. It is telling that some of the inhabitants (in particular the intelligentsia of the older generation) are complicit in Popenkov's ascension to power; though they are glad to be liberated when he departs, they are judged guilty of apathy by Aksenov.

Monsters thus serve as an effective device of characterization in portraying Stalin. On the one hand, the monster is alterior, originating from outside. On the other hand, the monstrous resides within the self and exists in a symbiotic relationship with the self. The monster—especially the dragon— is related to the serpent and shares its demonic connotations. Certainly associations with the devil are useful in casting Stalin as a monster. As we have seen, the monster is also bestial insofar as it has some animal characteristics. Although depictions of Stalin as a monster depend on different generic conventions, like portraits of the dictator as an animal they tend to interrogate his relationship with the human or the cultural self.

In considering the significant differences between Shvarts's and Aksenov's treatments of Stalin in their respective satirical portraits, one must keep in mind the disparate contexts in which they were written. *The Dragon* dates from the Second World War, when Stalinism was still very much in force but its full ramifications were not yet known. In casting Stalin as a dragon, Shvarts poses the possibility that he is an interloper, an outsider whose evil might be resisted. However, he also chastises readers and viewers for their complaisance, their willingness to appease the monster in exchange for peace and prosperity. True to fairy-tale convention, Shvarts ends on an optimistic note, expressing certainty that the townspeople (i.e., the Russian people) can be cured of their passivity and made strong enough to oppose totalitarianism. Aksenov wrote *The Steel Bird* when Stalinism was already in the past but threatening to return with the refreeze at the end of Khrushchev's Thaw. Here Stalin is a monstrous steel bird, an alien who inveigles himself into the house at 14 Fonarnyi Lane (i.e., the Soviet Union) and gradually achieves near-absolute power. The inhabitants of the apartment house are victims of his machinations and his strange, hypnotic force; they fail to oppose him actively until it is almost too late. Aksenov's tale represents a preliminary examination of popular complicity in the crimes of Stalinism, which will occupy an increasingly central place in the author's work.

5

The Devil Made Us Do It

Stalin as a literary character takes on features and characteristics of the devil or Antichrist in several satirical texts written in the Soviet period. This is perhaps unsurprising, for casting a target of satire as diabolical is a powerful, tried-and-true rhetorical device. However, the devil and Antichrist in Russian culture have peculiarities that make this characterization especially effective in satirizing Stalin. To some extent the works treated in this chapter share the conceit that the diabolical is alien and emanates from outside the Russian cultural self, so that Stalin's demonic qualities separate him from the healthy society he tyrannizes. Associating Stalin with the diabolical can exonerate the Russian people, for a force that is supernatural and vies with Christ for power cannot reasonably be resisted by mere mortals. As we shall see, this dynamic is complicated by the devil's ambivalent nature in Russian folklore and art; this ambivalence problematizes the image of Stalin and hence the question of complicity. Mikhail Bulgakov's masterpiece *The Master and Margarita* (*Master i Margarita*), completed in 1940, features a complex and polyvalent devil, who is on one level a portrait of Stalin. "Poem about Stalin" ("Poema o Staline"), a song-poem composed and popularized by the bard poet Aleksandr Galich in the seventies, is a bitterly satirical treatment of the dictator as a demonic character, the opponent and rival of Christ. Finally, Fazil Iskander's tale *The Feasts of Belshazzar* (*Piry Valtasara*), originally published in 1979 in the West as one of the component pieces of the epic cycle *Sandro of Chegem* (*Sandro iz Chegema*), is a fictional account of one of Stalin's nocturnal banquets.

The Devil and Antichrist

The devil (or Satan) and Antichrist are quite distinct concepts in theology, but the distinctions are often minimized in Russian satirical practice. The persona of the devil is not clearly delineated in Russian culture or literature; rather, he is "an extrapolation, a field of possibilities, a set of interwoven traditions."[1] In the Russian tradition the devil is most often plural and petty, not the singular archfiend Satan. Indeed, a Russian devil need not even look like a demon and may well assume the guise of a serpent, a beast or—most significantly—a foreigner. Portrayals of the devil in literary satire draw on multiple sources, ranging from folklore and the Bible to literature and art. Russian satirists frequently rely on Western literary models for depictions of the devil, such as those created by Dante, Milton, and Goethe. The most significant and influential Russian literary source is Dostoevsky, whose devils can be traced to the Christian apocalyptic tradition—specifically the Book of Revelation.[2] Much has been written about the nature and role of the devil in Russian culture and literature.[3] It will suffice here to emphasize that twentieth-century satirists draw on an extraordinarily rich and diverse demonic tradition.

With respect to satirical portraits of Stalin, the Antichrist legend is more pertinent than mythology connected with the devil. As Bernard McGinn notes, the concept of Antichrist has been more powerful in Russia than in any other Christian culture over the past three centuries.[4] Russians have long been familiar with the Antichrist myth not only through biblical texts but also through popular apocryphal texts such as the revelations of Saint Ephraem the Syrian, the Tracts of Hippolytus of Rome, and the *Revelations of the Pseudo-Methodius of Patara*.[5] Antichrist has been closely connected in the Russian tradition with the dragon, the serpent, and Satan (though his relationship with the latter is controversial). Thus, in its Russian interpretation the idea of an embodiment of boundlessly powerful evil at work in the world derives from a variety of sources, both religious and secular.

Antichrist's relationship with the devil is inconsistently represented in Russian literature. It is clear that Antichrist and the devil are related, but Antichrist is sometimes portrayed as a man controlled by the devil and sometimes as identical to Satan. In general, the tradition of Satan in Russia, as elsewhere, is distinct from the myth of Antichrist. The latter is widely regarded as "Satan's greatest accomplishment, his final trump card, to be revealed at the end of time."[6] The idea that Antichrist is the incarnation of evil (as Christ is the incarnation of good) informs some Russian representations of Antichrist. Vladimir Soloviev's influential "Short Story of the Anti-Christ" ("Kratkaia povest' ob Antikhriste") (1900) portrays him as the earthly embodiment of sin and apostasy, a supernaturally evil man. However, this conception of Antichrist as a reversed, negative incarnation has not been widely accepted. Indeed, viewing Antichrist as the incarnation of evil is theologically problematic, for only God can assume a human nature; the devil cannot become human because his power is not equal to God's. In the texts treated in this chapter the idea of Antichrist as the incarnation of evil is sometimes perceptible, coexisting and intermingling with other myths about the nature of Antichrist.

The myth of Antichrist is, of course, an essentially Christian tradition and parallels the story of Christ. It is, as McGinn writes, "inseparable from belief that Jesus of Nazareth . . . was the messiah."[7] Moreover, Antichrist is the rival of Christ, as Satan is the opponent of God. His coming is a parody of Christ's own promised return; he will rise from the abyss (whereas Christ will descend from heaven) and have boundless power to spread wickedness (while Christ will bring justice and goodness). He will attempt to usurp God's authority, to claim divinity for himself.

These beliefs about Antichrist have led observers to see him embodied in various historical figures—especially corrupt or vicious rulers. Antiochus IV, the king of Syria, is considered by many scholars as the original model of John's Antichrist; his savage persecution of the Jews in 168–164 B.C. epitomized imperial subjugation. Nero, who ruled from A.D. 54 to 68, may well have added some early characteristics to the popular conception of Antichrist, such as unmitigated cruelty and megalomania. Domitian (A.D. 81–96) also seemed a likely candidate; he augmented his infamy by insisting that his subjects address him as *dominus et deus*. Antichrist has subsequently been found in the Roman Empire as a whole, the Jews as a nation, the Ottomans, various popes or the papacy, France, and so on. Most significantly for Russian culture, Antichrist was identified as successive rulers after Patriarch Nikon's reforms of the mid-seventeenth century. The Old Believers considered Nikon and Tsar Alexis apostates: "Nikon, Alexis, and the bishops who obeyed them all signified the spirit of Antichrist. But, as holders of supreme power, Nikon and particularly Alexis had a greater responsibility. They were not just part of the general spirit of the times but were guiding the work of Antichrist; they were, in a sense, a part of Antichrist, or at least of the apocalyptic vision—being cast interchangeably as precursor, as Antichrist himself, or as the Beast of the Apocalypse."[8]

Ivan the Terrible, who radically extended Russian imperial hegemony and was notorious for his capricious cruelty, was compared to Antichrist by critical observers of the sixteenth century. In his turn, and perhaps most widely, Peter the Great was regarded as Antichrist. His westernizing campaign, his persecution of the church, his secular and religious reforms, and his personal eccentricities all pointed to the conclusion that the End Tyrant was ruling Russia. So broadly held was this conviction that Peter's actions and personality influenced later perceptions and expectations of Antichrist in Russia. Not coincidentally, Stalinist culture consciously and purposefully encouraged comparisons of Stalin with both Ivan the Terrible and Peter the Great. Indeed, Eisenstein's film *Ivan the Terrible* was commissioned to legitimate Stalin's despotism. These traditions—both demotic and propagandistic—have shaped representations of Stalin as Antichrist in the satirical texts examined here.

The presence of the devil or Antichrist in fiction generally and in satire in particular is a powerful device for expressing something about the human condition or human society. The devil may serve as a clever critic who focuses the reader's attention on the shortcomings and faults of the social structure he observes. Alternately, satiric antagonists assume epic proportions when they are characterized as diabolical. Likely candidates for casting as the devil or Antichrist are those guilty (in the satirist's view) of blasphemy, persecution of the faithful, or false leadership. Stalin was not only culpable on all three counts, but he also promoted a cult of personality during his lifetime that elevated him to almost divine status. Portrayal of the dictator as a god in official art and literature made the satiric reversal—his characterization as the devil or Antichrist—all the more powerful.

Biographers of Stalin and memoirists have speculated about his appearance and personality, often hinting at some preternaturally evil quality. He was, first of all, physically "marked" by attributes that could be interpreted as diabolical. Stalin's complexion was brownish and pockmarked, a result of smallpox that threatened his life when he was seven years old. Many biographers have noted his irregular complexion, and one admiring journalist wrote that his pockmarks suggested "his powers of resistance. He had fought a deadly disease . . . and had won."[9] Stalin was also lame, which is traditionally a sign of the devil; folk belief has it that the devil's leg was injured while falling from heaven, leaving him with a limp. The cause of

Stalin's limp is sometimes ascribed to his feet having been frozen in one of his escapes from exile.[10] More often biographers recount his having been run over by a horse-drawn carriage when he was ten, an accident that left him lame and convinced that his miraculous recovery heralded a special destiny.[11] Another feature that contributed to Stalin's identification with Antichrist was the fused second and third toes on his left foot. This characteristic was documented in police records and led, strangely enough, to the widespread rumor that he had six fingers. In addition, Stalin's left arm was several inches shorter than his right arm; he reportedly could not rotate it at the shoulder or bend it completely at the elbow. Again, the causes of this disability are disputed. His arm may have been damaged as a result of blood poisoning from an ulcer on his left hand in childhood, or he may have developed osteomyelitis as a result of his father's beatings. In either case Stalin was rejected for military service in 1916 on the basis of his crippled arm. Anna Allilueva (the aunt of Svetlana Allilueva) recalls Stalin dismissing this as a pretext: "'They thought I'd be an undesirable element in the army,' he told us, 'so they found fault with my arm.'"[12] Later in life Stalin habitually wore a glove on his left hand, claiming that he had rheumatism, or tucked the hand inside his jacket. Numerous sources (other than the Bible) offer descriptions of Antichrist. In at least one, the Midrash va-Yosha, Antichrist is described in some detail as a human monster with arms of unequal length: "He shall be bald-headed, with a small and a large eye; his right arm shall be a span long, but his left two and a half ells; on his brow shall be a scab, his right ear stopped, but the other open."[13] Stalin's physical appearance, then, provided considerable grist for the rumor mill, supporting the conclusion that the dictator was, in fact, Antichrist.

Information about Stalin's background, though sketchy and largely unsubstantiated, was further evidence for those eager to discern the End Tyrant in the USSR's ruler. Rumors that Stalin was illegitimate circulated widely; the Antichrist legend holds that Antichrist will be born of a defiled woman. Stalin's father, Vissarion, reportedly suspected his wife, Keke, of infidelity and doubted that Stalin was his son. It is possible that Stalin was the son of the priest Yakobi Egnatashvili, who married Vissarion and Keke and who later arranged Stalin's acceptance to the Tiflis Orthodox Seminary.[14] Although Stalin's years at the Gori Ecclesiastical School and the seminary were extremely important in forming his character, he ultimately rejected religion to become a revolutionary and, in time, an extraordinarily powerful secular ruler. Under the influence of Darwin and Marx, Stalin became persuaded that God is "sheer nonsense" and declared himself an atheist.[15]

Having consolidated his power, Stalin carried out a brutal campaign of persecution against the church; Antichrist's enmity toward the church is, of course, foretold in multiple sources.

Apocalyptic eschatology tends to externalize good and evil, to cast current events and conflicts in cosmic terms. This may be fallacious with respect to understanding history, but it is very effective in satirical practice. As McGinn notes, the apocalyptic worldview is absolutist; it posits clear opposition and permits no moral ambiguity.[16] Good is defined and affirmed through its opposition to evil. Thus, what is positive and healthy in Russian culture takes on clearer outlines and is reinforced by way of satirical conflict with the force of evil, embodied in Stalin as the devil or Antichrist. One should keep in mind that eschatology implies hope—indeed, surety in the ultimate triumph of good. The prophecy that underlies the Antichrist myth is that the End Tyrant, after causing great suffering and destruction, will be defeated and destroyed, setting the stage for the Second Coming and the establishment of heaven on earth. The satirical works examined here are in some sense protreptic, foreseeing (if only implicitly) a dawn to follow the darkness of Stalinism. The role of apocalyptic texts as "literature of consolation" is central to an understanding of satire depicting Stalin as a diabolical entity. Like earlier apocalypses, these satirical texts are directed toward readers living under or with the effects of persecution and tyranny (in this case Stalinism). They are meant to promise, to console, and to support faith in "the basic goodness of God and his control over history despite the evil so evident in the world."[17]

The dynamic of opposition described earlier is problematized by a reading of Antichrist as both an external threat and an internal force. Jung's view of Antichrist is unique yet significant with respect to Stalin's otherness. According to Jung, if the figure of Christ corresponds to the psychic manifestation of the self, then Antichrist corresponds to the shadow of the self, the "dark half of the human totality, which ought not to be judged too optimistically."[18] This latter element is as much a part of the self as the former, only the obverse side. Antichrist is material or chthonic, in contrast to and in balance with Christ's spirituality. If one accepts Jung's contention that the power of evil is part of the self, then the unconscious (where the shadow resides) is rendered even more formidable. The figure of Antichrist is a consequence of this realization, as is the tendency to find him active in current events. While Jung's explanation of Antichrist is not by any means a majority view, it offers important insight into the characterization of Stalin as a diabolical figure in satire. First, it suggests a preoccupation with the issue of self and other, with defining what is *svoi* and distinguishing what is *chuzhoi*. Second, it helps us to see how these satirical representations of Stalin are attempts to come to terms with the question of the locus of evil in Russian culture. Antichrist, the boundless power of evil that could create Stalinism, is both alien to the self and (as the shadow) inextricably part of the self.

Bulgakov's *The Master and Margarita*

The story of Bulgakov's relationship to Stalin, pieced together from biographical sources and memoirs, is fascinating, complicated, and somewhat inconsistent. Bulgakov wrote to Stalin as early as 1929, complaining of his treatment by critics and requesting permission to emigrate.[19] In letters dated 1931 and 1934 he again turned to Stalin for permission to travel abroad to relieve the pressure under which he was living and writing. Most of Bulgakov's letters went unanswered. One, which he wrote in March 1930 and addressed to Stalin and to other representatives of the Soviet government, elicited a telephone call three weeks later from the dictator himself. In response to Bulgakov's desperate complaint that he could not find work in the theater, Stalin promised him that he would be reinstated in the Moscow Art Theatre. In addition, Stalin questioned Bulgakov's desire to leave the Soviet Union. Bulgakov's reply (which he would later regret bitterly) was that he could not live outside Russia.[20] Why Stalin deigned to call Bulgakov is an open question. Anatoly Smeliansky asserts that the phone call was a carefully calculated step to increase Stalin's popularity and enhance his reputation in the artistic community. He quotes a report by an anonymous informer to GPU (the Soviet secret police) appraising the result of Stalin's phone call to Bulgakov: "It has to be said that Stalin's popularity has taken a really unusual form. He is being spoken about warmly and lovingly, telling the legendary history of Bulgakov's letter over and over again."[21] It is also significant that the phone call took place the day after Mayakovsky's funeral; given the shock waves that accompanied Mayakovsky's suicide, it may well be that Stalin was moving shrewdly to prevent the death of another highly visible member of the intelligentsia.[22] In the aftermath of the phone call, *The Days of the Turbins* (*Dni Turbinykh*) was restored to the repertory of the Moscow Art Theatre in January 1930 at Stalin's behest and despite his blanket condemnation of Bulgakov's plays in 1929.

It is probably true that Stalin's intervention—and, in particular, his phone call to Bulgakov—provided the writer with "safe passage" through the 1930s, when many less controversial writers were arrested and destroyed. Biographical and historical evidence suggests that Stalin regarded Bulgakov much the same as he did Akhmatova, Pasternak, Shostakovich, and a few others: creative artists who, by virtue of their genius, could be tolerated and preserved, left unharmed by the whirlwind of the purges. Moreover, Bulgakov may have held the status of legitimate opposition and been granted a certain latitude in his behavior and his writing. Stalin apparently considered it necessary to claim Bulgakov as *svoi*. In reference to the play *Batum* he is reported to have said: "We taught even Bulgakov to work for us."[23] However, Stalin's patronage of Bulgakov—if indeed that is what it was—remained insidious. At the end of their phone conversation Stalin had promised to meet with Bulgakov at some unstated future time, and Bulgakov pursued that promise obsessively. It must have been immensely frustrating to feel oneself a favorite yet to be unable to gain access to one's benefactor, to follow up on a brief, one-sided conversation about the state of literature and culture. Bulgakov's inability to secure Stalin's attention again reportedly poisoned the last decade of his life. Marietta Chudakova suggests that the story of Ieshua in *Master and Margarita* was an artistic response to his obsessive quest to talk to Stalin. In her view the final encounter between Pilate and Ieshua is a version of the exchange Bulgakov desperately wanted to have with Stalin.[24] One may also speculate that the Master's passionate assertion to Ivan Bezdomny that he would sacrifice everything—even the keys to the asylum—to meet Satan reflects Bulgakov's own overwhelming desire to talk with his patron.

Bulgakov declined physically during the thirties, the result of the kidney disease that would eventually end his life in 1940. Stalin's phone call may have exacerbated his illness, adding stress and anxiety. Then again some biographers (including his widow) claim that it may have saved or prolonged his life, if only by preventing his suicide. Stalin never again responded directly to Bulgakov, although he did take an interest in his physical decline and death. When a group of actors from the Moscow Art Theatre appealed to Stalin to visit Bulgakov on his deathbed, he apparently sent Aleksandr Fadeev (then secretary of the Soviet Writers' Union) as his emissary.[25] Following Bulgakov's death in March 1940, Stalin's secretariat called his home to confirm that he had died.

In assessing Bulgakov's tortured relationship with Stalin, it is essential to consider his play *Batum* (completed in 1939 though never staged), which dramatizes Stalin's revolutionary youth in the period 1898–1904. Although the play is far from hagiographic, it has long been considered as evidence of moral capitulation on Bulgakov's part. Smeliansky calls it "an intimation of compromise, and a prayer for deliverance."[26] Ellendea Proffer judges it to be "a shameful episode in Bulgakov's career,"[27] though she concedes that Bulgakov was certainly subject to enormous pressure. Other critics, such as Maiia Kaganskaia and Zeev Bar-Sella, simply dismiss it as an inferior work of art.[28] In writing the play Bulgakov may have been motivated by a desperate hope of salvaging his career as a playwright. As early as 1936—shortly before the premieres of his plays *Moliere* and *Ivan Vasilievich*—he discussed the possibility of authoring a play about Stalin with the director of the Moscow Art Theatre. Realizing that his health was failing, Bulgakov may have seen writing *Batum* as a way to secure his wife's future. However, based on his wife's diaries and his recorded conversations with friends and associates, it appears that Bulgakov was genuinely enthusiastic about undertaking this project.[29] In the final analysis, one should recall that Bulgakov's contemporaries—Mandelstam, Akhmatova, and Pasternak—all composed adulatory verses to Stalin. Rather than excise *Batum* from collections of Bulgakov's works, as has been done in the West as well as in the Soviet Union, it makes sense to ask what the play can tell us about the author's relationship to his protagonist.

Batum is not an example of obsequious flattery but a serious examination of the nature of tyranny. Indeed, a repetitive theme in Bulgakov's oeuvre is the relationship between a creative individual and a cruel tyrant. His plays *The Last Days* (*Poslednie dni*) and *A Cabal of Hypocrites* (*Kabala sviatosh*) treat the dynamic of power between Nicholas I and Pushkin (in the former) and Louis XIV and Moliere (in the latter); this same theme is prominent in *The Master and Margarita*. Miron Petrovskii's assertion that Bulgakov continuously examined his own position by depicting parallel historical relationships between artists and tyrants is persuasive: "[Bulgakov] reflected his relationship to Stalin not through *Batum* but throughout all of his creative work."[30] It is, of course, important to remember that by the late thirties many—perhaps most—creative artists regarded Stalin as the arbiter of their fate, as either their potential benefactor or the agent of their destruction. Bulgakov's case is complicated by his fascination with the relationship between creative genius and tyranny, which engendered his idea that Stalin should play the role of his "first reader." In obvious reference to Pushkin and Nicholas I, he explicitly invited Stalin to become his first reader in a letter that was never sent.[31]

It is possible to read *Batum* as an Aesopian text, but this requires that one look at the play within its historical context. The fact that Bulgakov describes Stalin in *Batum* as rather ordinary is striking: "Average build. An ordinary head . . . the appearance of the aforementioned person makes no particular impression."[32] In a period when the cult of adulation was at its zenith, to portray Stalin as merely human was bold. Moreover, the contrast between the revolutionary ideals espoused by Stalin in *Batum* and the harsh repression of the late thirties would have been palpable to readers or viewers. Several critics, including Smeliansky and Petrovskii, find traces of the demonic in Bulgakov's depiction of Stalin in *Batum*. According to Petrovskii, his role as a false prophet is suggestive of Antichrist.[33] More explicitly, Bulgakov has the prison governor in the play exclaim "Oh, damned demon!"[34] just before Stalin is beaten by the guards. (This beating, this treatment of Stalin as "a simple *zek* and not a divine being,"[35] was certainly one reason the play was impermissible.) Stalin's reference in the play to the legend of a black dragon that stole the sun from mankind recalls both the purges of the late thirties and the Apocalypse. Mariia Shneerson asserts that Aesopian writing was foreign to Bulgakov and that such a reading of *Batum* is unsupportable.[36] The issue of Bulgakov's intention may not be resolvable, but the ambiguity of Stalin's portrait in the play is crucial. It suggests an ambivalence on the author's part vis-à-vis Stalin, which is recapitulated in the character of Woland in *The Master and Margarita*.

Aside from issues of patronage, Bulgakov genuinely seems to have admired Stalin on some level. He may well have respected him as a strong leader or even sympathized with his burden of power. Like other intellectuals of his generation, Bulgakov may have seen Stalin as the embodiment of Hegel's universal historical genius.[37] Judith Mills hypothesizes that Bulgakov authored *The Master and Margarita* as a "tribute to Stalin as the significant creative irrational force that could change Russia's and perhaps even humanity's vision of reality."[38] While Mills's contention may be overstated, it seems clear that Bulgakov's fascination with Stalin was genuine. This preoccupation resulted neither in panegyrics (as in the case of Pasternak) nor diatribes (as in Mandelstam's poem "We live, not feeling the country beneath us" ["My zhivem, pod soboiu ne chuia strany"]).

We know from archival evidence that Bulgakov worked on *The Master and Margarita* from 1928 until his death in 1940. Whether the text was, in fact, completed by the author has been the subject of dispute; Bulgakov left some variant chapters and additions that were incorporated only after the first, heavily censored publication of the novel in the journal *Moskva* in 1966–67.[39] What was taken to be the restored full text was published by Posev in 1969, but this samizdat version was probably corrupted by corrections and emendations made by Elena Sergeevna, Bulgakov's widow. The most reliable full edition is the 1973 Soviet republication of the novel in a collection of Bulgakov's work.[40]

Bulgakov's portrayal of Stalin as the devil in the character of Woland is admittedly oblique. There is, however, strong cumulative evidence for an interpretation of Woland as Stalin in the descriptive details of the text. Like Stalin Woland has a lame leg, and Hella massages it with salve before the ball. Woland is perceived by Berlioz and Bezdomny as a foreigner, though their suppositions about his nationality vary wildly. Stalin, though not a foreigner (but rather a colonial subaltern as a Georgian), spoke Russian with a marked accent. Woland is a master of illusion who manipulates reality through his supernatural powers. Abram Terts points to Stalin's similar "magical powers" by way of arguing for an allegorical interpretation of Woland: "In [Woland's] character Stalin emerges as an amazing magician, unique in his profession, . . . who has devoted himself completely to the art of confusion and mockery of people, to the creation of all kinds of mirages and delusions."[41] The chaos Woland wreaks is blamed on hypnosis by skeptical Muscovites. When Likhodeev is transported to Yalta, he sends a telegram to his colleagues at the Variety Theater, asserting that Woland accomplished this through hypnotism. During Woland's performance at the theater, Bengalsky insists: "Citizens, we have just seen a case of so-called mass hypnosis" (540). Following Woland's departure, the conclusion of "cultured people" is that "a gang of hypnotists and ventriloquists, magnificently skilled in their art, had been at work" (800). Stalin's extraordinary rise to power and his hold on Soviet society have been attributed to some kind of mass hypnosis, an explanation Bulgakov surely found improbable.

Woland works behind the scenes to effect confusion and destruction. The reader is given to understand that he orders the disappearance of Likhodeev, and he is responsible (if only through the power of suggestion) for the death of Berlioz. By the late thirties it was obvious that Stalin was responsible for the arrest, imprisonment, and execution of thousands of people, though he remained in the background, to all appearances only a witness and not the actual executioner. In prefacing the story of Pontius Pilate and insisting that Jesus did exist, Woland tells his listeners that "no proof is required" (435). Mills draws a parallel between Woland's assurance in the power of faith and Stalin's imposition of his views of history: "When immersed in the ethereal realms of true belief, proofs are unnecessary."[42] D. G. B. Piper has traced Woland's dictum that "a fact is the most stubborn thing in the world" (689) directly to Stalin's writing.[43] Andrei Sinyavsky suggests that Woland's question to Margarita after the ball—"Well, have we really worn you out?" (691)—echoes Stalin's question to Bulgakov in his 1930 phone call: "So, are you really fed up with us?"[44] The Master tells Bezdomny that one of the articles denouncing his novel was signed with the initials N. E., which may mean *non esse*, the spirit of negation or the devil. It might also suggest Stalin's accented pronunciation of the negative particle *ne*, again linking Woland and Stalin.[45] Marsh asserts that the servility and obsequiousness displayed by Woland's retinue suggest the behavior of Stalin's underlings.[46] Woland's admonition to Margarita that she should never ask for anything from those more powerful, that "they themselves will offer and grant everything" (697), may echo a widespread belief—perhaps shared by Bulgakov—in Stalin's largesse.

There is considerable disagreement concerning the validity of an allegorical reading of the character of Woland as Stalin. Some critics have found the textual parallels convincing. For example, Sinyavsky demonstrates persuasively that "Woland, or Satan, favorably disposed toward the Master, is to a certain extent Stalin favorably disposed toward Bulgakov: a somber, black, and yet idealized Stalin."[47] Others dismiss the points of similarity as tenuous or too slight to support a consistent allegorical equation of Woland with Stalin. Milne rightly points out that the chronology of composition of the novel argues against such a reading; Bulgakov began planning and writing *The Master and Margarita* in the late twenties, before Stalin had assumed the role of intercessor for him.[48] Since the novel evolved over more than a decade, it is possible that Stalin may have gradually found his way into Woland's character. Recognizing that an extended or detailed allegorical interpretation is difficult to sustain,[49] it is nevertheless certain that the novel has been read this way since the 1960s.

The treatment of Stalin in Bulgakov's novel is broader and deeper than allegorical representation in the character of Woland. Stalinism provides the background for the action of the Moscow story, though Stalin is never mentioned by name. Nearly everyone acts out of fear and duplicity; the atmosphere is one of pervasive mistrust. Moreover, the Muscovites resolutely refuse to admit the truth of what they are experiencing. Although there is ample evidence of the presence of evil and irrationality, they insist on a vision of the world that does not recognize the existence of the devil. This situation certainly resonates with Soviet culture of the thirties, when Russians (and many westerners) resisted the reality of the terror.

Conversely, the Jerusalem strand of the novel includes a number of oblique references to Stalin and Stalinism. Pilate's toast to Caesar echoes panegyric addresses to Stalin (and was partially cut in the version of the novel published in the sixties): "To us, to you, Caesar, father of the Romans, the dearest and best of people!" (719). The conversation between Ieshua and Pilate about who has the ability to cut the thread by which one's life hangs may be an allusion to Stalin's power. Pilate's arranging the murder of Judas suggests Stalin's Machiavellian intrigues and his elimination of members of his retinue no longer useful to him. This broad but diffuse web of allusion to Stalin and Stalinism supports a conclusion that Bulgakov's allegory is neither direct nor simple. Stalin is, however, one aspect of Woland's character, so it is useful to ask what kind of a diabolical being Woland is.

Woland resembles the devil of the Old Testament in several important ways. He is a tempter, but as such he is an instrument of justice: he tempts only sinners and punishes only those who deserve retribution.[50] In meting out justice, Woland ensures balance and moral order and thus serves as God's agent in the earthly realm. His sphere of influence is limited to the globe he spins, while God's divinity is an all-embracing power. It is true that he saves the Master and Margarita, but it may be that he does not have the authority to harm them since they do not belong to his realm of darkness. This is extremely important if we regard the Master as an autobiographical character, for it means that Bulgakov has cast Stalin as a devil who does not have ultimate power over the creative artist. That Woland is the agent of good is underscored by the epigraph to the novel from Goethe's *Faust* (Part One, Scene 11): "I am a part of that power that eternally wishes evil and eternally does good." It is, finally, significant that Woland is a sympathetic and attractive character. He resembles a Romantic version of the devil and depends on the literary models of Pushkin, Lermontov, Odoevsky, Hoffmann, Tieck, and others. Woland exhibits a nobility, beauty, and freedom that, according to Thompson, are "fit only for the unusual and the strong."[51] However, Merritt Clifton's point that Woland derives more directly from a Russian literary prototype than from a Western model is pertinent here:

> Dostoevsky and Bulgakov, by wide contrast, coming not from proudly righteous western Christian tradition, but instead from less high-and-mighty Russian Orthodoxy, writing without the English or American author's everlasting consciousness of the Miltonic Satan looming over his shoulder, with Goethe's version of the Faust legend in place of Marlowe's far more conventional treatment as their great model story of demonic possession, addressing themselves to a nation made thoroughly aware by her Vissarion Belinskys and social upheavals that what she needs is not moral

justification but sharp criticism, clearly may exercise wider latitude in attacking political, religious, and human weakness.[52]

Bulgakov's devil shares with Gogol's demonic presences (e.g., in "The Portrait" ["Portret"], "Diary of a Madman" ["Zapiski sumasshedshego"], and "Viy" ["Vii"]) the pernicious traits of disorder and falsity. Bulgakov is at pains to deny the grandeur of evil, stressing the vulgarity and banality of Satan's works. The Muscovites who succumb to him are not magnificent sinners; they are merely petty and corrupt.[53] Woland also echoes Ivan's shabby devil in Dostoevsky's *Brothers Karamazov* (*Brat'ia Karamazovy*), whose evil lies in his utter banality. (Although Dostoevsky's devil is the model for the character of Koroviev, Woland's focus on quotidian, often trivial, issues derives from this source as well.) Stalin's scope of evil is implicitly diminished and, as in *Batum*, he emerges as ordinary despite his supernatural nature.

While recognizing the peculiarly Russian sources of Bulgakov's devil, it is impossible to ignore the many points of contact with Goethe's *Faust* embedded in the text. The borrowings from *Faust* include (aside from the epigraph) the names of Woland and Margarita, the recurrent references to a poodle, details of Woland's initial appearance, as well as other plot situations.[54] Goethe's influence on Bulgakov may be indirect. As I previously noted, Woland's portrait has Romantic models and the writers of the Romantic period were much affected by Goethe. In any case, the epigraph and the numerous allusions to *Faust* encourage the reader to identify Woland with Mephistopheles rather than with Satan. This turns out to be a false lead, for Woland is not Mephistophelean. He is cynical and he knows men's weaknesses, but he does not desire evil for the sake of evil, he does not seek to enslave men's souls, and he is not treacherous. The references to *Faust* are best understood as "open-ended and suggestive, rather than correlative."[55] Bulgakov uses Goethe's model creatively and independently, suggesting that we consider Woland/Stalin's traits as Mephistophelean while simultaneously frustrating any simple equation.

The devil is traditionally a trickster, and this aspect of Woland's character provides another link with Stalin. Woland, of course, does not himself play pranks; he delegates buffoonery to his subordinates Behemoth and Koroviev. He maintains his dignity and is unfailingly serious. Milne suggests that he is something of a satirist and Vladimir Lakshin notes that he emerges as a moralist.[56] Stalin loved practical jokes and humor, though it was often of a sardonic or even sadistic variety. Iurii Borev recounts many instances where Stalin told anecdotes and played practical jokes, often through the agency of his subordinates.[57] It is quite possible that Bulgakov sought to reconcile in his fictional creation the dictator's dignity and authority with his infamous proclivity for playing tricks.

I have suggested that the distinction made between Satan and Antichrist in satirical texts is blurry, and this is particularly true of Woland's character in *The Master and Margarita*. Bulgakov had used apocalyptic imagery extensively in his earlier works. In his 1924 novel *The White Guard* (*Belaia gvardiia*) Bulgakov has a religious zealot condemn Moscow as "the city of the devil" and "the kingdom of the Antichrist."[58] Father Alexander immerses himself in Revelation, and Petliura, whose arrival in Kiev is associated with Armageddon, is confined in a prison cell numbered 666.[59] His story "Diaboliad" ("Diaboliada") and tales "The Fatal Eggs" ("Rokovye iaitsa") and "Heart of a Dog" ("Sobach'e serdtse"), all written in the mid-twenties, have demonic and apocalyptic themes as well. In portraying Moscow of the thirties in *The Master and Margarita*, Bulgakov draws upon the tradition of a corrupt earthly kingdom that is materially rich but spiritually debased, and in limning Woland he utilizes details of the Antichrist legend.[60] Woland's appearance as a man parallels and parodies the Incarnation of Christ, who turns out to be his rival for influence in the novel. Woland tells Berlioz and Bezdomny that he has come to Moscow to study the manuscripts of Gerbert Aurillac, who was elected Pope Sylvester II in 999 and oversaw the coming of the millennium.[61] Moscow of the thirties is a most appropriate setting for the coming of Antichrist, for the city was predicted to be the locus of the final crisis of Christianity.[62] Stalin's terror might well have seemed to be the Great Tribulation foretold in Revelation; the persecution of the innocents and of the church fulfilled the prophecy. The members of Woland's retinue become the Four Horsemen of the Apocalypse after leaving Moscow, accompanying Woland back into the abyss. Marsh interprets this as a subversion of the popular portrayal of Stalin as a *bogatyr'* and thus "a particularly suitable image to suggest the apocalyptic nature of Stalinism."[63] It is worth noting that Woland's Four Horsemen are not individualized, but this would seem to be another instance of Bulgakov's creative adaptation of his model. In a farewell gesture to Moscow, Koroviev and Behemoth playfully whistle, and their whistles (especially Koroviev's) wreak havoc on the city, causing trees to be uprooted, the river to boil, and birds to fall dead from the sky. These are certainly references to the trumpets of the angels of Revelation who bring down hail and fire, turn the sea to blood, and make the stars fall from the sky. Abaddon, Woland's agent of retribution, and Azzazelo, his henchman, take their names from figures who are fallen angels (in the biblical Book of Revelation and in the parabiblical Book of Enoch, respectively).[64] All of these echoes suggest that Woland/Stalin shares traits with Antichrist of biblical and popular legend, and they strengthen Bulgakov's vision of Stalinism as apocalyptic. Nevertheless, Woland is not a fully delineated Antichrist and Bulgakov's portrait of Stalin does not represent him simply as the End Tyrant.

We have in Woland, then, an unconventional diabolical being, a composite figure derived from a variety of sources ranging from biblical to literary to folkloric. As A. C. Wright notes, this makes Woland's function more capacious: "Because Bulgakov's devil is not precisely defined, he becomes a more meaningful figure, in the same way that the concept of the devil can be meaningful in human lives however vaguely it is understood."[65] We know that Woland's character evolved during the novel's composition; the various working titles suggest this development ("The Consultant with a Hoof," "The Great Chancellor," "Satan," "The Black Magician," etc.). In his afterword to the 1966 publication of the novel in *Moskva*, A. Vulis notes that Bulgakov had written a number of common names for the devil—Mephistopheles, Lucifer, Asmodeus—in the margins of a draft notebook but ultimately rejected them in favor of Woland.[66] Andrew Barratt cautiously concludes, based on what we know of revisions that Bulgakov made in his manuscripts, that successive depictions of Woland reduced his conventionality.[67] Given Bulgakov's philosophical breadth and his dislike of dogma, it makes sense that he ultimately created a multivalent devil. Leaving aside the issue of intention, Woland's composite and ambiguous nature—if we accept the partial identification of Woland with Stalin—becomes very meaningful.

Despite the complexity of his lineage, Woland is undoubtedly and consistently a supernatural being who comes from elsewhere. Literally "demonizing" Stalin by casting him as the devil allows Bulgakov and his readers to locate the source of the evil of Stalinism outside of Russian culture. It permits a projection of culpability to the realm of the supernatural and absolves Russians (though they are guilty of petty sins) of the great crime of complicity in Stalinism. The devil has always been useful in this way; he is a traditional scapegoat, deflecting blame from the human race. This is not to say that the question of conscience is resolved by Bulgakov. Indeed, the issue of complicity is central to the novel; guilt for not actively resisting evil torments Pilate and must have preoccupied Bulgakov. Chudakova suggests that release from guilt is the peace that the Master has earned and that Bulgakov himself longed for: "In order to get rid of this burden a hero is needed whose guilt is of a higher order—a guilt of long standing. This new hero must be taken to the last frontier of the torments of conscience and—let go. . . . By his gesture of mercy (granting freedom to Pilate) the Master asks for absolution for himself and all those who need absolution and peace."[68]

Bulgakov's ambivalence about this key question of guilt helps to explain the paradox of Woland's character. Although he is the devil (with attributes of Antichrist), he accomplishes good and saves the Master and Margarita. Stalin was not only the agent of evil who needed to be satirically purged from Russian culture for Bulgakov. He was also a superhuman, mythologically grandiose figure who stood above the banal evil of everyday Stalinism, who could save or destroy lives and careers at will. Woland is charming and sympathetic as well as dangerous and frightening because Stalin himself embodied this duality for Bulgakov. He is other to the cultural self with which Bulgakov identified—but nevertheless a fascinating, attractive other.

Galich's "Poem about Stalin"

Galich's artistic development was shaped by Stalinism and much of his work responds to the times in which he lived. Born Aleksandr Arkad'evich Ginzburg in 1918, Galich became a successful, privileged playwright under Stalin. Blessed with both literary and dramatic talent, he studied simultaneously at the Literary Institute and in Stanislavsky's acting studio. Following Stanislavsky's death in 1938, Galich moved to the Moscow Theatrical Studio, where he had come under the tutelage of the director V. Pluchek and the playwright A. Arbuzov. He achieved early and considerable success. His plays *The Taimyr Is Calling You* (*Vas vyzyvaet Taimyr*) and *The Steamship They Call "Orlenok"* (*Parokhod zovut "Orlenok"*), and his film *On the Seven Winds* (*Na semi vetrakh*) enjoyed both popularity and official approval. According to Ruth Zernova, *The Taimyr Is Calling You* was even performed in labor camps by and for prisoners.[69] In all, ten of his plays were produced; three were rejected by the censors. Although he was exempt from military service because of a heart condition, Galich continued his theatrical work during the Second World War. He participated with Pluchek in a frontline theater company, writing scenarios, sketches, and *chastushki* (short popular ditties), as well as acting and directing. Initially Galich was not permitted to travel to the front on the grounds that he had relatives living abroad, but in 1943 this obstacle was removed and he spent the rest of the war at the western front.

In the postwar years Galich continued to build his career as a writer for stage and screen. His plays were produced in the best theaters in Moscow and other cities and his scenarios were filmed by well-known directors and actors. He became a member of the Soviet Writers' Union in 1955 and was a member of the Cinematographers' Union and the Literary Fund (appointed by the executive committee of the Soviet Writers' Union) as well. Galich's lifestyle at this time was, by Soviet standards, luxurious. As one of his contemporaries recalled, "Sasha was a member of all kinds of unions, societies, committees, sections. He had prizes, diplomas, and so on. Sasha was charming, witty and handsome; he loved elegant clothes of foreign cut; he traveled abroad. He played the piano well, he was great at billiards, and was a first-class hand at preference and poker. Sasha lived expansively, never having problems with money; he had a wonderful apartment in the writers' house on Aeroflot Street, in which I saw quite a few antiques."[70]

It was at this point that Galich began writing and performing his song-poems (*avtorskie pesni*), the works that would make him famous as one of the Bard poets of the late fifties and sixties, along with Bulat Okudzhava, Vladimir Vysotsky, Iulii Kim, and Novella Matveeva. The exact date of Galich's turn to this genre is not known, but one of his first songs, "Clouds" ("Oblaka"), can be dated with some certainty to 1962. His popularity as a Bard was never as great as that of Okudzhava or Vysotsky, but his songs were nevertheless widely known. That his works were published abroad from the late sixties on gave his work even broader currency. In turning to the song-poem, Galich was drawing on a rich Russian oral tradition that includes the narrative poems of Nekrasov as well as the romance and the anecdote. Gerry Smith speculates that the underworld song (*blatnaia pesnia*) also had a stylistic influence on Galich's work.[71] Given the massive return to major Soviet cities of many former prisoners of the camps in the mid-sixties, this seems plausible.

Galich's performance at a festival in Novosibirsk in 1968 marked a turning point in his career. His song "In Memory of Pasternak" ("Pamiati Pasternaka") created a stir since it expressed anger and bitterness at the treatment of the great poet by the Soviet authorities. A press campaign of vilification followed Galich's performance in Novosibirsk, with especially strident attacks appearing in *Literaturnaia gazeta* and *Sovetskaia kul'tura*. Although he was under increasing pressure and the shadow of disapprobation was widening, Galich continued to perform his song-poems at private gatherings; recordings of his works circulated widely. It was apparently the playing of a tape of Galich's songs at a private party that led to a formal denunciation by

D. Polianskii, a former member of the Politburo, who happened to hear the recording at a party given by his daughter and subsequently communicated his displeasure to the head of the Soviet Writers' Union.

In the same period *tamizdat* editions of Galich's works began to appear abroad. Posev published the collection *Songs* (*Pesni*) in 1969 without the author's permission; moreover, it contained the erroneous information that he had been a prisoner in the gulag for twenty years. The 1972 collection *Generation of the Doomed* (*Pokolenie obrechennykh*) was published with Galich's consent. Also issued by Posev, it includes the long work "Poem about Stalin."

Galich was expelled from the Soviet Writers' Union in 1971 and from the Cinematographers' Union the following year. He was also excluded from the Literary Fund, which deprived him of the social benefits afforded by membership in this organization. Along with Solzhenitsyn, Galich was made a corresponding member of the Sakharov-Chalidze Committee for Human Rights, a dissident organization operating in the West. Openly challenging the Soviet authorities, he signed numerous documents of protest and support for human rights.[72] In 1974 Galich was refused permission to attend a conference on Stanislavsky in Norway and was instead urged by a representative of the KGB to immigrate to Israel. Galich initially resisted this option and delayed for several years, insisting on the distinction between leaving willingly and being forced out.[73] His friends and associates stress that he was deeply patriotic and considered himself a Russian poet. I. Grekova writes: "I, a close friend of Aleksandr Arkad'evich, know well that he was no 'anti-Soviet.' He was, on the contrary, an intense patriot; he was tormented about the fate of his motherland; he rejoiced at her achievements; he suffered for her woes."[74] Two years before leaving the Soviet Union and after suffering his third heart attack, Galich was baptized in the Orthodox faith. He left the USSR in June 1974 and received a Nansen passport, which gave him international refugee status.

Like other dissident émigrés, Galich found the West uncomprehending and alien, and he continued to nurse hope of returning to his homeland. He traveled extensively throughout Europe, finally settling in Paris in 1976. Although he continued to travel and to perform actively, his biographers concur that he was suffering a spiritual crisis—probably connected with his emigration—during this period.[75] His poetry dating from these years is sparse; it was only toward the end of his life that he began to write as prolifically as he had previously. In addition to writing and performing, he broadcast a radio show called "Galich at the Microphone" ("U mikrofona

Galich") on Radio Liberty once or twice a week. Galich also became associated with the émigré journal *Kontinent,* under the editorship of Vladimir
Maksimov. In December 1977 Galich accidentally electrocuted himself while
testing a new amplifier. Rumors circulated about the cause of his death, and
even those writing after the fall of the Soviet Union still find it "strange and
frightening."[76] However, the French authorities ruled his death accidental,
and this has never been disproven. Galich was posthumously reinstated in
both the Soviet Writers' Union and the Cinematographers' Union in 1988
and his citizenship was restored in 1993. Beginning in 1987, his works have
been published in his homeland and his plays have been produced again;
public performances of his song-poems have been organized as well. A recording of his collection *When I Return* (*Kogda ia vernus'*) was issued in
1989 by Melodiia and articles about his life and work have appeared in
major journals in the former Soviet Union.

Why did Galich reject success and privilege to follow a course that
would obviously lead to official disapprobation, exclusion, and forced emigration? It seems there was no single event that precipitated Galich's disaf-
fection but rather an evolution toward dissidence. While Galich was never
arrested or imprisoned under Stalin, he did experience the purges directly
(as did nearly all Soviet citizens). His cousin Boris was arrested in 1935 and
imprisoned until Stalin's death in 1953. The 1948 murder of Solomon Mikhoels, the director of the Moscow Yiddish Art Theater, reputedly had a profound impact on Galich given the fact that Mikhoels had been a close friend
and mentor. Contact with former prisoners returning from the camps from
the mid-fifties on probably affected Galich's outlook. A watershed event
seems to have been a 1961 trip Galich made to Karaganda, where he met former inmates of camps for the orphaned children of "enemies of the people."
At some point the bargain Galich had made with the authorities—comfort
in exchange for obedience and submission—became untenable. Arguably
his three best plays, *Sailor's Silence* (*Matrosskaia tishina*), *August* (*Avgust*),
and *I Know How to Make Miracles* (*Ia umeiu delat' chudesa*), had been
banned by the censors. The history of *Sailor's Silence* was particularly painful for Galich. He had written the play in 1947–48 and read it in private
gatherings. Since its hero is a Jew, it was deemed unacceptable at that time.[77]
However, following the death of Stalin it was slated for production both at
the Studio of the Moscow Art Theatre and at the Lenin Komsomol Theater
in Leningrad. The sudden banning of the play in 1958 may have convinced
Galich that anti-Semitism still presented an insurmountable obstacle in
Russian culture.

Numerous references to Stalin and Stalinism in Galich's oeuvre suggest a preoccupation with the dictator and the regime that he created. In his autobiographical book *Dress Rehearsal* (*General'naia repetitsiia*) he uses typically hyperbolic titles in ironic references to Stalin. He refers to Mikhail Chiaurelli as the favorite director of "the genius of all times and peoples, the leader and teacher, our own father, Comrade Stalin." He recalls a toast made to "our own beloved, dear leader and teacher, the brilliant commander of all times and peoples, Comrade Stalin, who leads us from victory to victory."[78] Galich's most bitingly satirical songs include explicit references to Stalin. In "Ballad of How the Director Nearly Lost His Mind" ("Ballada o tom, kak edva ne soshel s uma direktor") he recounts the dilemma of the director of a secondhand shop who cannot decide what to do with old recordings of Stalin's speeches: "Is he a genius or not anymore?"[79] Galich exposes the ambivalence of de-Stalinization during the Thaw and captures the politically fraught situation through this single character sketch. The poem "Night Watch" ("Nochnoi dozor") is less humorous, positing a grotesque nocturnal ritual in which hundreds of thousands of statues of Stalin come to life and take to the streets. Galich raises the specter of a return of Stalinism, warning of a reanimation of the cult of personality. "A Dance Tune" ("Pliasovaia") also treats the possibility of Stalin's return. In this poem Galich ironically calls for sympathy toward Stalin's henchmen, the executioners who gather to share their nostalgia for the iron fist. "Ask Away, Boys!" ("Sprashivaite, mal'chiki!") expresses a firm insistence that the older generation be held accountable for the crimes of Stalinism. In "The Right to Rest" ("Pravo na otdykh") Galich boldly equates Stalin with Hitler, a comparison that remained taboo until glasnost.

"Poem about Stalin" is the most extensive and most direct treatment of Stalin in Galich's oeuvre. Discussion of this work—indeed, of any of Galich's works—should be prefaced by a caveat that there exists no truly definitive text. Indeed, some variants of the song-poem bear the alternative title "Meditations of a Long-Distance Runner" ("Razmyshleniia beguna na dlinnye distantsii"). Galich performed this work with variations, so that versions transcribed from different recordings naturally vary. Moreover, he sometimes performed the six individual parts of the work independently; this is especially true of the last and best known part, "Ave Maria." Of course, oral performance of the work either as a whole or as separate songs produces a very different effect from reading it as a poem. According to one critic, Galich toyed with phrasing, drawing out some syllables, adding extra vowels, shifting stress, and using nonstandard pronunciation—all to enhance the humorous effect.[80] For the purpose of elucidating the author's relationship to Stalinism, the poetic quality of "Poem about Stalin" is primary, and it will be analyzed here as a literary phenomenon.

"Poem about Stalin" treats both the dictator and the culture that developed around his dictatorship. Stalin appears as a character in the first three parts of the poem; we are introduced to him in the first, we see the scope of his evil in the second, and we witness his psychic torment in the third. In the last three parts of the poem Galich explores the consequences and effects of Stalinism. The parts of the poem are distinguished by varying rhythms and rhyme schemes, resembling a poetic pastiche. As Smith has observed of Galich's work in general, "Poem about Stalin" is "conducted on two or more narrative or thematic planes simultaneously."[81] With respect to the poem's treatment of Stalin, it is worth noting that early apocalyptic texts also represent history not through linear narrative but through a combination of legend, myth, and allegory.[82]

Galich takes as his epigraph for the poem the closing line of Aleksandr Blok's long poem "The Twelve" ("Dvenadtsat'"): "Ahead is Jesus Christ."[83] Like Blok in his poem about the Revolution, Galich draws a parallel between biblical accounts and current events. Blok's closing line has caused considerable debate among readers and critics, for the appearance of Christ before the Red Guard is not easily explained. In choosing this single line as his epigraph, Galich strikes resonances of ethical ambiguity and the impossibility of moral certitude. Although some critics interpret Galich's gesture as ironic,[84] I prefer to see it as expressing ambivalence. This reading of the epigraph is supported by the fact that ambivalence pervades and motivates the work as a whole.

The first part of the poem, subtitled "Nativity" ("Rozhdestvo"), sets the theme of competition between Stalin and Christ. The contest between good and evil or God and the devil is, of course, highly conventional. In introducing the plot of "Poem about Stalin," Galich begins in medias res, as he does in many of his song-poems. Jesus has already been born, and the associated events and characters—the shepherds, the Star of the Nativity, the Wise Men—are briefly mentioned. Into this scene Stalin appears, which Galich explains by means of the telescoping of time, a shift from historical to mythological time: "And losing meaning all at once / Centuries, saturnalia and instants / Closed up in an endless circle" (104). Drawing a parallel between Rome and Stalin's Soviet Union is an effective satirical device used previously by Bulgakov (*The Master and Margarita*) and Pasternak (*Zhivago* poems).[85] The juxtaposition of these temporal and situational planes is strikingly incongruous, which calls attention to the points of contact Galich wants to establish. References are made both to historical (biblical) events and to contemporary realia, and the narrative intertwines these allusions. This is an example of what Lev Kopelev calls polyphony in Galich's work, achieved through the combination and development of widely varied situations and characters.[86] The poem's supernatural quality derives from this unlikely conflation of time periods.

Stalin's appearance in the first part of the poem is preceded by portents of evil:

> It got quiet, quiet, quiet,
> Lips froze in a shout,
> That star hissed like a firework,
> And was extinguished.
>
> It got chilly, chilly, chilly,
> And in a premonition of the end
> The insects started humming,
> The ox began to bleat like a sheep.
>
> (103)

Although he is introduced simply as "he," Stalin's identity is immediately evident, for his persona is metonymically represented by Caucasian boots at the threshold and a "face spattered by smallpox" (104). His unpleasant smirk is concealed by a mustache, another obvious marker. That he is not named builds dramatic suspense and may also suggest Soviet citizens' reluctance to speak Stalin's name aloud.

In the second part, "The Leader's Oath" ("Kliatva vozhdia"), Stalin gains his own voice and addresses his monologue directly to Christ. Galich sets up an incongruous juxtaposition by combining the notion of a religious vow with the demonic character of Stalin (here called by his nickname *Vozhd'*). This relatively brief section effectively conveys Stalin's evil nature, for he cruelly ridicules Christ's teachings, asserting that his power is greater. The section ends with a suggestion that Stalinism—and perhaps even Stalin himself—is immortal: "If I die (which might happen), / My kingdom will be eternal!" (105). Stalin's monologue and Christ's silence are reminiscent of the parallel scene in Dostoevsky's "Legend of the Grand Inquisitor," where the Inquisitor reveals the scope of his cynicism and lust for power.

The third part of the poem, subtitled "Moscow Suburban Night" ("Podmoskovnaia noch'"), is an extended psychological portrait of Stalin that draws on earlier depictions of the dictator by Solzhenitsyn, Maximov, and others. We see him as a lonely, paranoid insomniac tormented by nausea and fear of death. His mercurial personality is revealed in his evocation of Ordzhonikidze's ghost:

> Let your face illuminate
> This unprepossessing room.
> Sing me something Georgian, Sergo—
> Sing me my favorite song, *katso*,
>
> The one that our grandfathers sang of old,
> Setting out on their last road . . .
> Sing, Sergo, and forget about the bullet,
> Forget for just ten minutes!
>
> But that's enough,
> Shut up, don't sing!
> You betrayed me basely—
> The hell with you!
>
> (107)

Although Galich's casting of Ordzhonikidze as a victim of Stalinism appears naïve, it reflects the popular distinction made in the sixties between "good" and "bad" Communists.[87] Galich ends this section with Stalin's epiphany, his sudden realization that his claim to divine status is worthless. He seems to acknowledge that God's power is greater than his own as he shifts to a prayer for forgiveness. The third part—in particular Stalin's questions, which remain unanswered—recalls Satan's soliloquy in Milton's *Paradise Lost,* thereby helping to establish the dictator's diabolical character.

Beginning with the fourth section, "Night Conversation in a Restaurant Car" ("Nochnoi razgovor v vagone-restorane"), Galich shifts his focus to the victims of Stalinism. The survivor of Magadan whose voice is heard articulates the suffering of prisoners in the camps yet also expresses the confusion engendered by de-Stalinization: "Our Father turned out to be / Not a father but a bitch" (*Okazalsia nash Otets / Ne ottsom, a sukoiu*) (109). Having the former prisoner call Stalin "Father" is, of course, ironic. Galich enhances his irony by means of the complete reversal in this line; he is merely *suka,* a strongly pejorative term meaning "bitch" or in camp jargon "informer" or "snitch." This victim is tormented not only by memories of the camps but by the knowledge that his father participated in the destruction of the Cathedral of Christ the Savior under Stalin. His own family was complicit in the crimes of Stalinism, serving as the agent of the devil against God. Significantly, memories of the demolition of the church and of Stalin's role in it lead the former prisoner to hallucinate: "Little demons [*beseniata*], little demons / Climb through the window into the train" (111).

Galich calls the fifth part of the poem an author's digression, and it is indeed an extended exhortation to the Russian people to resist the evil of totalitarianism. The last section or epilogue, subtitled "Ave Maria," echoes the first part in that it combines biblical elements with twentieth-century Soviet realia. Mary embodies the suffering of Russia under Stalin, a poetic device that was used effectively by Akhmatova in "Requiem" ("Rekviem"). Galich, too, insists on the moral imperative to remember the victims of Stalinism, though he notes that "Judea went on roaring all around / And did not want to remember the dead" (114). Joseph, who trudges disconsolately behind Mary, is of course her husband on the level of biblical narrative. However, his name also recalls the Father evoked and rebuked earlier by Galich (i.e., Stalin).

As one might expect in so allusive a work, it is difficult to pinpoint the nature of Stalin's evil as portrayed by Galich. His fictive Stalin certainly shares qualities with the devil or Satan, such as the sins of pride and envy. Stalin's professed competition with Christ (and, by extension, with God) is a characteristic often attributed to the devil. It is significant that Galich places his diabolical Stalin at the Nativity, for in Russian folklore pregnancy and birth were considered particularly dangerous times. Demons were thought to hover around the hut or bathhouse where births took place since pregnant women and infants were believed to be especially vulnerable to the unclean force.[88] Conversely, Stalin's claim of divine status and rejection of the sovereignty of God echo features ascribed to Antichrist, as does his implied role of false teacher and deceiver. Although Galich does not name Stalin as the deceptive leader in the fifth section of the work, the allusion is clear:

> Don't fear ashes and hell,
> Fear only the one
> Who says "I know the answers!"
>
> Who says "Everyone who follows me
> Will get heaven on earth as reward!"
>
> (112)

This describes the Soviet utopian mentality and, within that framework, any number of prophets and aspiring autocrats. Stalin is among those who duplicitously promised "heaven on earth" to Galich's generation.

Stalin's presence at the Nativity in Galich's poem links him to Antichrist as well.[89] In the version of the Nativity related in Revelation, the dragon is present at the birth of the Messiah and is frustrated in its attempt to seize and devour Him. The woman "clothed with the sun, and the moon under her feet, and upon her head a crown of twelve stars" (12:1) is sometimes interpreted as the people of Israel rather than Mary, but the child who is born and quickly taken up to heaven is Christ in either reading. The dragon, or Antichrist, is enraged, for the child's escape means the disallowance of his priority; his anger derives from his postponement (or the denial of his right to inheritance).[90] Turning his wrath upon the woman, the dragon pursues her into the wilderness. Galich borrows from Revelation the motif of the suffering mother representing the whole community, in this case Russia under Stalin. Stalin's blasphemy is emphasized by Galich's choice of imagery, for Stalin/Antichrist mocks and parodies Christ in his opposition to Him. Part of a diabolical trinity (with the beast and Satan),[91] Stalin/Antichrist is Christ's antipode for Galich.

It is significant for Galich's vision that Antichrist is both mortal and supernatural. As I previously noted, Antichrist is distinct from the devil; he is a human agent of evil, the human form in which the devil's designs are embodied. However, the devil cannot become human through incarnation simply because he is not God. Antichrist is inhabited and possessed by the devil, but he is fully human. Indeed, as McGinn writes, "The issue raised by belief in Antichrist . . . is that of the relation between human agency and evil, especially the possibility of a completely evil human being."[92] This ambiguity concerning the nature of Antichrist complicates Galich's characterization of Stalin in very interesting ways.

On the one hand, casting Stalin as Antichrist (with elements of Satan) supports his otherness, his being not of this world. Galich thus accomplishes a reversal of the cult of personality. Through its association with the regime of Antichrist, Stalinism is exposed as a false religion, a totalitarian regime that aspires to world domination through evil. The demonization of Stalin is an inversion of the glorification of the dictator that was standard practice during the cult period. Galich's representation of Stalin functions satirically to indict the Soviet political system in general and Stalinism in particular. As the power of Rome is concentrated in the hands of Antichrist, so Stalin appropriates all power in the Soviet Union and his person embodies the wickedness of the corrupt state. Stalin is the enemy of the faithful, God's children, the people of Russia. Thus, to some extent Russian culture is exonerated of the sins of Stalinism by Galich, for a dictator with the power of Antichrist can not reasonably be resisted.

However, "Poem about Stalin" is best understood in the context of Galich's oeuvre. Such a reading leads one to qualify the conclusion that the poet would absolve the Russian people of guilt; rather, this song-poem is a working out of the question of national and personal responsibility for Stalinism. In other works from approximately the same period Galich harshly condemns his countrymen's complicity in the crimes of Stalin. For example, in "Untitled" ("Bez nazvaniia") he expresses outrage that no one is held accountable:

> "Judge not, lest ye be judged . . ."
> Does that really mean not to judge?!
> Does that really mean to sleep soundly
> To drop five-kopek pieces in the metro box?!
> But to judge, to lay down the law—why should we?!
> "Don't touch us, and we won't tou——"
>
> No, this formula for living
> Is contemptible at its core!
> Only those who are chosen are judges?!
> Well, I'm not chosen, but I am a judge![93]

In *Dress Rehearsal* he insists that ordinary Russians (including himself) did, in fact, know about the excesses of Stalinism as they were being committed. It was, he suggests, "cowardly faith" that made people choose to ignore the truth of what was happening around them.[94] Many of Galich's song-poems convey his conviction that the Russian people were responsible for their own fate. Furthermore, complicity is not only active participation but also passivity in the face of evil. The notion that "silence is connivance"[95] is expressed both in *Dress Rehearsal* and in many of the song-poems that comprise *Generation of the Doomed*. For example, in "Goldminers' Waltz" ("Staratel'skii val'sok") he sarcastically excoriates those who kept silent:

> How many times we were silent in different ways,
> But not against, of course, means for!
> Where now are the loudmouths and moaners?
> They made a lot of noise and vanished in their youth . . .
> But the silent ones became the bosses
> Because silence is golden.[96]

In "Ask Away, Boys!" he insists that the truth be aired and counsels the younger generation not to spare its elders but rather to call them to account.

Galich himself seems ambivalent about assigning culpability for the crimes of the past. By casting Stalin as a diabolical other in "Poem about Stalin," he posits the source of his evil outside Russian culture. However, in many other works he finds his compatriots guilty of complicity in the creation and support of Stalinism. Several critics postulate a nagging conscience.[97] The suffering he expresses was experienced only vicariously; he escaped the vicissitudes of the gulag and outlived countless friends and relatives. Galich counts himself among those who were complicit through their failure to resist evil; he was, after all, a favorite son of the "generation of the doomed." In "Ballad about Clean Hands" ("Ballada o chistykh rukakh") he plays at conjugating the verb "to wash" (*umyvat'*) in order to assert collective responsibility for the crimes of Stalinism: "I wash my hands, you wash your hands, and he washes his hands / Saving our pitiful Rome."[98] In this poem ordinary Russians are like Bulgakov's Pilate, guilty of the crime of cowardice. In the end, "Poem about Stalin" should probably be seen as a stage in Galich's working out of his (and his compatriots') relationship with Stalin.

Iskander's *The Feasts of Belshazzar*

The Feasts of Belshazzar is a more explicit treatment of the dictator and his milieu than his portrayal as a python in Iskander's satirical novel *Rabbits and Boa Constrictors* (see chapter 2) since here Stalin and his closest associates are central characters. This tale, one of the original pieces that comprise *Sandro of Chegem*, was not included in the heavily censored version of the epic cycle that appeared in 1973 in *Novyi mir* (nos. 8–11). *Sandro of Chegem* is ostensibly a panoramic, fictionalized history of Abkhazia over the course of the last century. The individual tales are arranged very loosely with respect to chronology but are linked through the figure of Sandro. Stalinism lurks in the background in many of the stories and occasionally comes to the fore, as it does in *Uncle Sandro and His Pet*. In the preface to a 1999 edition of the cycle Iskander writes that his overarching purpose in authoring the work was "to cheer up my depressed countrymen. There was reason to be depressed."[99] The first part of *Sandro of Chegem* was published in the West in 1979, and a second volume entitled *New Chapters* (*Novye glavy*) appeared in 1981. Translations quickly followed in 1983 and 1984,[100] making Iskander better known in the West than many of his literary compatriots. In the glasnost period previously banned parts of the cycle were published in literary journals in the Soviet Union/ Russia. The cycle finally appeared in its entirety (at the time) in 1989.[101] Iskander has continued to add to the *Sandro* cycle; it remains—and may always remain—unfinished. Moreover, Sandro (and Stalin) appear in stories in another cycle entitled *Man and His Surroundings* (*Chelovek i ego okrestnosti*).

Because of its overtly satirical treatment of Stalin, the publication of *The Feasts of Belshazzar* in *Znamia* in 1988 was a watershed event of glasnost. In a brief preface to the tale, which appeared together with *Story of the Prayer Tree* (*Istoriia molel'nogo dereva*), Iskander notes that both were written fifteen years earlier but could not be published then, albeit "not through the capricious will of the author, as the reader will readily understand."[102] In *The Feasts of Belshazzar* Stalin is named and portrayed as a historical figure; no decoding of his identity is necessary. Iskander's literary portrait of Stalin relies on widely known historical and biographical details. In particular, he bases the conceit of the tale—a nocturnal banquet attended by Stalin and his associates—on memoiristic accounts of such events. Milovan Djilas provides a generalized description of Stalin's dinners. The seating arrangements, the food served, and dinner conversation as described by Djilas are all elements of the mythology that came to surround these evenings: "Such a dinner usually lasted six or more hours—from ten at night till four or five in the morning. One ate and drank slowly, during a rambling conversation which ranged from stories and anecdotes to the most serious political and even philosophical subjects. Unofficially and in actual fact a significant part of Soviet policy was shaped at these dinners. Besides they were the most frequent and most convenient entertainment and only luxury in Stalin's otherwise monotonous and somber life."[103]

The markers Iskander employs to characterize Stalin in this literary portrait are entirely typical, yet they also suggest the dictator's essential nature. His mustache and roguish smile figure prominently: "He smiled cunningly into his mustache."[104] While biographically accurate, these details are chosen to emphasize Stalin's craftiness. The pipe he clenches in his fist carries demonic associations of smoke and flames. Stalin's pockmarked face (Kalinin uses the dialectical *konopatyi* in addressing him) suggests the signs of Antichrist. His presence haunts those who experience it; Sandro (in a long flashback) senses that Sabid's Hollow is an unholy place after Stalin passes through it.

Although Stalin's identity is unambiguous in the tale, other characters avoid naming him and use third-person pronouns: "'Will he be here?,' asked Uncle Sandro quietly" (249). This linguistic practice reflects the folk belief that one should never refer to the devil by name lest he appear. The fact that both Judeo-Christian and Slavic pagan cultures impose a taboo on naming God (Yahweh) and a powerful force of nature (Medved) complicates Iskander's portrait. When Stalin's diabolical nature has been fully revealed at the end of the tale, Sandro refers to him simply as "That One" (*tot*): "That One had a very sloping shoulder" (292). The term "leader" (*vozhd'*), a title Stalin himself encouraged, is also used by Iskander's characters to avoid calling him by name. Devil oaths are playfully scattered throughout his narrative as well; although not directly referring to Stalin, they nevertheless hint at demonic presence. For example, the narrator tells us that Sandro was making good money and ends by exclaiming: "Devil take it!" (236). A digression about the philosophy of cannibalism is linked to Stalin's portrait as well, for the terms "cannibal" (*liudoed*) and "hangman" (*palach*) are used repeatedly in the passage; both nicknames were used by camp prisoners and others to refer to Stalin.

Some of the details Iskander supplies in his text support an interpretation of Stalin as the devil, while others echo the Antichrist myth. Stalin's imminent arrival and his possible presence at the banquet are the subjects of speculation and rumor among the dancers; unnamed and unbidden, he is nevertheless much anticipated. Here is how Iskander conveys Sandro's speculation about Stalin's "withered arm" and its significance: "It seemed to Uncle Sandro that the Leader's left arm didn't move entirely smoothly. He has a withered arm, thought Sandro, and, looking carefully, decided yes, a little bit. . . . He should get together with Bad Arm, he thought for no apparent reason. In general Uncle Sandro felt that this slight impairment somehow lowered the image of the Leader. Just a little bit, but all the same" (261–62). Like his sloping shoulder, Stalin's deformed arm strengthens his connection with Antichrist. Stalin's eyes are described several times in the tale. Their "oily gleam" (257) reminds Sandro of the gleam of Stalin's boots, and his gaze is so "resplendent" (262) that one cannot look directly at him. Within the flashback passage Iskander explicitly expresses Stalin's evil nature through a description of his eyes: "[He] looked at the blue-eyed youth with such malice as no one had ever looked at him" (288). Fury and malevolence are perceptible in his gaze, reminding us of the prophecy of Antichrist in the Book of Daniel: "And in the latter time of their kingdom, when the transgressors are come to the full, a king of fierce countenance, and understanding dark sentences, shall stand up" (8:23).

After the dance troupe has performed, Stalin rewards them by ripping apart a roasted chicken and distributing pieces to the dancers. His treatment of the chicken, recounted graphically by Iskander, is certainly metaphorical: "Noticing that the food was late in coming, Stalin gave up waiting and, using both hands, decisively took the chicken by the legs and, with enjoyment (as Uncle Sandro noticed), ripped it into two parts. Then he ripped each of these again. The fat ran down his fingers, but he paid no attention" (261). His violent treatment of the chicken suggests his destruction of human beings, with his gestures displaying his sadistic cruelty combined with his famous generosity. The devil is often represented devouring or gnawing sinners; the notion of the "Jaws of Hell," pictorially represented by the gaping mouth of a serpent, involves ingestion. It is noteworthy that Stalin does not himself eat the chicken he rips apart, but another passage depicts him chewing the meat of a lamb prepared in milk: "Slathering a piece of lamb thickly with the purple condiment, he placed it in his mouth and crunched the milky gristle" (266). The lamb has connotations of Christianity and milk suggests maternity and humanity, so that Iskander's description links Stalin with Antichrist (the opponent and rival of Christ).

Stalin's powers of magnetism or telepathy have been noted by many memoirists. As James E. Abbe writes: "As soon as I saw the whites of his eyes, I recognized that Stalin has the surgical ability to remove a man's thoughts from his head and sort them out on the table."[105] In this tale Sandro recalls that Stalin could drive horses without a whip or stick because the animals instinctively sense his evil: "This man didn't need any stick or whip. . . . [H]e was one of those whom horses feared without any kind of goading" (289). Stalin communicates with Sandro in Sabid's Hollow by projecting his thoughts, threatening to return and kill the boy if he tells his elders what he has witnessed. Iskander endows Stalin with this trait elsewhere in his oeuvre, most notably in *Uncle Sandro and His Pet*.

Iskander alludes to Stalin's illegitimacy in a digression that represents the character Stalin's fantasy or daydream. Having withdrawn into a state of mental solitude, feeling gloomy and alienated from his associates, Stalin imagines what his life would have been like if he had not become the General Secretary of the Communist Party and a ruthless dictator. The alluring fantasy is disrupted when he tries to extend it to include his aged mother: "His dear old mother with the wrinkled face. Only in old age have respect and plenty come to her at last. . . . Dear . . . Damn you!!!" (279). Stalin remembers an old insult when he overheard two village men chuckling obscenely about his mother. As I previously noted, Antichrist's origins are equally dubious; in some versions of the myth he is born of an immoral, depraved woman. It is also significant that Stalin imagines himself as a simple grape farmer; he believes that his "essential greatness" (278) is clear to all, but he is modest and content with his lot. This is "pride that apes humility," to use Coleridge's formulation in his poem "The Devil's Thoughts," and pride is the devil's favorite sin.

The title of Iskander's work encourages us to read the tale within a biblical context, and such a reading strengthens the demonic characterization of Stalin. The Belshazzar of the title is the king of the Chaldeans (Daniel 5), and Iskander's allusion implies that Stalin, too, is a corrupt ruler. According to the Book of Daniel, Belshazzar hosted a great feast for a thousand of his lords and "drank wine before the thousand" (5:1). He brought in the gold and silver vessels that his father, Nebuchadnezzar, had taken from the temple in Jerusalem and encouraged his guests to drink from them. As his guests caroused and praised pagan gods, a hand appeared and inscribed words on the wall, which only the wise Daniel could interpret: "And this is the writing that was written, Mene, Mene, Tekel, Upharsin. This is the interpretation of the thing: Mene; God hath numbered thy kingdom, and finished it. Tekel; Thou art weighed in the balances, and art found wanting. Peres; Thy kingdom is divided, and given to the Medes and Persians" (Daniel 5:25–28). Belzhazzar is a frivolous king who thoughtlessly commits sacrilege, and he is guilty of pride and idolatry as well.[106] Stalin and his works, by analogy, are weighed and found wanting by Iskander. Like Belshazzar he is denigrating the religious and cultural customs of his subjects through his great arrogance. The tradition of holding a sumptuous banquet the night before the fall of a city or kingdom is found in prebiblical sources, such as Herodotus and Xenophon.[107] Iskander is not only satirizing Stalin but also warning his readers of the consequences of complicity.[108]

There is in *The Feasts of Belshazzar* a Faustian subtext that complicates the interpretation of Stalin's character in interesting ways. Sandro initially "worships" Stalin and symbolically enters into a kind of bargain with him. He demonstrates his loyalty, his willingness to serve Stalin, by sliding on his knees, blindfolded, across the dance floor and right up to him. Iskander describes the tableau this way: "Stalin frowned in surprise. He even slightly waved the pipe gripped in his fist, but Uncle Sandro's pose, which expressed bold devotion, and the touching defenselessness of the outstretched arms and the blindness of the head proudly thrown back—and, at the same time, the mysterious stubbornness of the whole figure, as if saying to the Leader, 'I won't stand up until you bless me'—made him smile" (258). Sandro is duly "blessed" by Stalin, recognized, and rewarded. One of Sandro's fellow dancers verbalizes the terms of the pact he has witnessed, shouting to Sandro: "Good going . . . now you're set for life" (260). Sandro, however, realizes the danger in time and backs out of the deal. He slips out of the snare set by Stalin and (significantly) thanks God for his own quick-wittedness. While driving home, the dancers distribute candy and sweets left over from the banquet to children. Iskander ironically calls these treats "a divine gift" (*bozhii dar*) (288), and the dancers' smiles confirm the ambiguity of Iskander's characterization: "'If they only knew whose table they were from,' [thought] the dancers wearily" (288).

The biblical subtext of *The Feasts of Belshazzar* suggests an indictment of Stalin's blasphemy on a cultural level as well. The banquet depicted is a desecration of Abkhazian table ritual, for it becomes a political event. Men's careers—indeed, their lives—are here subject to Stalin's whims and shifts of mood. As the honored guest at the banquet, Stalin presides over a scene of excess. The devil, of course, loves drunkenness and gluttony and encourages men to indulge in these sins. Iskander's banquet is thus a blasphemous parody of the Last Supper as well. His mock-Homeric description of the feast conjures up images of hell. The table has two wings "laden with fruit" (253), suggesting temptation and the Fall. The roast chickens expose their bare rumps "with a certain appetizing indecency" (253). Iskander describes the pomegranates in lavish detail: "Split pomegranates, as if cracked by an inner heat, revealed their sinful caverns, stuffed with jewels" (253). Pomegranates are associated with the underworld in classical mythology. Persephone's eating of the seeds of a pomegranate seals an unbreakable contract, leading to her compulsory residence in Hades for half of each year. Lambs are roasted for the banquet, which suggests an offering to God prescribed by the Torah but also (in this context) triumph over Christ. The roasted piglets (already carrying diabolical associations) here clench radishes in their teeth "with devilish glee" (253). Nestor Lakoba's drinking horn is a "scepter of power at table" (254). Both the ram and the goat—and, by extension, their horns—are symbols of power in the Old Testament,[109] and the horn (*roga*) is associated with Antichrist through Daniel. While sitting at the feast, Stalin muses that only singing brings him true pleasure, and Iskander's formulation at this point is very significant: "No, not power, not an enemy's blood, not wine ever gave him such enjoyment" (277). The mixing of blood and wine in Stalin's indirect speech is a parodic reference to the Eucharist. Similarly, his calling Kalinin his "All-Union goat" (*vsesoiuznyi kozel*) (267) is a double entendre; while the goat conveys biblical connotations of power, it also bears the sense of "lecher" in colloquial Russian.

Iskander's closing assessment of Stalin carries a biblical tone; it echoes the vision contained in the Book of Daniel, in which "the judgement was set, and the books were opened" (7:10). In the final paragraph of the tale the authorial narrator steps forward to assert his faith in divine justice: "The very fact that he died a natural death (if, of course, he did die a natural death) prompts me personally to the religious thought that God demanded to see the dossier with his deeds in order to judge him Himself with the highest judgement and to punish him Himself with the highest punishment" (293). In his digression on cannibalism Iskander hypothesizes that baseness always requires "overcoming humanity" (271), and it is not coincidental that in his self-pitying gloom Stalin curses mankind: "Damn life, damn human nature!" (281). Since Stalin's nature is not fully human, it follows that only God can judge and punish him fairly. In his reference to Stalin's "natural death" Iskander is alluding, on one level, to the rumor that Stalin's end was hastened in some way (e.g., by tampering with his medication or simply by delaying aid following his stroke).[110] On another level he is hinting at the possibility of God's manifest judgment, for he has shown that Stalin exceeded all limits of earthly wickedness.

Linking Stalin to Belshazzar, the devil, and Antichrist elevates the dictator to a cosmic plane. The spirit of evil that he embodies is essentially external and uncontrollable, and it is up to God to terminate his rule. Antichrist and those associated with him are destined to be overthrown and cast into hell, but the timing of this divine justice is controversial.[111] Nevertheless, the message of the Book of Daniel, upon which Iskander clearly relies, is that God can be counted upon to carry out judgment.

Although Iskander has been outspoken in his condemnation of Stalin and Stalinism, he has been cautious about assigning blame. It would seem that placing the evil wrought by Stalin on a superhuman plane shifts culpability away from the Russian people. Keenly interested in avoiding the division and dissension that Antichrist is supposed to effect, Iskander tends toward irony in his conclusions about Stalinism. In a 1994 interview he questioned the possibility of understanding Stalin's evil and said that he "mostly feared lapsing into speculations on hatred for Stalin."[112] It is in this context that the embedded digression on the nature of cannibalism becomes meaningful: "Man is given the choice of becoming an executioner, just as he is given the choice of not becoming one. In the final analysis the choice is ours. And if the cannibal's stomach just didn't accept human flesh, this would be a simplified and dangerous path of humanizing the cannibal. Who knows where this proclivity of his might lead. There is no humanity without triumph over baseness and no baseness without triumph over humanity. In each instance the choice is ours, as is the responsibility for that choice" (271). Couched as they are within a tale about Stalin and Stalinism, these musings suggest a didactic insistence on the role of free will in assessing culpability. Iskander's emphasis on personal responsibility for moral choices crucially qualifies his characterization of Stalin as the devil or Antichrist. While Stalin's evil may have been of a cosmic order, man (i.e., the Soviet populace) is not exculpated for participating in the crimes of Stalinism. This does not prevent one's reading of Iskander's tale as an affirmation of faith in divine justice. Rather, it grounds his apocalyptic treatment of Stalinism in a strongly humanistic moral vision.

Conclusion

Rendering Stalin as the devil or Antichrist is a powerful satirical device that depends in part on positioning the dictator beyond the boundaries of Russian (or, in the case of Iskander, Soviet) culture. If his power and influence over the Russian people are supernatural in origin, no effective resistance is possible and the nation is absolved of guilt for the crimes of Stalinism. To some extent this device positively strengthens the signification of *svoi*, for it emphasizes Stalin's otherness, his belonging to the realm of *chuzhoi*. This dynamic is complicated in satire, however, by the tradition of the diabolical in Russian culture. The devil is a foreigner, but he is also plural and petty; moreover, he is part of human nature. Antichrist, too, has peculiarly Russian features in satirical portraits of Stalin. The theological concept of Antichrist is strongly colored by folk interpretations of the Apocalypse, including the habit of detecting Antichrist in the person of cruel tyrants (such as Peter the Great). Thus, casting Stalin as diabolical is an ambiguous gesture that does not definitively resolve the issue of moral culpability.

Bulgakov's *Master and Margarita* is the richest and most complex example of satirical texts depicting Stalin as the devil. I have suggested that Woland's character derives from the author's own deep ambivalence toward Stalin. Galich's Stalin, who resembles Antichrist more than the devil, is thoroughly evil. Read in the context of Galich's oeuvre, the protagonist of "Poem about Stalin" functions as a satiric goad to the collective conscience of the Russian people. Iskander's tale *The Feasts of Belshazzar* replays one of

Stalin's nocturnal banquets as a version of the biblical feast in the Book of Daniel, so that his satire functions as both excoriation and warning.

The diabolical is fascinating and attractive because it tempts and seduces, inclining one to capitulate. In the Romantic tradition—and in the conscious comparisons made by official Stalinist culture—diabolical characteristics are closely linked with the creative and revolutionary aspects of power. The figure of Stalin inspires awe and admiration as well as dread. These satirical texts by Bulgakov, Galich, and Iskander address this duality of the demonic explicitly or implicitly. Casting Stalin as the devil or Antichrist is certainly effective in exposing the depth and breadth of his evil, but it leaves unresolved the larger question of guilt. As Dostoevsky so persuasively argued, the Russian people are drawn to mysticism and grandeur, and their quasi-deification of Stalin has popular roots and is supported by official ratification. Characterizing Stalin as the devil or Antichrist in satire thus contributes to the ongoing dialogue about guilt and complicity in twentieth-century Russian culture. Satirical portraits of Stalin as a demonic figure serve to question the limits of volition and ethical choice under the Stalinist regime.

6

The Corpse and the Revenant

Stalin is effectively cast in some works of Russian satire as the unquiet or unclean dead, another category marked as other. To some extent this follows from Stalin's mysterious death and the mythology that grew up around this event. The fact that his body was not buried and was displayed for eight years in the mausoleum together with Lenin's corpse certainly contributed to his being regarded as a potential or actual revenant. As we shall see, the idea of the unquiet dead (*zalozhnye umershie*) is rooted in beliefs both universal and specific to Slavic folk culture, so that satiric characterization of Stalin as a revenant is a powerful device. In this chapter I examine three works in which Stalin is portrayed as the unquiet dead. Evgenii Evtushenko's 1962 poem "The Heirs of Stalin" ("Nasledniki Stalina") questions the ramifications of removing Stalin's body from the mausoleum and suggests the lingering threat of Stalinism in Soviet society. Anatolii Gladilin's story "Rehearsal on Friday" ("Repetitsiia v piatnitsu"), published in 1977, has Stalin reanimated in the Brezhnev period after prolonged sleep in an anabolic state. Andrei Siniavsky's autobiographical 1984 novel *Goodnight* (*Spokoinoi nochi*) features Stalin's spirit returning after his death to seek absolution and peace.

The Unquiet Dead and Stalin

Questions about whether Stalin's death was "natural" have lingered, with various accounts advanced by historians and biographers. It is generally agreed that his aides were slow in discovering that he had suffered a stroke on February 28, 1953; none of them dared enter his room unbidden for an entire day. There have also been allegations that he was poisoned or that someone tampered with his anticoagulant medicine. Another version has it that Lavrenty Beria, the head of the NKVD, or his henchmen beat Stalin after his stroke, hastening his end.[1] Moreover, the press did not report his death for two days, instead informing the public that he had suffered a stroke, that he was weak, and that his condition was serious. It is little wonder that rumors about the circumstances of his death circulated—and continue to circulate—widely, given the fact that it may have effectively been a coup d'état.

Even before Stalin had died, attempts were made to revive him by a brain surgeon specializing in reanimation.[2] Immediately following his death, his corpse was embalmed and laid out in the Hall of Columns, where it lay in state for three days. During that period, such enormous crowds pressed in to view the body that a stampede ensued, and five hundred people were crushed to death.[3] In the weeks following Stalin's death, posthumous appearances of the dictator were reported and misfortunes were attributed to his influence. Stalin thus continued to exercise mysterious power over people's lives even in death.[4] Folkloric accounts of Stalin's life after death recapitulated similar stories told about Lenin and, before him, Alexander I. It was rumored that Stalin, like his predecessors, had not really died but was wandering the Russian countryside disguised as a peasant or hermit.[5]

On March 9 Stalin's body was placed in a glass catafalque next to Lenin's body in the mausoleum and Stalin's name was added to the inscription in marble on the facade. The decision to exhibit Stalin's body in the mausoleum was based on the cult of Lenin, already an established fact of Soviet culture. Following the Revolution, funerary customs had been minimized in accordance with the atheist tenet that the dead body is merely a useless husk. The treatment of dead leaders' bodies was a striking exception to this rule, perhaps because Lenin's and Stalin's personae had both become emblematic of the "body politic." If the leader's health is tightly intertwined with the health of society as a whole, it is deeply problematic when he dies and his body begins to decay.[6] In the case of Lenin, the commission charged with the question of his funeral ostensibly based its original decision to delay burial on popular demand to view the body. However, there were many who felt that it was unthinkable simply to consign his body to the earth. Within a short time the plan to embalm Lenin's body for forty days was changed and it was decided to preserve and display it indefinitely. Once this precedent was established, it followed that Stalin's body should also be preserved for posterity.

Many observers of Soviet culture have noted that this treatment of the two leaders' bodies implies the creation of holy relics and that the mausoleum functions as a religious edifice.[7] The body as a relic becomes a symbol of the state and can be used to instill national pride and loyalty. The successful embalming of Lenin's corpse—staving off decomposition—was both evidence of his divinity and a demonstration of the capabilities of Soviet science. These political purposes were certainly operative in the embalming and display of Stalin's corpse as well. Aside from the prototype of Orthodox relics (a link that the Soviets strenuously denied), an obvious model was Egyptian mummification. The tomb of Tutankhamen had been discovered only fifteen months before Lenin's death, and an analogous treatment of the Soviet leader's body seemed appropriate. A. V. Shchusev, the architect chosen to construct Lenin's tomb, proposed the cube as the basis of the structure, and both the original wooden mausoleum opened in August 1924 and the granite building that replaced it in 1930 are based on Shchusev's design. Like the pyramid, the cube symbolized immortality. As Kazimir Malevich wrote in 1924, "The cube is no longer a geometric body. It is a new object with which we try to portray eternity, to create a new set of circumstances, with which we can maintain Lenin's eternal life, defeating death."[8] Thus, a secular cathedral containing the founder's preserved corpse stood at the geographical and symbolic center of the Soviet state, promising immortality albeit not an afterlife.

Another influence on the Immortalization Committee's original decision to preserve Lenin's body may well have been Nikolai Fedorov's concept of the "common task" current in the early years of the twentieth century. Fedorov's project of reanimating the dead through (future) advanced technology supported the preservation of Lenin's corpse, for it promised that on Resurrecting Day the whole person will rise from the dead. There are certainly traces of Orthodoxy in Fedorov's thinking; his project emphasizes the Eastern notion of Christ as Resurrection as opposed to the Western idea of Christ as atonement.[9] For Fedorov the most important act performed by Christ was the raising of Lazarus, proving that death and decay could be reversed in an ordinary man.[10] It is likely that Leonid Krasin, the engineer-diplomat in charge of the disposition of Lenin's body, believed that the leader's body should be preserved for reanimation in the future. While Fedorov soon fell out of favor with the Bolsheviks, his ideas about controlling nature were incorporated into Soviet ideology.[11] In particular, the Bolshevik god-building movement—embraced by Krasin along with Gorky, Lunacharsky, and Bogdanov—sought a new human-centered religion in the Soviet experiment.[12] Technology was to be the source of miracles, such as limiting the power of death over humankind.

Ideas about the possibility of reanimation of the dead through science coexisted in twentieth-century Russian culture with the lingering belief in the unquiet or unclean dead. It was thought that those who die unnatural deaths—by accident, murder, or suicide—become revenants. Since they have not lived out their allotted time on earth, they are consigned to a troubled existence beyond the grave. *Zalozhnye umershie* were believed to remain in close proximity to their families, either at the place of their deaths or near their graves. Another category of people who are at risk of becoming revenants are those who do great evil, such as murderers or sorcerers. The earth will not accept the bodies of grievous sinners and casts them out; they must then exist as *zalozhnye umershie*.[13] Those who have been cursed are also likely to become revenants, as are people who die alone and unattended. Not receiving the last rites and thus dying with a guilty conscience can cause the dead to be unquiet. The funeral is very important in popular belief as a means of avoiding unquiet death, for through the funeral rite a society carries out "disaggregation" (removal of the corpse, recovering what was so-cially invested in the dead person) and "reinstallation" (through which the collective triumphs over death).[14] Failure to observe funerary rituals can short-circuit this process, with the dead presenting a danger to the collective as a potential revenant. Indeed, those denied proper funeral rites are the most dangerous of the unquiet dead. They want to be reincorporated into this world, and because they cannot be they are hostile toward the living.[15]

Fear of corpses is nearly universal, and Slavic culture is no exception. Embalming—especially cremation—serves to render the corpse harmless, to neutralize its power before it is buried. Burial must be accomplished in a timely manner; allowing a corpse to remain in the house longer than is pre-scribed may bring about another death.[16] During the time between death and burial, the corpse is particularly susceptible to the influence of evil forces. Some of the rituals associated with the treatment of the corpse, such as ablutions and closing of the eyes, are meant to protect the soul of the dead. Family members or others who were close to the dead person must keep vigil, fending off diabolical forces. Improper burial—notably not being buried or not being buried deeply enough in the earth—is believed to cause unquiet death in some cultures.[17] Complete decomposition of the body within the earth is required for passage of the dead into the other world. According to some folk beliefs, the bodies of *zalozhnye umershie* cannot decay even when buried properly.[18] Cause and effect are intertwined: the unquiet dead may become unquiet because they are not buried properly, or they may defy proper burial (and decomposition) because they are unquiet.

A common element in all of these ideas about the unquiet dead is the perception of the revenant as other. As Paul Barber states, "Lists of potential revenants tend to contain people who are distinguished primarily by being different from the people who make the lists."[19] The unquiet dead are suspended in a state of transition, and because they are not admitted to the other world, they remain uncontrollable and malevolent spirits in this world. Until the spirit finds peace in the world of the dead, it will continue to return of its own volition and cause terror among the living. *Zalozhnye umershie* disturb especially those who were close to them in life, often visiting them in their sleep. The living are safe only when the spirit loses its liminal and frightening character, when it is firmly ensconced in the other world.

The foregoing discussion is intended to demonstrate the effective functionality of satirically characterizing Stalin as a revenant. Having suffered a debilitating attack (through natural or unnatural causes), Stalin was left alone and died, reportedly in agony, without any rites of passage. His body was then embalmed but not buried; his corpse was displayed for an unusually long time in the Hall of Columns (causing many additional deaths) and then installed in the mausoleum. The facts surrounding his death encourage superstitious extrapolation in literature. Stalin was a great and unrepentant sinner and was thus consigned to the unquiet dead.

Evtushenko's "The Heirs of Stalin"

Evgenii Evtushenko made an enormously successful career for himself as a Russian poet by conforming to changing political exigencies. His life, like that of virtually all Russians of his generation, was shaped by Stalinism. Born in Siberia in 1933, he claimed that he was by background "half an intellectual and half a peasant."[20] Both his grandfathers were arrested during the purges. His maternal grandfather, a committed revolutionary, was arrested in 1938 for high treason; his paternal grandfather, a mathematician of Latvian origin, was accused of being a foreign spy.[21] As a young man Evtushenko lived within the parameters of Stalinism and did not question the legitimacy of the regime. In his autobiography he recalls that Stalin "exercised a sort of hypnotic charm,"[22] and that he, like other Soviet children, adored the dictator. Beginning his career as a poet, he quickly learned that every poem required mention of Stalin and adapted to this requirement for the purpose of publication. He has explained his youthful poetic worship of Stalin as typical of his generation: "We grew up in a hypnotic state, we waved little flags at demonstrations, passing by the mausoleum where stood the one by whose order our grandfathers and fathers were sentenced and shot; we wrote laudatory verses dedicated to him."[23] Evtushenko's poetry, however, is by and large not overtly political; commentators noted early on that most of his verse was ideologically neutral.[24]

In the early sixties, at the height of his popularity, Evtushenko was acknowledged as his generation's poetic spokesman. His fame, like that of his fellow poet Andrei Voznesensky, approached that of film stars; Evtushenko constituted a "phenomenon" in that era.[25] Thousands of people flocked to hear him give poetry readings, and his work was published widely not only in the Soviet Union but in translation in Europe and America. Literary scholars—notably Andrei Sinyavsky—have pointed out that his work suffers from "haste, instability, and diffuseness,"[26] and the critical consensus is that he is not a great poet. Nevertheless, his influence and cultural centrality during the Thaw period are undeniable.

Evtushenko has published prolifically since his literary debut in 1949. He studied at the Gorky Literary Institute beginning in 1954 and was accepted into the Soviet Writers' Union. Evtushenko briefly fell from favor in 1957 after speaking out at a meeting in defense of Vladimir Dudintsev's novel *Not by Bread Alone* (*Ne khlebom edinym*) and was expelled from the Komsomol and the Literary Institute (ostensibly for spotty attendance); he was later reinstated in both.[27] He served on the editorial board of the liberal journal *Iunost'* from 1962 to 1969 and became a member of the Praesidium of the Soviet Writers' Union in 1967. A measure of his official stature was reflected in his extensive travel abroad, serving as a kind of cultural ambassador for the Soviet Union in the sixties.

By his own account Evtushenko came to doubt the validity of the cult of Stalin while still a young man. Although he did not voice his doubt at the time, he later admitted that "inside me the conviction that it was my duty to fight to remove the dirt that was about to drown the ideals of my two vanished grandfathers was growing."[28] As he acknowledges in his autobiography, Stalin's funeral marked a turning point for him, for he understood that the stampede in which hundreds of people were killed (and which he witnessed) was a direct result of the paranoia engendered by Stalinism. Evtushenko here also asserts that Khrushchev's Secret Speech in 1956 was a genuine revelation, and that the Russian people (including himself) did not know what was happening during the purges: "They sensed intuitively that something was wrong, but no one wanted to believe what he guessed at in his heart. It would have been too terrible."[29] Moreover, for the Soviet people Stalin's name was linked with Lenin's, and this legacy lent him legitimacy.

Evtushenko's rejection of Stalinism—however late and tentative—has been expressed in some of his most memorable poems. "Winter Station"

("Stantsiia Zima"), published in 1956, touches on the theme of Stalinism and conveys the pain that Stalin's crimes caused the poet personally. The publication of "Babii Yar" in 1961 aroused tremendous controversy in the Soviet Union; although primarily an exposé of anti-Semitism, it is implicitly an indictment of Stalin's policies as well. "Bratsk Hydoelectric Station" ("Bratskaia gidrostantsiia"), written in 1965, is ambivalent in its approach to Stalinism. Sinyavsky notes that in this poem Evtushenko criticizes Stalin for not trusting and valuing the innate patriotism of the Russian people yet celebrates the gulag as "a stronghold of our military and industrial might . . . which sounds altogether blasphemous."[30] One must be careful to contextualize these poetic treatments of Stalinism. While they appear timid from our vantage point, they did express opinions and attitudes shared by the younger generation of Soviets that were still taboo. In short, although his "civic muse" is very cautious, the fact that he treats the painful theme of Stalinism should not be devalued.

A Precocious Autobiography, published in France in 1963, was more outspoken in its critique of Stalin and Stalinism and aroused vociferous official disapproval. Evtushenko here revealed that he was ashamed for Stalin and lamented that the dictator so distrusted the people. The latter, by contrast, had profound faith in communism and extended that faith to Stalin.[31] In Evtushenko's view, Stalin was guilty of distorting Lenin's ideas and thus was more damaging to the cause of communism than its overt enemies. His greatest crime was not the purges but "the corruption of the human spirit," which led to widespread "careerism, servility, spying, cruelty, bigotry [and] hypocrisy."[32] As in his poems, Evtushenko here insists that Stalinism was a cancerous growth on the essentially healthy civic body of Soviet society. By 1990, when he was filming Stalin's Funeral (Pokhorony Stalina), he had become much more outspoken about Stalin's crimes, while still emphasizing the positive effects of his generation's rejection of Stalinism: "If one is to speak of Stalinism, then we are still digging down to the roots of the poisonous tree of totalitarianism, of which Stalin was the gardener. But this film is not about the roots and not about the gardener but rather about the green shoots sprouting in the evil shade of that tree and yet straining toward the light—about our generation."[33]

"The Heirs of Stalin" merits close attention as Evtushenko's attempt to exorcise Stalin satirically by casting him as a revenant. This poem was controversial enough to require direct authorization by Khrushchev; with his permission, it appeared in Pravda in 1962. Evtushenko had performed the poem publicly for a year before its publication and it was most likely regarded by the authorities as a useful weapon in the current campaign of de-Stalinization. It was, however, excluded from later collected editions of Evtushenko's poetry, presumably because criticism of Stalin was no longer advantageous to the regime. The occasion of the poem's composition was the removal of Stalin's body from the mausoleum in 1961 in accordance with a resolution of the Twenty-second Party Congress of 1956, where Khrushchev is reported to have said: "The mausoleum stinks of Stalin's corpse."[34] Consequently the body was removed and sealed under concrete under the ramparts of the Kremlin Wall, along with the remains of other Soviet leaders. The name "Stalin" subsequently disappeared from the facade of the mausoleum.

In Evtushenko's poem Stalin is richly endowed with features of the unquiet dead. He silently watches everyone, as the newly dead or the undead are thought to do: "He wanted to remember all of those, / who carried him out—the young Riazan and Kursk recruits."[35] Moreover, the coffin emits smoke and "breath flowed from the coffin" (343). Stalin threatens "to rise from the earth" (*vstat' iz zemli*) (343) to take revenge on those who have dishonored him. In the context of this poem, Stalin's rising from the dead suggests the return of Stalinism, for his body is emblematic of the state. He has left many followers behind, as does a vampire. They are located specifically "on the earth" (*na share zemnom; na zemle*) (343, 344), still active among the living.

According to Russian folklore, the newly dead are "half-dead" (*polupokoiniki*) for some period, certainly in the days before the corpse is buried. Thus, funeral and commemorative ceremonies include the dead as if they were present. Failure to appease the dead and demonstrate respect may arouse their anger and cause them to take revenge upon the living.[36] During this period of liminality it is important to bestow due honor on the newly dead so that they may pass on to the other world and not become revenants. Evtushenko positions Stalin in this space between the living and the dead. Unburied—and, by implication, with none of the other funerary rituals performed—Stalin has remained partially animate, threatening the living with his return as a vengeful revenant.[37] He is grotesque and frightening as the unquiet dead in this poem, but the real power of Evtushenko's denunciation of Stalin lies in his suggestion that there are some—perhaps many—who would welcome a return to Stalinism. "The Heirs of Stalin" exculpates honest Soviet patriots—as Evtushenko judges them—but indicts those of his countrymen who were and are complicit in the crimes of Stalinism.

Gladilin's "Rehearsal on Friday"

Anatolii Gladilin (born 1935) was a successful writer in the Soviet Union for ten years and published frequently in *Iunost'* from the mid-fifties on. He was one of the most promising of the "New Voices" of the sixties, gaining initial fame with the appearance in 1956 of *The Chronicle of the Times of Viktor Podgurskii* (*Khronika vremen Viktora Podgurskogo*). Accepted into the Soviet Writers' Union in 1960, he was the organization's youngest member and enjoyed a favored position in the literary bureaucracy.[38] Like other figures prominent in the Youth Prose movement of this period, Gladilin was patriotic and "pro-Soviet by inclination."[39] Beginning in 1965, however, Gladilin's career trajectory took a sharp downward turn. Certainly his signing an open letter of protest against the prosecution of Sinyavsky and Daniel contributed to his fall from grace. Moreover, in 1966 he was arrested, together with a group of writers, on Red Square, where they had gone to observe a rumored rally of Old Bolsheviks on the anniversary of Stalin's death. The last straw, it seems, was the samizdat circulation and *tamizdat* publication of his novel *Forecast for Tomorrow* (*Prognoz na zavtra*) in 1972. Gladilin left the Soviet Union in 1976 and settled in France, where he remained active in émigré literary circles.

Gladilin remarks in his autobiography that the typical Soviet citizen sincerely mourned the death of Stalin. He explicitly poses the question of how his countrymen are to come to terms with Stalinism: "In the hall sits Vanya Petrov, or Petya Ivanov, power supply sources student, or university graduate, or young engineer—our coeval, our confederate. One problem disturbs him, as it does us: How are we to live now? When we were growing up, two schizophrenics slaughtered sixty million people. These leaders and führers exchanged experience in the areas of repression and concentration camp management."[40] He explores this theme of reconciliation in his story "The First Day of the New Year" ("Pervyi den' Novogo goda"), published in 1963. The hero's relationship to his father is complicated by their inability to communicate; their life experiences are completely different as a result of Stalinism.

"Rehearsal on Friday," a story that features Stalin as a character, was published in 1977 in *Kontinent* and in 1978 in an émigré edition of Gladilin's works. When it finally appeared in Russia in 1991 (in *Iunost'*), a review by Vladimir Abashev took note of the tale's "depressing resonance with the mood of today."[41] The conceit of Gladilin's tale is that Stalin has been preserved in an anabolic state since his death and finds it timely to return in the

Brezhnev period. This plot is loosely based on the rumor that Stalin did not actually die but was living incognito as a simple peasant. Gladilin's science fiction plot twist involves cryogenics, whereby the body is preserved immediately at death. By means of rapid cooling and the administration of blood thinners, calcium channel blockers, and so forth, the body is preserved in a frozen state and stored, awaiting regeneration in the future. Stalin himself explains the successful application of this technology in "Rehearsal on Friday": " 'I was seriously ill,' continued the speaker, 'and medical science came to the conclusion that the only way to cure me was to put me to sleep and freeze me for a long period, that is, scientifically speaking, to put me in an anabolic condition. . . . Now I've awakened and I'm absolutely healthy.' "[42] Thus, he has been lying frozen in the mausoleum for twenty-one years, and now, in 1974, he returns and attempts to claim his former authority. In this tale he is a kind of technologically enhanced revenant, having become one of the unquiet dead through medical science.

Even before Stalin is called by name in Gladilin's text, he is referred to by a number of titles and nicknames that make it clear who he is. He is called "the old man" (starikan), "the Mustached Boss" (Usatyi Khoziain), "he" (on), "the leader" (vozhd'), "the Leader and Teacher" (Vozhd' i Uchitel'), "the Very One" (Samyi), "Our Teacher and Leader, the Greatest Genius of mankind" (Nash Uchitel'i Vozhd', Velichaishii Genii chelovechestva) and "the great scholar" (bol'shoi uchenyi). The very first reference to him is as "the Object" (Ob "ekt), meaning his preserved body (5). According to Ilya Zbarsky, this was a euphemism used to describe Lenin's corpse during the debates concerning its embalming and display.[43] It is also noteworthy that Gladilin names one of his characters Krasavin, perhaps based on the historical figure of Leonid Krasin. Initially Stalin's body is merely an inert object that needs dusting once a week and holds no particular terror for those watching over it: "The gray mustache of the Boss moves under the stream of air [of the vacuum cleaner] . . . and you don't understand why he frightened the people so much that they cowered before him" (8).

Stalin's eyes are a clear marker of his identity in Gladilin's text. Vasilii Ivanovich, the guard who is on duty when Stalin returns to life, recognizes him precisely because of his unique eyes: "The eyes! The eyes lit up and the harmless little old man disappeared and HE arose, the real Boss" (11). Stalin's eyes, as Ziolkowski notes, are a feature frequently emphasized in satirical portraits of the dictator, "virtually a sine qua non of negatively portrayed literary Stalins, one of the signposts of an evil personality."[44]

Gladilin's Stalin smokes a pipe, and his manner of breaking a cigarette and filling his pipe with the tobacco is peculiar to (the historical) Stalin. Stalin's speech is initially heavily accented; moreover, Gladilin tells us explicitly that Stalin speaks with a Georgian accent. It is interesting that his accent disappears later in the text, perhaps because Gladilin considered the point made with a few brief passages of direct speech. Just as significant is Stalin's reliance on propaganda clichés and folksy adages: "Without a doubt certain exaggerations and instances of breaking Leninist legality took place. But, as the folk saying goes, you chop wood, and the chips fly [*les rubiat—shepki letiat*]" (37). A long speech he delivers is full of his characteristic verbal mannerisms, including his tendency to use lists, his proclivity for rhetorical questions, and his reliance on formulae (37–38).

The psychological traits with which Gladilin endows Stalin are also clear markers of his identity. As a regional secretary observing him notes, he neither forgets nor forgives, nursing grudges until he can take revenge. He is explicitly anti-Semitic: "Let the remnants of the Jewish bourgeoisie that we haven't finished off go off to their Palestine; as they say among the people, it's easier for the mare with the woman off the cart [*baba s vozu, kobyle legche*]" (27).

With the aid of a science fiction plot device Gladilin's Stalin becomes a revenant in the most literal sense; he rises from his technologically induced, deep-freeze sleep and returns to life. Stalin's body has not decayed, although it has been dormant for two decades. The guard assigned to stand watch feels a rush of cold from the crypt. The source is left ambiguous, but we understand that Stalin's body exudes cold: "In the silence the window glass tinkled slightly and Vasilii Ivanych felt a draft of cold air" (9). When Stalin first appears, he is standing on a threshold, "in the doorway" (10), which is a liminal space, a symbolic boundary between the other world and this world. He returns from the dead on a Friday, which connotes a carnivalesque reversal of the Resurrection.

Gladilin's description of the space Stalin's body inhabits in its frozen state is strongly suggestive of the mausoleum. The crypt is equipped with a double-thick steel door, luminescent lamps that cast a bluish light on the cadaver, screens, and shades. It is below ground level, as is the room where Lenin's body is still displayed (and where Stalin's body was once displayed).[45] Underground spaces (caves, catacombs, crypts) are viewed by many cultures as suitable for housing the spirits of the dead; they provide space where the soul may be made comfortable.[46] On the mythic level, spaces beneath the earth function as the "universal uterus"[47] and are thus appropriate to house the dead, who are returning to the womb. In Russian folklore it is believed that *zalozhnye umershie* inhabit space beneath the earth since their bodies cannot decay.[48]

Keeping the unquiet dead Stalin in a crypt may be connected to the mythological trope of imprisoning or restraining a rebel god. Ahriman, who opposed Ormuzd in Persian mythology, was bound for a thousand years; Prometheus, who set himself against Zeus in Greek myth, was chained to a rock; and Loki, who fought against the Scandinavian gods, was restrained with thongs of iron.[49] Satan, too, is bound for a certain period of time, which varies according to the source. Stalin's prolonged stay in the crypt in Gladilin's text may also suggest the dangers connected with failure to bury a body appropriately. While the deceased is still unburied, the soul wanders restlessly, recalling injuries done to it and seeking revenge.

In casting Stalin as a revenant, Gladilin expresses the fear—common to his generation—of a return to Stalinism. In a dialogue between the KGB officers Surikov and Potapov the author embeds an indictment of Stalin as the most destructive enemy of the Soviet people imaginable. Surikov lists his crimes: the purges; the destruction of the officer corps of the Red Army; lack of preparation for the Nazi attack; and the terrible losses of the Russo-Finnish War of 1939-40. He refutes the traditional defense of Stalin, namely, that at least he led the Soviet Union to victory in the Second World War: "Any fool can be victorious at such a cost. Not Stalin but the Soviet people won the war, and they won it not thanks to Stalin but in spite of Stalin. That's why after the war Stalin shouldn't have been honored as a national hero but prosecuted as a state criminal" (54-55). It is ironic, of course, that it is representatives of the KGB who successfully conspire to thwart Stalin's bid to return to power. Even the secret police reject the possibility of a return to the past, so harmful was Stalinism.

While most people are not nostalgic for Stalinism in Gladilin's text, there are those who sincerely rejoice at his return. When he first appears, an old man cries out: "Our own Father, glory to you, Lord, he's alive!" (*Otets rodnoi, slava Te, Gospodi, zhiv!*) (26). That his outburst is markedly religious in tone emphasizes the degree to which Stalin was still regarded as a deity by some of Gladilin's compatriots. The press is implicated as well; the sycophantic editor Gladilin creates is quick to switch allegiances and composes the headline "Stalin Is Lenin Today" (46). The hack poet Zaikin turns to writing verses praising Stalin before he is even asked to do so. He is a

representative of the cynical careerists Gladilin savaged in his autobiography: "If tomorrow the papers were to say that Comrade Brezhnev himself
was a spy for one of the imperialist intelligence organizations, the writers
would begin in concert to fling mud at him. They will serve any sovereign
'faithfully and true,' because the authorities pay them generously to do so.
And that's the sort of writers, if one may call them so, who are numbered in
the ranks of true patriots in our country."[50] It is telling that when Stalin delivers a speech to party functionaries, they respond with enthusiasm to his
cliché-ridden diatribe.[51] During a performance of an operetta celebrating
Stalin's leadership in the war, the public literally sings along, picking up the
refrain; thus they "demonstrated their loyalty to the Leader and Teacher"
(69). Stalin himself muses on his rise to power (71), asserting that he is the
only one who understands that Russia does not need theoretical communism but an iron fist. The Russian people, he believes, must be held firmly
in check. Stalin genuinely inspires some—both old and young—with unquestioning adulation and loyalty. A Komsomol secretary, presumably too
young to have experienced Stalinism directly, is completely enamored of
Stalin: "[He] looked at Stalin with the eyes of a dog, and the words no longer
reached him. He simply knew that from now on every cell of his body belonged to the wise Leader and Teacher. And if Comrade Stalin—our military glory—sent him into battle, then he would go to the end, to the grave,
he would gnaw the throat of anyone . . ." (30). Despite the enthusiastic celebration of the dictator's return by some, Stalin's bid for power is ultimately
thwarted. The televised speech he demands to make is purposefully scheduled at the same time as a major hockey game, ensuring a very small audience. Stalin is effectively silenced and put back into storage, thanks to the
intervention of his own KGB henchmen. Gladilin's portrayal of Stalin as a
revenant thus intensifies his criticism of his countrymen for complicity in
Stalinism. Preserved in a half-frozen slumber for two decades, Stalin is still
a powerful animus and his subjects—former and potential—are all too
ready to embrace him again.

Sinyavsky's *Good Night*

Andrei Sinyavsky came to maturity at the height of Stalinism. Born in
1925, he graduated from Moscow State University in 1949 and achieved the
status of *kandidat nauk* (candidate of science) in 1952. His formative years
thus coincided with *Zhdanovshchina*, the most repressive phase of socialist

realism.[52] As a young man (1947–50) Sinyavsky was a *komsomolets* and—according to those who knew him in that period—a Soviet patriot. He quickly built a remarkably successful career as a literary critic, publishing numerous articles and reviews through the Academy of Sciences and the Institute of World Literature. During this early period he published a series of critical articles in *Novyi mir* and coauthored an important book on Picasso with the art historian I. N. Golomshtok.

Even while his professional fortunes were on the rise, Sinyavsky apparently was growing disillusioned with the Soviet regime—and Stalinism in particular. His father, who occupied a high post in the party apparatus, was arrested in 1951, which undoubtedly affected Sinyavsky's outlook. The Twentieth Party Congress and Khrushchev's denunciation of Stalin in 1956 were further blows to Stalinism, yet Sinyavsky has stated that none of the revelations of the immediate post-Stalin period were news to him.[53] As Richard Lourie notes, his reaction to the events of the Thaw and de-Stalinization was unusually intense and spurred his creativity.[54] Even within the parameters of his professional life, Sinyavsky was firmly in the liberal camp, focusing on writers who had been repressed and unpublishable under Stalin.[55] Together with Iulii Daniel he served as a pallbearer at Boris Pasternak's funeral in 1960, which, in light of Pasternak's official status as a literary pariah, was an act of great courage. It subsequently became known that, beginning in the mid-fifties, Sinyavsky had been sending his literary manuscripts abroad, publishing them under the pseudonym Abram Terts. In 1959 his works began to appear in *tamizdat*, including his seminal essay "On Socialist Realism" ("Chto takoe sotsialisticheskii realizm?"), three novels, a collection of "fantastic tales," and a compilation of aphorisms.

Abram Terts's true identity was eventually discovered by the KGB[56] and Sinyavsky was arrested in late 1965. The trial of Sinyavsky and Daniel (who was also arrested for publishing his works abroad) the following year became an international cause célèbre. Their prosecution and conviction effectively signaled the end of the Thaw, sending a clear message of renewed repression and intolerance to the Russian intelligentsia. It is significant that Sinyavsky and Daniel were indicted and prosecuted for anti-Soviet agitation and propaganda under the infamous Article 70. In an article entitled "Turncoats" ("Perevertyshi"), published in *Izvestiia* in January, a month before the beginning of the trial, Dmitrii Eremin, secretary of the Moscow Section of the Soviet Writers' Union, attacked Sinyavsky and Daniel for denigration of the Soviet Union. By offending the values of Soviet society,

Sinyavsky and Daniel placed themselves outside its boundaries; they became "internal émigrés" (*vnutrennie emigranty*).[57] Moreover, they attempted to conceal their foreignness by pretending to be loyal Soviet citizens, publishing their work under pseudonyms. The writer Mikhail Sholokhov went even further in labeling Sinyavsky and Daniel as alien in his speech to the Twenty-Third Party Congress following the trial. Suggesting that the convicted writers may have received lenient sentences—Sinyavsky was sentenced to seven years of hard labor, Daniel to five—Sholokhov asserted that in previous periods these "werewolves" (*oborotni*) would have been dealt with much more harshly.[58] Sholokhov's introduction of the idea of the changeling is intriguing, for it illustrates the Russian proclivity to separate the world into *svoi* and *chuzhoi* and to regard the latter with suspicion and hostility.

Not coincidentally, in the spring of 1966, at about the same time as the trial, the Brezhnev regime began a campaign to slow down the process of de-Stalinization. The positive achievements of Stalin were again emphasized in the media and in pronouncements by the party. In this much chillier political climate the trial signaled a major change in the regime's attitude toward nonconformists. By refusing to admit their guilt or repent, Sinyavsky and Daniel effectively flouted the rules of Soviet political trials. Their resistance fueled the nascent dissident movement and encouraged others to defy political authority. Sinyavsky served all but fifteen months of his sentence in a labor camp in Mordovia. Following his release in 1971, he returned to Moscow.

Granted permission to leave the Soviet Union in 1973, Sinyavsky immigrated to France. Although he was initially welcomed by the Russian émigré community, Sinyavsky soon found himself at odds with his compatriots in the diaspora. After early involvement with the journal *Kontinent*, Sinyavsky noisily broke with its editor, Vladimir Maksimov, and founded his own rival journal, *Sintaksis*, with his wife Mariia Rozanova. His polemic with Solzhenitsyn, the leader of the "Russophile" camp, was also a source of public controversy in the seventies. Sinyavsky and Rozanova were self-styled "pluralists" who rejected what they regarded as Great Russian chauvinism on the part of Maksimov, Solzhenitsyn, and their followers.

Sinyavsky remained productive in exile, publishing under the names of both Sinyavsky (the literary critic and polemicist) and Terts (the fiction writer and author of "fantastic literary criticism" [*fantasticheskoe literaturovedenie*]). His adoption of the pseudonym Abram Terts—after the Jewish hero of an Odessa thieves' song—placed him in the position of other; the fact that he continued to use the pseudonym after emigrating suggests that it represented a part of his creative personality and was not simply a disguise to elude the Soviet authorities. As Sinyavsky himself put it in an interview, "Abram Tertz is a criminal and he's a Jew. . . . And to be a Jew means to be an alien, a renegade, an apostate in Russian society."[59] By insistently embodying this duality of *svoi* and *chuzhoi*, Sinyavsky defies any attempt on the part of Russian culture to repress or discourage literature's painful but necessary work of disclosure.[60]

A major scandal followed the publication in 1976 (under the name of Terts) of *Strolls with Pushkin* (*Progulki s Pushkinym*), written while Sinyavsky was still imprisoned in a Soviet camp. His treatment of Pushkin—which amounts to humanization and skeptical reconsideration—aroused the wrath of the émigré intelligentsia and earned him the pejorative title "the second d'Anthès." Rumors circulated claiming that he had never been in the camps and that the KGB had supplied him with a special library.[61] When an excerpt from *Strolls with Pushkin* was published in the Soviet Union in 1989, the controversy was reignited and a campaign of vilification ensued, led by the conservative spokesman Igor Shafarevich. Sinyavsky was (once again) accused of denigration of his homeland and of putting himself in the position of a hostile outsider. With the collapse of the Soviet Union, he began to make periodic visits to his homeland, most notably in 1989 to pay his respects at Daniel's death. Sinyavsky died in France in 1997.

Sinyavsky has written that treating Stalin requires exaggeration: "Stalin seemed to be specially made for the hyperbole that awaited him: mysterious, omniscient, all-powerful, he was the living monument of our era and needed only one quality to become God—immortality."[62] His essay "On Socialist Realism" is an exposé of Stalinism, in particular the damage done to Russian literary and artistic culture by the enforcement of the tenets of socialist realism. Stalin figures only peripherally in *The Trial Begins*, but the atmosphere of Stalinism is pervasive and insidious in that early text. Sinyavsky implies that the distortion of values and personalities described in this work is a result of Stalinism. His "fantastic prose" is an effective vehicle for expressing lived reality under Stalin, for it had indeed become surreal. By including elements of the phantasmagoric and the grotesque, Sinyavsky conveys the weird, irrational universe of Stalinism. In *Good Night*, published in the West in 1984,[63] these techniques are applied to autobiographical themes, notably the author's relationship with Stalin.

The figure of Stalin pervades *Good Night*, though his character is not a historical portrait but rather a presence. Sinyavsky[64] refers to him by many standard—and nonstandard—pejorative nicknames, clearly identifying him. He is variously called "the Mustache" (*Us, Usatyi*),[65] "the damned" (*okaiannyi*) (235), "the Murderer" (*Dushegub*) (235), "an old wolf, a were-wolf, a dragon" (*staryi volk, oboroten', drakon*) (238). In a letter that Sinyavsky imagines Beria circulating to summon up loyalty to the now dead leader, Stalin is ironically called "the true anointed one, Tsar and Lord" (*istinnyi Pomazannik, Tsar' i Gosudar'*) (255). Sinyavsky's autobiographical narrator recalls seeing Stalin on the reviewing stand during a May Day parade: "I remember only—the stout Vaska the Cat in Krylov's fable. With a mustache. The Cat and the Cook. And that's all?" (265). Stalin's language, presented in reported direct speech, is unaccented—a detail the narrator specifies: "By the way, there was strangely nothing Georgian in his accent. Only the phrases familiar since childhood" (233). In the fourth chapter, entitled "Dangerous Liaisons" ("Opasyne sviazy"), Sinyavsky treats the image of Stalin in depth.

Sinyavsky—or, rather, Terts—is obviously ambivalent about Stalinism. On the one hand, his autobiographical narrator experiences what Beth Holmgren calls "an attraction to the macabre aura of Stalinism."[66] He insists that his growing up under Stalin benefited him as a writer:

> Philosophically speaking, as a writer connected with a definite period (the end of the forties, the beginning of the fifties), the epoch of mature, late, and flowering Stalinism, I cannot help remembering *my time* with a certain pleasure and a sense of filial gratitude. Yes, I'm not ashamed to say that I am a child of that dark time. All these trivial machinations and bits of madness and horror that I describe here with such knowledge, those that run through everyday life with the electricity of an imminent end of the world, all these witches and vampires that to this day don't let me fall asleep peacefully—created then a kind of worldwide radioactive current or, more precisely, a shield to which I was bound, like it or not. That time is dear to me if only because then and only then, and not anywhere else, I understood something contrary to it and, gritting my teeth, broke with society, gnashed my teeth, shut myself up in a shell, and retreated in horror in order to live and think at my own risk and terror. (267)

He associates Stalin in *Good Night* with the mystery and the temptation of a miracle offered by Antichrist (292–93). This allusion to Dostoevsky's "Legend of the Grand Inquisitor" is extremely apt since it casts Stalin in the position of omnipotent (and thus attractive) monster.[67] Stalin, he suggests, was less free than anyone else, for he could not shave off his mustache or cease smoking his pipe. He had become a puppet controlled by others, who

needed him. Sinyavsky expresses empathy for his lack of freedom: "How difficult it must be to turn into one's own portrait while one is still alive and to
have to do everything that is ordained by the worshipers of their deity" (274).

Yet Sinyavsky is explicit in expressing his fear and discomfort at con-
fronting Stalin's image. He describes the intense physical reactions he experiences when he considers writing about him: "My hand refuses. My knees,
so to speak, turn watery. I throw everything in the wastebasket. My pulse
has risen. My urine reeks of acetone" (230). Sinyavsky feels Stalin's constant
presence threatening him as he writes and asserts that he causes hallucinations and can respond to people's dreams. An inescapable companion, Stalin's ghost accompanies everyone: "Stalin was in everyone like a hammer,
together with a sickle, in the head" (227). Sinyavsky denies that he hated
Stalin. Although he claims indifference toward him he confesses that he was
curious about his actions and motivations: "Into what new nightmare
would he hurl the country next? From him all you could expect was death.
Your own. Everyone's. Prison. Plague. War" (238–39). Sinyavsky theorizes
that Stalin was a kind of evil magician who worked behind the scenes yet
inspired faith in his powers.[68] The language of Stalinism—the metaphors
employed in the purges and show trials, the phrases of invective coined by
Stalin—worked like spells and conjured reality. For Sinyavsky the great destructive power of Stalinism was that it transformed the world into text that
could be manipulated and distorted by Stalin, the artist-magician. As Olga
Matich notes, this portrayal of Stalin is a polemical response to Solzhenitsyn's satirical portrait of the dictator in *The First Circle*.[69] Instead of a
senile, paranoid megalomaniac, we have in Sinyavsky's text a fakir: "Well,
Stalin in general is most mysterious. . . . Perhaps a poet in his soul, a film
director" (232).

In *Good Night* Stalin is associated by Sinyavsky with revenants; he refers
to the werewolves and vampires of Stalinism that still disturb his peaceful
sleep (267). In one extended passage in the novel Stalin appears to the actress
and medium Alla immediately following his death. Prefacing her account of
this apparition, the authorial narrator muses that she is an appropriate person for Stalin's ghost to visit, for she is sensitive and receptive, "magnetic,
a pure personification of the victim" (227). Living in exile in Siberia, Alla
senses from the disturbances in nature that Stalin has died, though it has not
been announced by the Soviet authorities. His appearance to her is presaged
by signs, most notably by the complete silence that descends around her:
"And suddenly everything grew still. She was awakened by the uncanny still-
ness that surrounded her from all sides. Even the grandfather clock wasn't

ticking. Not a cricket was chirping. Not a floorboard creaked. The wind over the slate roof seemed to have dropped. And she understood from the silence that the beloved had arrived. The damned had bayed themselves out. He stands like a pillar, in silence, next to her little bed. He himself. The Mustache" (228). Alla's encounter with Stalin as a revenant is one of the "dangerous liaisons" referred to in the title of the chapter. The meeting of the living and the dead is a metaphor for the intersection of the worlds of reality and art.[70] Alla's discourse with Stalin thus becomes an act of creation.

Stalin appears to Alla as a huge column of cold air, the embodiment of death. When he leaves, she senses a change in the elements: "Over the roof something seethed and crashed" (235). This image echoes a folk belief Sinyavsky mentions much earlier in the novel. According to this superstition, whirlwinds are devils and witches playing and dancing. When Stalin appears to Alla, he is devoid of human features; she experiences him as "absolute negation expressed in positive form" (228). He has no shape at all, casts no shadow, and does not breathe. Nevertheless, Alla feels his presence to be unbearable, powerful, and threatening. He speaks to her, asking her to forgive his "debts" (*dolgi*) and pardon him in the name of all his victims. Rather than request absolution outright, he plays a verbal game with Alla, making her guess the meaning of the riddle he expounds. The first letters of all of his clues spell out "my sins" (*moi grekhi*), but she stubbornly pretends not to understand what he is asking of her. Arousing his fury, she senses his rage and impotence, which finally erupts in the cry "Forgive me!" (*Prosti!*) (230). Stalin does not want to seek forgiveness but is compelled to do so in his state of unquiet death. Even as a revenant, he tries to reduce human beings to abstract signs, naming his victims as part of a riddle but failing to acknowledge his guilt in destroying their lives.[71] Alla reasonably replies that she does not have the right to grant him absolution on behalf of all of his victims, although she herself will forgive him. Echoing Sonya in *Crime and Punishment,* she directs him to go and seek forgiveness from everyone, both the living and the dead. Stalin abruptly disappears, perhaps overwhelmed at the enormity of the task: "To go around to everyone individually— everyone injured or destroyed by Stalin—that's a real job, you know. Eternity isn't long enough" (235–36).

Stalin's corpse also has power in this text. For Sinyavsky, the stampede around the Hall of Columns was caused directly and purposefully by the dead dictator. He uses a metaphor evoking an image of Stalin as the unquiet dead, continuing to wreak havoc following his death: "The dead man strode through Moscow reaping a blind harvest, leaving big tracks with his iron boots. And everywhere he passed, ribs cracked, eyes popped out, and hair was easily—like a sock—peeled off together with skin" (252). Sinyavsky describes Moscow on the day of Stalin's funeral as smoky ("*Moskva dymilas'*") (251). Sinyavsky's synesthetic evocation of the atmosphere of the city has overtones of apocalypse: "Smells of incense, it seems, emanated from the black and scarlet flags in the light of the street lamps and the breathing of the compressed masses, which had been pressing around the clock to bid farewell to the leader" (251). Stalin's body, still present in the city, affects—indeed, directs—the actions of the living. It is noteworthy that Sinyavsky examined the centrality of the corpse in Pushkin's work and found it strange: "The peculiar begins when the dead body is moved to the center of the work and breaks up the plot with its unnatural intrusion, and suddenly it turns out that, strictly speaking, the action as a whole unfolds in the presence of a corpse."[72] One might, by analogy, position Stalin's corpse as central to *Good Night*.

The theme of the pretender or imposter is related to that of the unquiet dead in Sinyavsky's novel. The autobiographical narrator remembers researching the Time of Troubles at the time of Stalin's death, so that the pretender takes on particular meaning for him. It is significant that in his embedded text the mother of the murdered tsarevich Dmitrii does not recognize her son in the body she sees, concluding that the dead body is not the tsarevich but an alien (*chuzhoi*) (243). Although there are numerous ideological and political analogies between the Time of Troubles and Stalinist Russia,[73] Sinyavsky chooses to focus on this particular detail. Murdered and still unburied, Tsarevich Dmitrii is already other. This is due, in part, to his mother's need to deny the truth of his death, but also to his status as unquiet dead. Stalin, like Dmitrii, has the power to return as an imposter, and Sinyavsky imagines this scenario in *Good Night*: "If not tomorrow, then the day after tomorrow an imposter will appear in the Caucasus—a False Stalin" (*Lzhestalin*) (254). As in the Time of Troubles, a plot to deny the leader's death and place a pretender in power is engineered by enemies of the regime. In Sinyavsky's vision Stalin is consigned to a "living death,"[74] for he exists only insofar as he functions as a symbol around which to consolidate power. A grotesque extension of this plot into the realm of the fantastic is the plan to reanimate Stalin. Beria plans to circulate a document promising that Stalin will be brought back to life "through the successes of progressive, patriotic medicine" (255). Sinyavsky's portrayal of Stalin as a revenant, temporarily dead and waiting to return to the living, is remarkably like Gladilin's fictional account. Like the figure of Stalin in "Rehearsal on Friday," in

Sinyavsky's novel Stalin is threatening and vengeful: "Isn't that why the sovereign Deceased is angry with us, his sinful subjects, and is spilling buckets of blood on the streets of Moscow? 'Do you realize who you're burying, you dogs?! It's coming, remember. The Second Coming, Stalin! . . .' He set to work. Pounded his fist" (266). Stalin's Second Coming is a blasphemous reversal of Christ's promised return in that Sinyavsky envisions his return as a triumph of evil.

In addition to the extended treatment of Stalin as a revenant in the fourth chapter, Sinyavsky includes a number of references to the unquiet dead elsewhere in his novel. The title of the first chapter, "The Turncoat" ("Perevertysh"), is taken from Eremin's 1966 article. This term, originally meaning "werewolf," was applied to Sinyavsky and Daniel during their trial. As Olga Matich notes, *perevertysh* has connotations of rebirth, albeit with diabolical overtones.[75] Eremin also applies the term *oboroten'* to Sinyavsky and Daniel in his article.[76] Sinyavsky speculates that Stalin himself deserves this appellation, whose approximate meaning is "werewolf" or "shapeshifter" (238). He is for the author still a palpable presence, capable of terrorizing the living.

Sinyavsky expresses his belief in the power of the dead to influence the living in graphic terms. In general, the dead actively participate in the events of this world: "Think about it: if the things living next to us can take on an indelible spiritual inflexion, then why can't someone from over there try to exert physical pressure on us? And they do try! . . . They're just waiting for a chance. They leap at every word. Grab you by the hand" (222). Stalin in particular leaves physical traces and manipulates the actions of the living. After he visits Alla, she finds a circular spot on the floor where his spirit had been. This spot is both literal and figurative; Sinyavsky compares it to an outline left by a pedestal or base. Stalin—both as a person and as an image (a statue)—has left perceptible scars on Russian culture. It is significant that one can also see the souls of the good in Sinyavsky's fictional world. His narrator envisions the Frenchwoman Hélène's spirit as an infant, perhaps a cherub. The spiritual world is thus not necessarily frightening and diabolical. The forces of kindness, generosity, and creativity can also wield power. Sinyavsky's final vision of night is of a peaceful darkness exorcised of the demons of Stalinism.

Sinyavsky unflinchingly acknowledges that there are those who would welcome a return of Stalin and Stalinism. In his article "The Literary Process in Russia" he evokes the controversy surrounding the Soviet national anthem and suggests that the very absence of words praising Stalin is significant: "Every historical fact is symbolic and twenty years of brassy booming instead of words, which many people are still itching to sing, are also symbolic."[77] The void left by Stalin's death has not been filled, which is dangerous. Perhaps his most pessimistic statement on this subject is the following passage in his book *Unguarded Thoughts*: "We are capable of putting Europe in our pocket or of stunning it with a fascinating heresy but quite incapable of creating a culture. As with a thief or a drunkard, people never know what to expect of us. We are easy to drive, to govern by administrative measures (a drunk is inert, incapable of managing his own affairs; he can be dragged anywhere) but also—unstable as we are—so difficult to cope with. What a job for our administrators!"[78] He asserts that what is Soviet is readily accepted as *svoi* in Russia, while outsiders and ideas perceived as *chuzhoi* are rejected and shunned.[79] Moreover, Russian anti-Semitism is a proven means of externalizing evil and projecting it onto a scapegoat, for what is harmful or pernicious in Russian culture cannot be caused by those who are *svoi*; it must be blamed on foreigners and outsiders. He charges that Russians are intent on assigning blame for the past to the Jews in order to exculpate themselves and retain their vision of the order of the world. According to this reasoning, the Jews are the "enemy within," who have secretly risen to power and supported the persecution of the Russian people. Sinyavsky notes that in Soviet prison camps "simple peasants (especially among the long-term prisoners) are to this day [the seventies] convinced that the entire government of present-day Russia—all the judges, all the state prosecutors, and above all the KGB—consists entirely of Jews."[80] Sinyavsky reserves judgment about whether the crimes of Stalinism were caused by Stalin or performed to give him pleasure and support (269–70). In either case, as he makes explicit in his discussion of scapegoating, the Russian people are far from innocent victims. In Sinyavsky's view, Russian—and particularly Soviet—culture has tended to project its shortcomings and its excesses onto his image rather than confront issues of guilt and complicity.

Conclusion

Portraying Stalin as the unquiet dead has the potential to render him comfortably *chuzhoi*, alien to Russian culture. Deprived of proper funeral rites and unburied, he is a prime candidate to haunt the living, to do harm to them in his quest for revenge. History conveniently supplied the details that supported his becoming a fictional revenant: he died alone, under suspicious circumstances, and his body was embalmed and displayed in a public mausoleum for eight years alongside Lenin's corpse. As a great sinner, Stalin could scarcely hope to find peace among the dead and is thus consigned to inhabit the liminal space between this world and the next in accordance with Russian folk beliefs and superstitions. In the three works examined in this chapter, satirists adopt the imagery of the unquiet dead and postulate Stalin's return following his death. However, his characterization as a revenant does not provide absolution for the society he tyrannized. Indeed, his literary exposure as a revenant leaves us questioning the vestiges of Stalinism in post-Stalinist Russian culture.

Evtushenko's poem "The Heirs of Stalin" is the most straightforward evocation of Stalin's spirit as unclean and vengeful. Still fuming as he is taken out of the mausoleum, Stalin is sharply differentiated from the Russian people, who were betrayed by his mistrust and who remain committed to the goal of building communism. However, even in Evtushenko's poetic universe there are some who harbor a nostalgia for Stalinism. In his story "Rehearsal on Friday" Gladilin imagines Stalin's return from prolonged anabolic suspension. As a revenant Stalin is revealed to be irrelevant and potentially dangerous to post-Stalinist Soviet culture. However, Gladilin suggests that there are many who would welcome Stalin's return and who still regard him as *svoi*. Sinyavsky's treatment of Stalin as the unquiet dead in his novel *Good Night* is deeply ambivalent. On the one hand, his disembodied spirit is consigned to wander the world seeking absolution from his multitudinous victims. On the other hand, Sinyavsky's narrator expresses a fascination with Stalin, a sense of awe before the power of his evil. Moreover, like Gladilin, he is keenly aware that there are many who would celebrate a return to Stalinism and he fears for the soul of his country.

As the unquiet dead, Stalin is a highly ambiguous figure in these satirical works. Following de-Stalinization, the corpse has been removed and the collective is left to reaggregate, to affirm its health. However, genuine catharsis has not been achieved: the body remains unburied; Stalin's crimes have not been examined thoroughly; and the guilt of the collaborators has not been fully acknowledged. Stalin still threatens Russian culture as a potential revenant, and this fictional danger reflects a cultural preoccupation. Not reconciled to death—or not accepted in the world of the dead—Stalin can still do enormous harm to the living.

Conclusion

More than fifty years after Stalin's death, Russia is still coming to terms with Stalinism and the Russian people's role in the crimes it sanctioned. During Stalin's lifetime and for some years following his death those crimes were literally unspeakable; there was no true reckoning and hence no lustration. While Beria and a few other high-ranking minions were dispatched in the power struggle following Stalin's demise, most of the police, guards, executioners, bureaucrats, informers, and other collaborators remained unexposed and unpunished. For the most part questions of complicity and responsibility were left unasked and unanswered. Unlike postwar Germany, post-apartheid South Africa, or post-genocide Rwanda, Russia was not allowed to confront the truth of its past. De-Stalinization was limited and carefully controlled—at least within the Soviet Union—until well into the glasnost period. A generation had to pass before the archives could be opened both literally and figuratively.

It has been seductively easy, it seems, to regard Stalin as an evil genius, a dictator devoid of human compassion or moral principles and able to bend everyone and everything to his will. His capacity for manipulation was so enormous that he achieved an undisputed position of authoritarian power, which he held for a quarter of a century. Yet this view of Stalin and the regime he headed is certainly too simplistic. Given the enormity of the country he ruled, the vast scope of his activities(e.g., agricultural collectivization, the purges, the gulag, the Second World War), and the sheer number of people killed during his reign (the figure of twenty-six million is credible), the evidence for collaboration is inescapable. A complex apparatus supported Stalinism, with many hundreds of thousands of Russians involved in the functioning of the system. Moreover, millions of citizens failed to oppose the crimes of Stalinism and thus were complicit through their passivity. Whether the Russian people's participation was voluntary and enthusiastic (the system materially benefited some segments of the population) or whether they were coerced is a question that cultural historians continue to debate. Although it has not been the purpose of this study to decide such questions, it is nevertheless crucial to recognize the centrality of these unresolved issues of guilt and responsibility in contemporary Russian culture.

Literature in general and satire in particular has always played a significant role in social and political debates in Russia. In the absence of a free press, literary satire has traditionally served as a venue for exposure, criticism, and dissent. Of course, many works that functioned in this way were not published in the Soviet Union, but their existence is evidence of a contrarian, anti-Stalinist mind-set dating from the earliest years of Stalinism. Satire concerns itself with the painful questions of how Stalin came to occupy a position of absolute power and why the Russian people participated in the crimes that were committed. Stalin's relationship to Russian culture is a key element in satirical discourse. If he can be shown to be liminal, alterior, or other vis-à-vis Russian culture, then it is possible to absolve the Russian people to some extent. His presence and his influence are thus aberrations, a kind of illness that befell an otherwise healthy nation. One approach of Russian satire has been to establish Stalin's otherness; he is portrayed as alien, excluded, and repudiated. Following this literary exorcism, the cultural self is left to heal and regenerate itself. Other satirical texts are more ambivalent about Stalin's relationship to Russia and explore the ramifications of his being part of the self, a genuine product of Russian culture. The works examined here are actively engaged in questioning Stalin's belonging/not belonging and concomitant issues of complicity and absolution.

Stalin's mental state—paranoid, megalomaniacal, narcissistic, perhaps unstable—has provided ample material for satirists. On one level, magnifying and exaggerating his madness serve to establish his otherness, his separation from the healthy norms of reason and sanity. This dynamic, however, does not offer straightforward absolution for the Russian people since at the very minimum they were complicit in supporting (or not resisting) a regime shaped by a madman's whims. Nabokov, Solzhenitsyn, Zinoviev, and Maksimov create fictional portraits of Stalin that reveal varying degrees of mental pathology. For Solzhenitsyn and Maksimov he is a paranoid megalomaniac,

an evil spider spinning a web of madness that holds Russia prisoner. Nabokov questions the nature of infectious madness and postulates that murderous and self-destructive insanity may have taken root in Russia under
his regime. Zinoviev's treatment of Stalin is both the most cerebral and the
most disturbing, for his fictional tyrant is eerily sane, a rational and focused
theoretician of an insane social system.

Animals signify otherness for us, and certain animals carry particularly
negative connotations in addition to signs of alterity. Stalin is made subhuman and his evil nature is emphasized when he is cast as a cockroach, a
black tomcat, or a boa constrictor. For the most part, the dynamic of exclusion is operative when Stalin appears as a beast; he cannot be part of the
healthy Russian cultural self if he is soulless, amoral, and predatory. However, the authors who treat Stalin as an animal in their works—Chukovsky,
Okudzhava, and Iskander—create complex allegories by situating their Stalinesque characters within fantastical settings. With the exception of Okudzhava's song-poem, the Russian people are likewise portrayed as animals.
Their tolerance and support of the beast-dictator implicates them in Stalinism and satirically tests the integrity of the cultural self.

The Russian cultural self is strongly male and misogyny has had a long
tradition in both Russian life and literature. Feminizing Stalin or blurring
his gender identity in satire thus has the powerful effect of diminishing the
stature of the dictator. Because androgyny is unsettling, calling binary oppositions into question, it also complicates issues of responsibility for the
crimes of Stalinism. Voinovich uses this device in a dream sequence, pictur-
ing Stalin in women's clothing. The appearance of the transvestite is disturbing and serves to call into question the nature of the self as well. Aleshkovsky's procedure involves dismembering Stalin's fictional body and granting
his right foot independence. This feminine aspect of the dictator's psyche—
a rebellious anima—defies and denounces him in a deliciously profane
manner.

The monstrous, existing as it does in the realm of myth and fantasy, is a
locus of alterity. Rendering Stalin as a monster casts him out of the world
of the natural and helps to absolve his victims, for monsters are always far
stronger than humans. However, Russian satirical monsters include elements of the human, so that their relationship to the world they terrorize is
complicated in that they are other, albeit an other that partakes of the self.
In his satirical treatment Shvarts questions both the nature of Stalin's power
over the Russian people and their complicity in supporting his regime.

Aksenov's portrayal of Stalin as a monster traces his rise to power, his coercive reign, and his demise. He, too, is interested in how it came to pass that Russian culture was distorted by monstrous evil.

It was suspected in some quarters that Stalin was an agent of the devil—perhaps even Antichrist. This supposition plays a role in several of these satirical texts, where he is characterized as demonic. Portraying Stalin as the devil or Antichrist is often a clear statement of moral judgment and a gesture of absolution, for the demonic emanates from outside a Russian cultural self that defines itself as faithful, as believing in and obeying God. Moreover, the demonic is not subject to control and cannot easily be repelled precisely because it is supernaturally powerful. Casting Stalin as the devil or Antichrist thus supports a satirical exorcism; Galich and Iskander rely on this dynamic in their work. Bulgakov's novelistic portrayal of Stalin as the devil is more multivalent, with the author's own troubled relationship vis-à-vis the dictator reflected in his fictional rendition of Stalin.

Revenants, or the unquiet dead, are imagined as liminal, alterior beings in many societies, but they have an especially strong presence in Slavic cultures. The fact that Stalin's body was not buried immediately following his death but instead was preserved and displayed encourages satirists to depict him as a revenant. Evtushenko and Gladilin proceed from the historical fact of the installation of his body in the mausoleum to fantastical scenarios in which he returns to haunt and bedevil the Russian people. In Sinyavsky's text Stalin's thoroughly evil spirit is incorporeal yet still threatening and powerful. Just as Stalin has found no peace after death (and thus is condemned to be a revenant), the Russian nation suffers his continued presence as the unquiet dead. These satirists suggest that the collective conscience is uneasy, having not yet come to terms with issues of guilt and complicity.

These texts belie the truism that there are some topics that are too terrible to serve as the subject of humor and satire. Stalin and Stalinism would seem too serious, too painful to contemplate satirically, yet satire has played a tremendously productive role in the process of cultural de-Stalinization. In the absence of a public, official reckoning with the crimes of Stalinism, satire functioned to pose critical questions about responsibility, guilt, and the possibility of reconciliation. This is not to say that the texts examined here have definitively answered these questions. Although Stalin is repeatedly expelled from the healthy Russian cultural self in these works, his relationship (as other) to the self is never neatly resolved. Indeed, the real work of de-Stalinization performed by these texts is in recognizing that the other embodied by Stalinism was part of the self.

Notes

Introduction

1. Margaret Ziolkowski, *Literary Exorcisms of Stalinism: Russian Writers and the Soviet Past* (Columbia, S.C.: Camden House, 1998), 172.

2. Andrei Sinyavsky, *Soviet Civilization: A Cultural History*, trans. Joanne Turnbull (New York: Arcade, 1988), 111.

3. Kathleen E. Smith, *Remembering Stalin's Victims: Popular Memory and the End of the USSR* (Ithaca, N.Y.: Cornell University Press, 1996), 39.

4. Derek Spring, "Stalinism—The Historical Debate," in *Stalinism and Soviet Cinema*, ed. Richard Taylor and Derek Spring (London: Routledge, 1993), 4.

5. Walter Laqueur, *Stalin: The Glasnost Revelations* (New York: Charles Scribner's Sons, 1990), 255.

6. Adam Hochschild, *The Unquiet Ghost: Russians Remember Stalin* (New York: Viking, 1994), xxiii.

7. There are many alternative terms used in the scholarship on collective or social memory, including "official memory, vernacular memory, public memory, popular memory, local memory, family memory, historical memory, cultural memory." Jeffrey K. Olick and Joyce Robbins, "Social Memory Studies: From 'Collective Memory' to the Historical Sociology of Mnemonic Practices," *Annual Review of Sociology* 24 (1998): 112.

8. For an excellent bibliography of scholarship on collective memory, see Andrew Witmer, "A Bibliographical Review on the Uses of the Past," *Hedgehog Review* 9 (Summer 2007): 81–87.

9. R. N. Bellah et al., *Habits of the Heart: Individualism and Commitment in American Life* (Berkeley: University of California Press, 1985), 153. Quoted in Olick and Robbins, "Social Memory Studies," 122.

10. Hochschild, *The Unquiet Ghost*, 140.

11. Spring, "Stalinism—The Historical Debate," 9.

12. Ibid.

13. Laqueur, *Stalin,* 227.

14. Spring, "Stalinism—The Historical Debate," 9.

15. Smith, *Remembering Stalin's Victims,* 9.

16. Margaret Ziolkowski, "A Modern Demonology: Some Literary Stalins," *Slavic Review* 50 (Spring 1991): 61. Two important critical works on literature about Stalin and Stalinism are Margaret Ziolkowski, *Literary Exorcisms of Stalinism,* and Rosalind Marsh, *Images of Dictatorship: Portraits of Stalin in Literature* (London: Routledge, 1989).

17. Smith, *Remembering Stalin's Victims,* 4.

18. Brian A. Connery, "Theorizing Satire: A Retrospective and Introduction," in *Theorizing Satire: Essays in Literary Criticism,* ed. Brian A. Connery and Kirk Combe (New York: St. Martin's Press, 1995), 2.

19. Ibid., 5.

20. Hochschild, *The Unquiet Ghost,* 281.

21. Ibid., 115.

22. Iurii M. Lotman and Boris A. Uspenskii, "Binary Models in the Dynamics of Russian Culture (to the End of the Eighteenth Century)," in *The Semiotics of Russian Cultural History,* trans. and ed. Alexander D. Nakhimovsky and Alice Stone Nakhimovsky (Ithaca, N.Y.: Cornell University Press, 1985), 31.

23. Ibid.

24. Ziolkowski, *Literary Exorcisms of Stalinism,* 7.

25. Yuri Glazov, *The Russian Mind since Stalin's Death* (Dordrecht, Neth.: D. Reidel, 1985), 226.

26. Machiel Karskens, "Alterity as Defect: On the Logic of the Mechanism of Exclusion," in *Alterity, Identity, Image: Selves and Others in Society and Scholarship,* ed. Raymond Corbey and Joep Leerssen (Amsterdam: Rodopi, 1991), 87.

27. Raymond Corbey and Joep Leerssen, "Studying Alterity: Backgrounds and Perspectives," in *Alterity, Identity, Image: Selves and Others in Society and Scholarship,* ed. Raymond Corbey and Joep Leerssen (Amsterdam: Rodopi, 1991), vii.

28. Julia Kristeva, *Strangers to Ourselves,* trans. Leon S. Roudiez (New York: Columbia University Press, 1991), 51–52.

29. René Girard, *The Scapegoat,* trans. Yvonne Freccero (Baltimore: Johns Hopkins University Press, 1986), 24.

30. Richard Shusterman, "Understanding the Self's Others," in *Cultural Otherness and Beyond,* ed. Chhanda Gupta and D. P. Chattopadhyaya (Leiden, Neth.: Brill, 1998), 112.

31. Ernst van Alphen, "The Other Within," in *Alterity, Identity, Image: Selves and Others in Society and Scholarship,* ed. Raymond Corbey and Joep Leerssen (Amsterdam: Rodopi, 1991), 15.

32. Emmanuel Levinas, *Totality and Infinity: An Essay on Exteriority,* trans. Alphonso Lingis (Pittsburgh, Pa.: Duquesne University Press, 1969).

33. Gisela Brinker-Gabler, introduction to *Encountering the Other(s)*, ed. Gisela Brinker-Gabler (Albany: State University of New York Press, 1995), 3.

34. Dylan Evans, *An Introductory Dictionary of Lacanian Psychoanalysis* (London: Routledge, 1996), 132.

35. Tzvetan Todorov, *On Human Diversity: Nationalism, Racism, and Exoticism in French Thought*, trans. Catherine Porter (Cambridge, Mass.: Harvard University Press, 1993), 19.

36. Ibid., 21.

37. Todorov, *On Human Diversity*, 23–24.

38. Girard, *The Scapegoat*, 33.

Chapter 1. The Insanity Defense

1. Michel Foucault, *Madness and Civilization: A History of Insanity in the Age of Reason*, trans. Richard Howard (New York: Vintage, 1988), 27.

2. On the question of Stalin's sanity, see the following biographical accounts: Adam B. Ulam, *Stalin: The Man and His Era* (New York: Viking, 1973), 685; Andrei Sinyavsky, *Soviet Civilization: A Cultural History* (New York: Arcade, 1988), 85; Roy A. Medvedev, *Let History Judge: The Origins and Consequences of Stalinism*, trans. Colleen Taylor (New York: Knopf, 1971), 306, 308, 311.

3. Medvedev, *Let History Judge*, 306.

4. Robert C. Tucker, *Stalin as Revolutionary, 1879–1929: A Study in History and Personality* (New York: Norton, 1973), 431. Daniel Rancour-Laferriere, *The Mind of Stalin: A Psychoanalytic Study* (Ann Arbor, Mich.: Ardis, 1988).

5. In their study of Stalin's psychology, D. Jablow Hershman and Julian Lieb come very close to concluding that Stalin was psychotic and suffered delusions (*A Brotherhood of Tyrants: Manic Depression and Absolute Power* [Amherst, N.Y.: Prometheus Books, 1994], 98). This seems largely speculative and has no basis in biographical or historical fact.

6. Gustav Bychowski, "Joseph V. Stalin: Paranoia and the Dictatorship of the Proletariat," in *The Psychoanalytic Interpretation of History*, ed. Benjamin B. Wolman (New York: Basic Books, 1971), 145.

7. Sinyavsky, *Soviet Civilization*, 99.

8. Rancour-Laferriere, *The Mind of Stalin*, 53, 55; Philip Pomper, "Nechaev, Lenin, and Stalin: The Psychology of Leadership," *Jahrbücher für Geschichte Osteuropas* 26 (1978): 17–18; Svetlana Klishina, "Stalin na prieme u psikhoanalitika," *Moskovskie novosti*, 22 February–1 March 1988.

9. Charles Prince, "A Psychological Study of Stalin," *Journal of Social Psychology* 22 (1945): 121.

10. Gustav Bychowski, *Dictators and Disciples: From Caesar to Stalin; A Psychoanalytic Interpretation of History* (New York: International Universities Press, 1948), 225; Hershman and Lieb, *A Brotherhood of Tyrants*, 89; Prince, "A Psychological Study of Stalin," 122.

11. Tucker, *Stalin as Revolutionary*, 423.

12. Bychowski, *Dictators and Disciples*, 224–25.

13. Tucker, *Stalin as Revolutionary*, 437.

14. Rancour-Laferriere, *The Mind of Stalin*, 45.

15. Bychowski, *Dictators and Disciples*, 233.

16. Adam B. Ulam, "The Price of Sanity," in *Stalinism: Its Impact on Russia and the World*, ed. G. R. Urban (London: Maurice Temple Smith, 1982), 113.

17. Margaret Ziolkowski, *Literary Exorcisms of Stalinism: Russian Writers and the Soviet Past* (Columbia S.C.: Camden House, 1998), 31.

18. Robert C. Tucker, "The Dictator and Totalitarianism," *World Politics* 17 (1965): 579.

19. Hershman and Lieb, *A Brotherhood of Tyrants*, 169. Brent Rutherford's work on paranoia and political decisionmaking helps to define the term: "In the official classification of the American Psychiatric Association (1956), paranoid reactions are defined as disorders which exhibit persistent delusions, usually persecutory or grandiose, without the presence of hallucinations. Intelligence is well-preserved; behavior and emotional response are consistent with the patient's ideas. . . . The paranoid does not conform to the popular conception of mental illness—loss of contact with reality, loss of control of elementary impulses, and regressive behavior and attitudes. . . . The paranoid maintains his intelligence, personality, and logical powers" ("Psychopathology, Decision-Making, and Political Involvement," *Journal of Conflict Resolution* 10 [1966]: 401–2).

20. Tucker, "The Dictator and Totalitarianism," 578.

21. Ulam, "The Price of Sanity," 103.

22. Sinyavsky, *Soviet Civilization*, 94.

23. Bychowski, "Joseph V. Stalin: Paranoia and the Dictatorship of the Proletariat," 146.

24. Rancour-Laferriere, *The Mind of Stalin*, 21.

25. Tucker, "The Dictator and Totalitarianism," 557, 566; Rutherford, "Psychopathology, Decision-Making, and Political Involvement," 390.

26. Prince, "A Psychological Study of Stalin," 125.

27. Medvedev, *Let History Judge*, 305.

28. Anton Antonov-Ovseyenko, *The Time of Stalin: Portrait of a Tyranny*, trans. George Saunders (New York: Harper and Row, 1981), 254.

29. Ewa M. Thompson, *Understanding Russia: The Holy Fool in Russian Culture* (Lanham, Md.: University Press of America, 1987), 26.

30. Ibid., 27–29.

31. Ibid., 30–44.

32. Ibid., 45.

33. Kristin Thompson, "*Ivan the Terrible* and Stalinist Russia: A Reexamination," *Cinema Journal* 17 (1977): 33.

34. Ulam, "The Price of Sanity," 105.

35. Maureen Perrie, *The Image of Ivan the Terrible in Russian Folklore* (Cambridge: Cambridge University Press, 1987), 116.

36. Vladimir Nabokov, *Speak, Memory: An Autobiography Revisited* (New York: Vintage, 1989), 241.

37. Ibid., 262.

38. Ibid., 272.

39. O. Mikhailov, "Korol' bez korolevstva," in Vladimir Nabokov, *Istreblenie tiranov* (Minsk: Mastatskaia literatura, 1989), 9.

40. Dan E. Burns ("*Bend Sinister* and 'Tyrants Destroyed': Short Story into Novel," *Modern Fiction Studies* 25 [1979]: 510) asserts that the most significant difference between these two works is the degree to which the "world" of the text is particularized.

41. Vladimir Nabokov, *Tyrants Destroyed and Other Stories* (New York: McGraw-Hill, 1975), 2.

42. Vladimir Nabokov, "Tyrants Destroyed," in *Tyrants Destroyed and Other Stories*, 6; "Istreblenie tiranov," in *Vesna v Fial'te i drugie rasskazy* (New York: Izdatel'stvo imeni Chekhova, 1956), 168. This English translation is used as the source of all quotations from Nabokov's text because it is Nabokov's own. Subsequent citations from this edition are acknowledged parenthetically in the text. The first page number refers to the English version, while the second refers to the Russian original.

43. Nina Allan, *Madness, Death and Disease in the Fiction of Vladimir Nabokov* (Birmingham, Eng.: University of Birmingham, 1994), 3.

44. Donald E. Morton, *Vladimir Nabokov* (New York: Frederick Ungar, 1978), 11.

45. Allan, *Madness, Death and Disease*, 33.

46. Aleksandr I. Solzhenitsyn, *A World Split Apart: Commencement Address Delivered at Harvard University June 8, 1978*, trans. Irina Ilovayskaya Alberti (New York: Harper & Row, 1978), 9–11.

47. Aleksandr I. Solzhenitsyn, *The Oak and the Calf: Sketches of Literary Life in the Soviet Union*, trans. Harry Willetts (New York: Harper and Row, 1980), 283.

48. Important exceptions are Rosalind Marsh's extensive analysis of *Circle-96* in *Images of Dictatorship: Portraits of Stalin in Literature* (London: Routledge, 1989) and Daniel Rancour-Laferriere's article "The Deranged Birthday Boy: Solzhenitsyn's Portrait of Stalin in *The First Circle*," *Mosaic* 18 (1985): 61–72.

49. Solzhenitsyn, *The Oak and the Calf*, 32–33.

50. K. Filips-Juswig, "New Chapters for Solženicyn's В круге первом: Indirect Modes of Expression," *Russian Language Journal* 29 (1975): 104.

51. Marsh, *Images of Dictatorship*, 138–40.

52. Ibid., 136; Georges Nivat, "Solzhenitsyn's Different *Circles*: An Interpretive Essay," in *Solzhenitsyn in Exile: Critical Essays and Documentary Materials*, ed. John B. Dunlop, Richard S. Haugh, and Michael Nicholson (Stanford, Calif.: Hoover Institution Press, 1985), 220.

53. Marsh, *Images of Dictatorship*, 136.

54. Nivat, "Solzhenitsyn's Different *Circles*," 220.

55. There are also critics (e.g., Zhores Medvedev, "Russia under Brezhnev," *New Left Review* 117 [1979]: 25) who believe the new chapters are inferior and distort the meaning of the novel.

56. Michael Scammell, *Solzhenitsyn: A Biography* (New York: Norton, 1984), 260.

57. Marsh, *Images of Dictatorship*, 142.

58. Brown, "Solženicyn's Cast of Characters," 162.

59. Marsh, *Images of Dictatorship*, 186.

60. Gary Kern, "Solzhenitsyn's Portrait of Stalin," *Slavic Review* 33 (1974): 10.

61. Aleksandr Solzhenitsyn, *V kruge pervom*, in *Sobranie sochinenii*, vol. 1 (Paris: YMCA-Press, 1978), 116. Subsequent citations from this edition are acknowledged parenthetically in the text.

62. Marsh, *Images of Dictatorship*, 194.

63. Brown, "Solženicyn's Cast of Characters," 162–63.

64. Susan Layton, "The Mind of the Tyrant: Tolstoj's Nicholas and Solženicyn's Stalin," *Slavic and East European Journal* 23 (1979): 483–84.

65. Kern, "Solzhenitsyn's Portrait of Stalin," 16.

66. Marsh, *Images of Dictatorship*, 152–56.

67. Rancour-Laferriere, "The Deranged Birthday Boy," 62.

68. Vladislav Krasnov, *Solzhenitsyn and Dostoevsky: A Study in the Polyphonic Novel* (Athens: University of Georgia Press, 1980), 31.

69. Rancour-Laferriere speculates that Stalin's narcissism was the result of a psychic wound inflicted early in life and that his later pathology stemmed from this psychological trauma. Conflating Solzhenitsyn's fictional Stalin with the historical Stalin, he suggests that his illegitimacy and lower-class origin damaged his psyche (Rancour-Laferriere, "The Deranged Birthday Boy," 68).

70. Brown, "Solženicyn's Cast of Characters," 164.

71. Marsh, *Images of Dictatorship*, 167–68.

72. Ibid., 162, 179.

73. Ibid., 163.

74. Rancour-Laferriere, "The Deranged Birthday Boy," 65.

75. Stalin's loneliness is emphasized significantly more in *Circle-96* than in the earlier version of the novel. See Marsh, *Images of Dictatorship*, 182.

76. Rancour-Laferriere, "The Deranged Birthday Boy," 67.

77. James F. Pontuso, *Assault on Ideology: Aleksandr Solzhyenitsyn's Political Thought* (Lanham, Md.: Lexington Books, 2004).

78. Michael Kirkwood, *Alexander Zinoviev: An Introduction to His Work* (Houndmills, Eng.: Macmillan, 1993), 10.

79. George Urban and Alexander Zinoviev, "Portrait of a Dissenter as a Soviet Man," *Encounter* 62 (1984): 22.

80. Aleksandr Zinov'ev, *Nashei iunosti polet* (Lausanne: L'Age d'Homme, 1983), 75.

81. Ibid., 13.

82. Ibid., 77.

83. Alexander Zinoviev, "From Yawning Heights to Radiant Future," *Survey* 23 (Summer 1977–78): 2.

84. Kirkwood, *Alexander Zinoviev: An Introduction to His Work*, 12.

85. Ibid., 15.

86. Zinoviev, "From Yawning Heights to Radiant Future," 2.

87. Michael Kirkwood, "Alexander Zinoviev: Seer or Scientist?" in *Ideology in Russian Literature*, ed. Richard Freeborn and Jane Grayson (Houndmills, Eng.: Macmillan, 1990), 178.

88. Urban and Zinoviev, "Portrait of a Dissenter," 10.

89. Charles Janson, "Zinoviev on Paradoxes of Stalinism," *Soviet Analyst* 12 (28 September 1983): 8.

90. Zinov'ev, *Nashei iunosti polet*, 27.

91. Aleksandr Zinov'ev, *My i zapad* (Lausanne: L'Age d'Homme, 1981), 13.

92. Zinov'ev, *Nashei iunosti polet*, 9.

93. Zinov'ev, *My i zapad*, 7.

94. Zinov'ev, *Nashei iunosti polet*, 97.

95. Zinov'ev, *My i zapad*, 9.

96. Mike Kirkwood, "Elements of Structure in Zinov'ev's *Zheltyi dom*," *Essays in Poetics* 7 (1982): 87.

97. Aleksandr Zinov'ev, *Zheltyi dom*, vol. 1 (Lausanne: L'Age d'Homme, 1980), 5. Subsequent citations from this edition are acknowledged parenthetically in the text, with a colon separating volume and page numbers.

98. Philip Hanson, "Alexander Zinoviev on Stalinism: Some Observations on *The Flight of Our Youth*," *Soviet Studies* 40 (1988): 133.

99. Sigmund S. Birkenmayer, *Nikolaj Nekrasov: His Life and Poetic Art* (The Hague: Mouton, 1968), 174–78.

100. N. A. Nekrasov, "Komu na Rusi zhit' khorosho," in *Polnoe sobranie stikhotvorenii v trekh tomakh*, vol. 3 (Leningrad: Sovetskii pisatel', 1967), 241.

101. Kirkwood, *Alexander Zinoviev: An Introduction to His Work*, 142.

102. Helen von Ssachno, "Zinoviev's Paradoxes," *Encounter* 52 (1979): 85.

103. Ulam, "The Price of Sanity," 112.

104. Ibid., 106–7.

105. Vladimir Maximov, "Vladimir Maximov's Visa: An Interview in London," *Encounter* 42 (1974): 55.

106. Ibid., 51–52.

107. Ibid., 52.

108. Vladimir Maksimov, "Literatura tam, gde est' bol'," *Literaturnaia gazeta*, 9 March 1994.

109. Ibid.

110. A. Krasnov-Levitin, *Dva pisatelia* (Paris: Poiski, 1983), 269.

111. Violetta Iverni, "Kazhdyi raven svoemu vyboru . . . ," *Grani* 116 (1980): 189–90.

112. Petr Ravich, "Nachalo eposa," in *V literaturnom zerkale: O tvorchestve Vladimira Maksimova* (Paris: Third Wave, 1986), 59.

113. V. Maksimov, *Kovcheg dlia nezvannykh,* in *Sobranie sochinenii,* vol. 6 (Frankfurt: Posev, 1979), 36. Subsequent citations from this edition are acknowledged parenthetically in the text.

114. Anatolii Krasnov-Levitin, "Vl. Maksimov," in *V literaturnom zerkale: O tvorchestve Vladimira Maksimova* (Paris: Third Wave, 1986), 190.

115. This version of the formation of Stalin's character is also recounted by Ronald Hingley in *Joseph Stalin: Man and Legend* (London: Hutchinson, 1974), 32–33.

116. Ziolkowski, *Literary Exorcisms of Stalinism,* 34–36.

117. Iverni, "Kazhdyi raven svoemu vyboru . . . ," 191.

118. Ibid., 188.

119. Maximov, "Vladimir Maximov's Visa," 55.

120. Iverni, "Kazhdyi raven svoemu vyboru . . . ," 184.

Chapter 2. A Bestiary of Stalins

1. Robert Glen, "Man or Beast? English Methodists as Animals in 18th Century Satiric Prints," *Connecticut Review* 14 (Spring 1992): 83.

2. Roger Sale, *Fairy Tales and After: From Snow White to E. B. White* (Cambridge, Mass.: Harvard University Press, 1978), 78.

3. Arnold Clayton Henderson ("Animal Fables as Vehicles of Social Protest and Satire: Twelfth Century to Henryson," in *Proceedings: Third International Beast Epic, Fable, and Fabliau Colloquium, Muenster, 1979,* ed. Jan Goossens and Timothy Sodmann [Cologne: Böhlau Verlag, 1981], 160–63) argues that the bestiary is not primarily a satiric genre. The allegory of bestiaries is "a notch too high for satire." Henderson's focus, however, is the medieval bestiary. Our own century has seen the renewal of the bestiary form, especially in Latin American literature, and the modern variant is decidedly satiric. See D. Curtis Pulsipher, "The Use of the Fantastic, Neo-Fantastic, Animals and Humor as Vehicles for Satire in the Works of Juan Jose Arreola and Murilo Rubias" (Ph.D. diss., University of Illinois, Urbana-Champaign, 1985), 229–30.

4. Willene B. Clark and Meradith T. McMunn, eds., *Beasts and Birds of the Middle Ages: The Bestiary and Its Legacy* (Philadelphia: University of Pennsylvania Press, 1989), 1.

5. For a history of the development of the *lubok,* see Dm. Moldavskii, *Russkii lubok XVII–XIX vv.* (Moscow: Gosudarstvennoe izdatel'stvo izobrazitel'nogo iskusstva, 1962), and Alla Sytova, *The Lubok: Russian Folk Pictures: 17th to 19th Century* (Leningrad: Aurora Art Publishers, 1984), 5–17.

6. Arthur O. Lovejoy, *The Great Chain of Being: A Study of the History of an Idea* (Cambridge, Mass.: Harvard University Press, 1950).

7. Clark and McMunn, *Beasts and Birds of the Middle Ages*, 2. This seminal text of animal literature probably dates from the second century A.D. and may have originated in Alexandria. Each chapter of the *Physiologus* describes a different animal, drawing on popular sources as well as direct observation.

8. Tzvetan Todorov, *The Conquest of America: The Question of the Other* (New York: Harper & Row, 1982), 153 –54.

9. Thomas Keith, *Man and the Natural World: A History of the Modern Sensibility* (New York: Pantheon, 1983), 48.

10. Ibid., 40.

11. René Girard, *The Scapegoat*, trans. Yvonne Freccero (Baltimore, Md.: Johns Hopkins University Press, 1986), 22.

12. Lauren G. Leighton, "Homage to Kornei Chukovsky," *Russian Review* 31 (January 1972): 47.

13. Nadezhda Mandelstam, *Hope Abandoned*, trans. Max Hayward (New York: Atheneum, 1981), 88.

14. Leighton, "Homage to Kornei Chukovsky," 48.

15. Vera T. Reck, trans. and ed., "Excerpts from the Diaries of Korney Chukovsky Relating to Boris Pilnyak," *California Slavic Studies* 11 (1980): 192.

16. Jeffrey Brooks, "The Young Kornei Chukovsky (1905 –1914): A Liberal Critic in Search of Cultural Unity," *Russian Review* 33 (January 1974): 51.

17. Lev Loseff, *On the Beneficence of Censorship: Aesopian Language in Modern Russian Literature* (Munich: Otto Sagner, 1984), 199.

18. Rosalind Marsh, *Images of Dictatorship: Portraits of Stalin in Literature* (London: Routledge, 1989), 18 –19.

19. M. Petrovskii, *Kniga o Kornee Chukovskom* (Moscow: Sovetskii pisatel', 1966), 252.

20. Kornei Chukovskii, *Stikhi* (Moscow: Khudozhestvennaia literatura, 1961), 12–13.

21. Kornei Chukovsky, *The Poet and the Hangman* (*Nekrasov and Muravyov*), trans. R. W. Rotsel (Ann Arbor, Mich.: Ardis, 1977), 23, 39.

22. Quoted in Mikhail Vaiskopf, *Pisatel' Stalin* (Moscow: Novoe literaturnoe obozrenie, 2001), 31.

23. Ibid.

24. Mark Lipovetskii, "Skazkovlast': 'Tarakanishche' Stalina," *Novoe literaturnoe obozrenie* 45 (2000): 132.

25. Ibid., 136.

26. Kornei Chukovskii, "Tarakanishche," in *Sobranie sochinenii v shesti tomakh* (Moscow: Khudozhestvennaia literatura, 1965), 174. Subsequent citations from this edition are acknowledged parenthetically in the text.

27. Loseff, *On the Beneficence of Censorship*, 199.

28. Iurii Borev, *Staliniada* (Moscow: Sovetskii pisatel', 1990), 20.

29. Marsh, *Images of Dictatorship*, 19.

30. Peter Mason, *Deconstructing America: Representations of the Other* (London: Routledge, 1990), 53; W. Arens, *The Man-Eating Myth: Anthropology and Anthropophagy* (New York: Oxford University Press, 1979), 28. Both Mason and Arens note that cannibalism is often associated with incest in accounts of "uncivilized," alien cultures. It is noteworthy that a rumor circulated claiming that Stalin's second marriage to Nadezhda Allilueva was incestuous. Edvard Radzinsky (*Stalin* [London: Hodder & Stoughton, 1996]) notes that "there is a horrid legend that this passionate woman [Nadezhda's mother] was not unmoved by Koba's arrival on the scene and that the birth of her younger daughter, Nadya, who was to be Koba's second wife, may have been the result of this infatuation. It is only a legend" (53).

31. Andreas Bode ("Humor in the Lyrical Stories for Children of Samuel Marshak and Korney Chukovsky," *The Lion and the Unicorn* 13 [December 1989]: 46) suggests that the sparrow represents the ordinary man or the working class.

32. Most of the factual information about cockroaches included here is taken from P. B. Cornwell, *The Cockroach*, vol. 1, *A Laboratory Insect and an Industrial Pest* (London: Hutchinson, 1968), 11–13.

33. Cornwell (*The Cockroach*, 14) attests to this; see also Petrovskii, *Kniga o Kornee Chukovskom*, 247.

34. Loseff, *On the Beneficence of Censorship*, 201; Roman Jakobson, "Marginalia to Vasmer's Russian Etymological Dictionary (Р-Я)," *International Journal of Slavic Linguistics* 1–2 (1959): 272.

35. Loseff, *On the Beneficence of Censorship*, 202.

36. V. P. Adrianova-Peretts, ed., *Narodno-poeticheskaia satira* (Leningrad: Sovetskii pisatel', 1960), 58.

37. Louis Fischer, *The Life and Death of Stalin* (New York: Harper, 1952), 6; J. Bernard Hutton, *Stalin, the Miraculous Georgian* (London: Neville Spearman, 1961), 23; Radzinsky, *Stalin*, 56, 61.

38. Maxim Gorky, *My Childhood*, trans. Ronald Wilks (London: Penguin, 1966), 67.

39. Barry P. Scherr, *Maxim Gorky* (Boston: Twayne, 1988), 81.

40. In response to Chukovsky's criticism of Gorky, Trotsky published his 1923 essay "K. Chukovskii," in which he charged that Gorky's socialism was repugnant to Chukovsky and his art was incomprehensible to him. See also Bode, "Humor in the Lyrical Stories," 41; Brooks, "The Young Kornei Chukovsky," 52.

41. It is interesting to contrast Solzhenitsyn's use of cockroaches in his tale "Matrena's Home" ("Matrenin dvor"), which on one level may also be a response to Gorky's *Childhood*. Matrena, his heroine, is also a grandmotherly figure, but she is content to cohabitate with the cockroaches in her home. She does not poison them because she considers them part of the natural world and—significantly vis-à-vis Gorky—because they are innocent of the Lie of Communism. Although Solzhenitsyn's didactic point is thus quite different than Chukovsky's, he also finds the image of the cockroach effective.

42. N. Tarasova, "Bulat Okudzhava—sovremennyi baian," in Bulat Okudzhava, *Bud' zdorov, shkoliar: Stikhi* (Frankfurt: Posev, 1966), viii.

43. Il'ia Medovoi, "Ia vnov' povstrechalsia s nadezhdoi," *Moskovskie novosti*, 31 May 1987, 11.

44. Boris Chichibabin, "Slovo o Bulate," in *Kol'tso A* (Moscow: Moskovskii rabochii, 1993–94), 13.

45. N. Korzhavin, "Poeziia Bulata Okudzhavy," in Bulat Okudzhava, *Proza i poeziia*, 7th ed. (Frankfurt: Posev, 1984), 332.

46. Martin Dewhirst and Robert Farrell, eds., *The Soviet Censorship* (Metuchen, N.J.: Scarecrow Press, 1973), 91.

47. The poem was published in the West in Bulat Okudzhava, *Proza i poeziia* (Frankfurt: Posev, 1968) and in *Bulat Okudzhava. 65 Songs*, ed. Vladimir Frumkin (Ann Arbor, Mich.: Ardis, 1980).

48. Medovoi, "Ia vnov' povstrechalsia s nadezhdoi," 11.

49. Bulat Okudzhava, "Arbatskoe vdokhnovenie, ili vospominanie o detstve," in "Iz liricheskoi tetradi," *Druzhba narodov* 1 (1988): 114.

50. Ibid.

51. I. I. Medzhakov-Koriakin, "Osobennosti romantizma v poezii Bulata Okudzhavy," *Melbourne Slavonic Studies* 7 (1972): 70; Tarasova, "Bulat Okudzhava—sovremennyi baian," 13–14.

52. Bulat Okudzhava, "Chernyi kot," in *Proza i poeziia* (Frankfurt: Posev, 1984), 220. Subsequent citations from this edition are acknowledged parenthetically in the text.

53. Solzhenitsyn, e.g., writes in *Cancer Ward* (trans. Nicholas Bethell and David Burg [New York: Farrar, Straus and Giroux, 1992]): "In the camps, Oleg had met an old political prisoner who had once been in exile in Turukhansk. He had told Oleg about those eyes—they were not velvet black, they were yellow" (510).

54. Todorov, *The Conquest of America*, 132.

55. Mason, *Deconstructing America*, 54.

56. In the poem "The Old House" ("Staryi dom"), for example, the mice all leave the courtyard in a gesture of abandonment of the home. In the poem "Arbat Inspiration, or Memories of Childhood" ("Arbatskoe vdokhnovenie, ili vospominaniia o detstve"), Okudzhava writes that his Arbat courtyard "raised" (*vospityval*) him and he metaphorically equates this courtyard with Russia: "I still love my courtyard / its poverty and its expanse, / and the smell of a cheap dinner" (*Eshche liubliu svoi dvor— / ego ubogost' i ego prostor, / i aromat groshovogo obeda*).

57. Klaus Dieter Seemann, "Bulat Okudžavas 'Černyi kot' als antistalinistische Parodie," *Die Welt der Slaven* 31 (1986): 139–46.

58. Katharine M. Briggs, *Nine Lives: Cats in Folklore* (London: Routledge, 1980).

59. Bulat Okudzhava, "My iz shkoly XX veka," *Literaturnoe obozrenie*, nos. 5–6 (1994): 13.

60. M. Oldfield Howey, *The Cat in the Mysteries of Religion and Magic* (New

York: Castle Books, 1956), 167; Beryl Rowland, *Animals with Human Faces: A Guide to Animal Symbolism* (Knoxville: University of Tennessee Press, 1973), 51.

61. Howey, *The Cat in the Mysteries of Religion and Magic*, 224; Rowland, *Animals with Human Faces*, 52.

62. Rowland, *Animals with Human Faces*, 52.

63. For an authoritative version of this fairy tale, see *Narodnye russkie skazki: Iz sbornika A. N. Afanas'eva* (Moscow: Khudozhestvennaia literatura, 1989), 28–30.

64. Moldavskii, *Russkii lubok XVII–XIX vv.*

65. This *lubok* was used as a cover illustration for the seventh edition of Okudzhava's *Proza i poeziia* (Frankfurt: Posev, 1984).

66. The *lubok* "Myshi kota pogrebaiut" also influenced Sumarokov's fable "The Mouse and the Cat" ("Mysh' i koshka"), about a tyrannical cat and a cowardly mouse. It is possible that this well-known fable represents an additional source of influence on Okudzhava's work.

67. The *povest'* was first published serially in *Kontinent* (nos. 22 and 23) in 1980. It was published in book form by Ardis in 1982. It first appeared in the Soviet Union in *Iunost'* (no. 9) in 1987.

68. Iskander made this comment during an interview cited in Natal'ia Ivanova, *Smekh protiv strakha, ili Fazil' Iskander* (Moscow: Sovetskii pisatel', 1990), 19. See also Sergei Ivanov, "O 'maloi proze' Iskandera, ili chto mozhno sdelat' iz nastoiashchei mukhi," *Novyi mir* 1 (1989): 255.

69. Mark Lipovetskii, "Usloviia igry," *Literaturnoe obozrenie* 7 (1988): 46–49; Ivanova, *Smekh protiv strakha*, 272.

70. Zhanna Golovchenko, "Otstupleniia byt' ne dolzhno," *Sovetskii ekran* 14 (1988): 5.

71. Yevgeny Ambartsumov, "Zinovyev, Kamenev, Others Rehabilitated," *Current Digest of the Soviet Press* 15, no. 24 (1988): 7.

72. Elena Veselaia, "Esli ostanovimsia, nas poneset nazad," *Moskovskie novosti*, 12 March 1989, 16.

73. Fazil' Iskander, "Pis'mo druz'iam," in *Poety i tsary (Sbornik)* (Moscow: Ogonek, 1991), 5.

74. Yuri Krokhin, "Fazil Iskander: Ideas and Images," *Moscow News*, 25 February–3 March 1994, 11.

75. Fazil' Iskander, *Diadia Sandro i ego liubimets*, in *Sandro iz Chegema* (Ann Arbor, Mich.: Ardis, 1979), 303. In his eclectic 1990 compendium of Stalin lore entitled *Staliniada*, Borev recounts this same anecdote (23). In the 1994 interview cited earlier (see n.74), Iskander asserts that this was an actual reminiscence told to him by one of Stalin's bodyguards.

76. Fazil' Iskander, *Pshada*, *Znamia* 8 (1993): 3–36.

77. Ibid., 30.

78. Lesley Milne, "Fazil' Iskander: From 'Petukh' to *Pshada*," *Slavic and East European Review* 74 (July 1996): 460.

79. Fazil' Iskander, *Kroliki i udavy* (Ann Arbor, Mich.: Ardis, 1982), 7. Subsequent citations from this edition are acknowledged parenthetically in the text.

80. Ivanova, *Smekh protiv strakha*, 281.

81. Iuliia Troll', "*Kroliki i udavy* Fazilia Iskandera," *Novyi zhurnal* 151 (1983): 302.

82. Richard L. Chapple, "Fazil Iskander's *Rabbits and Boa Constrictors:* A Soviet Version of George Orwell's *Animal Farm,*" *Germano-Slavica* 5, nos. 1–2 (1985): 38. Laura Beraha notes that Iskander's *samopoedanie* is "an obvious send-up of the self-criticism inculcated by the former seminarian [Stalin]." Paper presented at the annual meeting of the American Association for the Advancement of Slavic Studies, Phoenix, Arizona, November 1992.

83. Troll', "*Kroliki i udavy* Fazilia Iskandera," 301.

84. C. G. Jung, *Nietzsche's Zarathustra: Notes of the Seminar Given in 1934–1939,* ed. James L. Jarrett (Princeton, N.J.: Princeton University Press, 1988), 748.

85. Roi Medvedev (*Sem'ia tirana* [N. Novgorod: Leta, 1993]) discusses the rumors that Stalin was illegitimate and recounts his visit to an Ossetian village where the inhabitants proudly insisted that "Stalin's father was the Ossetian Prince Dzhugaev" (8).

86. Oleg Dolzhenko, "Den' zhizni otlichat' ot nochi," in *Khronograf: Ezhegodik 89* (Moscow: Moskovskii rabochii, 1989), 48. In the popular imagination Africa seems to be the habitat of the largest and most dangerous snakes. Albert the Great cites a case from Roman history where a boa 120 feet long appeared in Africa: "Regulus, the Roman general, ordered that the beast be attacked with ballistae and other military engines customarily employed in the siege of fortified towns; when the snake was killed, Regulus brought its stripped skin and jaws to a spectacle at Rome" (*Man and the Beasts,* trans. James J. Scanlan [Binghamton, N.Y.: Medieval and Renaissance Texts and Studies, 1987], 398–99). For another interpretation of the significance of Africa as the setting of *Rabbits and Boa Constrictors,* see Karen Ryan-Hayes, *Contemporary Russian Satire: A Genre Study* (Cambridge: Cambridge University Press, 1995), 29.

87. See Fazil Iskander, *Rabbits and Boa Constrictors,* trans. Ronald E. Peterson (Ann Arbor, Mich.: Ardis, 1989). There is phonetic similarity between the two words *pitomtsy pitona* that gives the phrase the quality of a spell or mantra in Russian; this quality is lost in English translation.

88. See chapter 10, "The Fascination of the Serpent," in M. Oldfield Howey, *The Encircled Serpent: A Study of Serpent Symbolism in All Countries and Ages* (New York: Arthur Richmond, 1955).

89. Medvedev, *Sem'ia tirana,* 6.

90. The verb *dushit'* ("to smother") is also used in the text to describe the snakes' technique of killing rabbits. This word also has a secondary, figurative meaning that facilitates political allegory.

91. Iskander's interest in biblical themes is of long standing. The *povest'* The *Feasts of Belshazzar* takes its name from a story recounted in the Book of Daniel.

One of his books of poetry (laden with biblical images) is called *Put'* (*The Way*), a word often used as a synonym for the Bible. Lastly, the hero of his recent story *Pshada* is moved to reexamine his life after reading a Christian leaflet handed to him on the street.

92. Roland Mushat Frye, ed., *The Reader's Bible: A Narrative* (Princeton, N.J.: Princeton University Press, 1965), 6.

93. Hilda Simon, *Snakes: The Facts and the Folklore* (New York: Viking, 1973), 16, 24.

94. I am indebted for this insight to an anonymous reader for the University of Wisconsin Press.

95. Rowland, *Animals with Human Faces*, 143.

96. Ibid.

97. Frank J. Miller, *Folklore for Stalin: Russian Folklore and Pseudofolklore of the Stalin Era* (Armonk, NY: M. E. Sharpe, 1990), 63–64.

98. Ovid, *Metamorphoses*, trans. Rolfe Humphries (Bloomington: Indiana University Press, 1955), 16.

99. Joseph Fontenrose, *Python: A Study of Delphic Myth and Its Origins* (New York: Biblo & Tannen, 1974), 9–10.

100. Ibid., 10.

101. Helmut W. Pesch, "The Sign of the Worm: Images of Death and Immortality in the Fiction of E. R. Eddison," in *Death and the Serpent: Immortality in Science Fiction and Fantasy*, ed. Carl B. Yoke and Donald M. Hassler (Westport, Conn.: Greenwood Press, 1985), 92–93.

102. Jack Lindsay, *The Origins of Alchemy in Graeco-Roman Egypt* (New York: Barnes & Noble, 1970), 261.

103. Jung, *Nietzsche's Zarathustra*, 1287.

104. Natal'ia Ivanova, "Smekh protiv strakha," in Fazil' Iskander, *Kroliki i udavy* (Moscow: Knizhnaia palata, 1988), 9.

105. Friedrich W. Nietzsche, *Thus Spoke Zarathustra*, trans. R. J. Hollingdale (Harmondsworth, Eng.: Penguin, 1961), 180.

106. Jung, *Nietzsche's Zarathustra*, 1292–93.

107. Michel Foucault, *Madness and Civilization: A History of Insanity in the Age of Reason*, trans. Richard Howard (New York: Vintage, 1988), 76.

Chapter 3. Stalin in a Dress

1. Dorothy Atkinson, "Society and the Sexes in the Russian Past," in *Women in Russia*, ed. Dorothy Atkinson, Alexander Dallin, and Gail Warshofsky Lapidus (Stanford, Calif.: Stanford University Press, 1977), 4.

2. Jane T. Costlow, Stephanie Sandler, and Judith Vowles, eds., *Sexuality and the Body in Russian Culture* (Stanford, Calif.: Stanford University Press, 1993), 18.

3. Matthew Hodgart, *Satire* (New York: McGraw-Hill, 1969), 79.

4. William Shakespeare, *Hamlet*, in *Four Tragedies*, ed. David Bevington (Toronto: Bantam, 1988), 90–91.

5. Katharine M. Rogers, "The Fear of Mom: The Twentieth Century," in *The Troublesome Helpmate: A History of Misogyny in Literature* (Seattle: University of Washington Press, 1966), 226–64.

6. Francine du Plessix Gray, *Soviet Women: Walking the Tightrope* (New York: Doubleday, 1989), 131.

7. Dorothy Atkinson, "Society and the Sexes in the Russian Past," in *Women in Russia*, ed. Dorothy Atkinson, Alexander Dallin, and Gail Warshofsky Lapidus (Stanford, Calif.: Stanford University Press, 1977), 14–16. Francine du Plessix Gray cites Joanna Hubbs's work in speculating that the misogyny of the Orthodox Church may have been a response to paganism in Slavic culture, in particular to the matriarchal roots of pagan religion (*Soviet Women*, 116).

8. Rosalind Marsh, introduction to *Gender and Russian Literature: New Perspectives* (Cambridge: Cambridge University Press, 1996), 12–13.

9. Tzvetan Todorov, *The Conquest of America: The Question of the Other*, trans. Richard Howard (New York: Harper and Row, 1984), 91.

10. Emmanuel Levinas, *Time and the Other and Additional Essays*, trans. Richard A. Cohen (Pittsburgh, Pa.: Duquesne University Press, 1987), 85.

11. Simone du Beauvoir, *The Second Sex*, trans. H. M. Parshley (New York: Vintage, 1989), xxii.

12. In *The Conquest of America* Todorov writes: "It is futile to speculate whether the image of woman has been projected on the foreigner or the foreigner's features on woman: both have always been there, and what matters is their solidarity, not the anteriority of one or the other. That such oppositions are made equivalent with the group relating to the body and the soul is also revealing: above all, *the other* is our body itself; whence, too, the identification of the Indians, as of women, to animals, creatures which, though animate, have no soul" (154).

13. Julia Kristeva, *Strangers to Ourselves*, trans. Leon S. Roudiez (New York: Columbia University Press, 1991), 42–50.

14. W. Arens, *The Man-Eating Myth: Anthropology and Anthropophagy* (New York: Oxford University Press, 1979), 26. It is noteworthy that one of the nicknames bestowed on Stalin by prisoners in the camps was "cannibal" (*liudoed*); see Vladimir Kozlovskii, "I. V. Stalin v russkoi zhargonnoi leksike," *SSSR: Vnutrennie protivorechiia* 3 (1982): 104–11.

15. Pamela Chester, "Engaging Sexual Demons in Marina Tsvetaeva's 'Devil': The Body and the Genesis of the Woman Poet," *Slavic Review* 53 (Winter 1994): 1034. On the issue of the gender of Tsvetaeva's devil, see also Lily Feiler, "Marina Cvetaeva's Childhood," in *Marina Tsvetaeva: Trudy 1-go mezhdunarodnogo simpoziuma (Lozanna, 30.VI.–3.VII.1982)*, ed. Robin Kemball (Bern, Switz.: Peter Lang, 1991), 37–45; Lily Feiler, "Tsvetaeva's God/Devil," in *Marina Tsvetaeva, 1892–1992,*

ed. Svetlana Elnitsky and Efim Etkind (Northfield, Vt.: The Russian School of Nor-wich University, 1992), 34–42. Especially pertinent is Mara Négron Marreo's discus-sion of Tsvetaeva's devil in her article "Crossing the Mirror to the Forbidden Land (Lewis Carroll's *Alice in Wonderland* and Marina Tsvetaeva's *The Devil*)," in *Writing Differences: Readings from the Seminar of Hélène Cixous,* ed. Susan Sellers (Milton Keynes, Eng.: Open University Press, 1988), 67.

16. Sam B. Girgus, "The Devil and the Demon Woman: Symbols of Freedom in Isaac Bashevis Singer," *Angloamericana* 6 (1985): 132.

17. Luce Irigaray, *Speculum of the Other Woman,* trans. Gillian C. Gill (Ithaca, N.Y.: Cornell University Press, 1985); de Beauvoir, *The Second Sex*; Kristeva, *Strang-ers to Ourselves.*

18. Vladimir Voinovich, *The Anti-Soviet Soviet Union,* trans. Richard Lourie (San Diego: Harcourt Brace Jovanovich, 1986), x.

19. Robert Porter, "Animal Magic in Solzhenitsyn, Rasputin, and Voynovich," *Modern Language Review* 82 (1987): 681–82.

20. Voinovich, *The Anti-Soviet Soviet Union,* 293.

21. Vladimir Voinovich, "The Trouble with Truth," *New Republic,* 28 November 1983, 28.

22. It is interesting that Voinovich toys with crossing gender boundaries in this story as well. Daniel Rancour-Laferriere considers Stalin's habit of cutting pictures of people out of *Ogenek* and rearranging men's and women's heads and bodies to be a form of cross-dressing ("From Incompetence to Satire: Voinovich's Image of Stalin as Castrated Leader of the Soviet Union in 1941," *Slavic Review* 50 [Spring 1991]: 39).

23. The first two parts of *Zhizn' i neobychainye prikliucheniia soldata Ivana Chonkina* (translated as *The Life and Extraordinary Adventures of Private Ivan Chonkin*) were published in *Grani* in 1969 and as a separate edition in Paris in 1975. The third and fourth parts (*Pretendent na prestol,* translated as *Pretender to the Throne*) were published in 1979. The fifth and final part of *Ivan Chonkin* has not yet appeared.

24. Vladimir Voinovich, *Zhizn' i neobychainye prikliucheniia soldata Ivana Chon-kina: Litso neprikosnovennoe* (Ann Arbor, Mich.: Ardis, 1985), 55. Subsequent cita-tions from this edition are acknowledged parenthetically in the text.

25. As Irina Vasiuchenko writes ("Chtia vozhdia i armeiskii ustav," *Znamia* 10 [October 1989]), "By the way, Stalin doesn't appear in the novel in person. This is a sort of magic word of the kind that mean more than reality in the world of terror and deception. If at the beginning of time 'the Word was God,' then here—corrupt and soulless—it becomes the devil or at least some mischievous demon whose ca-price despotically controls the fates of characters" (215–16). Violetta Iverni ("Kome-diia nesovmestimosti," *Kontinent* 5 [1975]: 450) also notes Stalin's absence from the novel but suggests that Gladishev is a kind of substitute figure, scaled down but con-nected to Stalin through a series of parallels (a penchant for experimentation, infor-mal education, an interest in the sciences, a proclivity for making grand speeches).

26. Leon Trotsky, *Stalin: An Appraisal of the Man and His Influence*, trans. Charles Malamuth (New York: Stein and Day, 1967), 160.

27. I am indebted to an anonymous reader for the University of Wisconsin Press for this insight.

28. Peter Petro, "Hašek, Voinovich, and the Tradition of Anti-Militarist Satire," *Canadian Slavonic Papers* 22 (1980): 21; Sally Anne Perryman, "Vladimir Voinovich: The Evolution of a Satirical Soviet Writer" (Ph.D. diss., Vanderbilt University, 1981), 136–37; Evgenii Gollerbakh, "Neprilichnyi anekdot: O proze Vladimira Voinovicha," *Novyi zhurnal* 184–85 (1991): 335; Grigori Svirski, *A History of Post-War Soviet Writing: The Literature of Moral Opposition*, trans. Robert Dessaix and Michael Ulman (Ann Arbor, Mich.: Ardis, 1981), 382; R. C. Porter, "Vladimir Voinovich and the Comedy of Innocence," *Forum for Modern Language Studies* 16 (1980): 102; Rancour-Laferriere, "From Incompetence to Satire," 39.

29. Winfried Schleiner, "Cross-Dressing, Gender Errors, and Sexual Taboos in Renaissance Literature," in *Gender Reversals and Gender Cultures: Anthropological and Historical Perspectives*, ed. Sabrina Petra Ramet (London: Routledge, 1996), 94.

30. Wendy Doniger O'Flaherty, *Women, Androgynes, and Other Mythical Beasts* (Chicago: University of Chicago Press, 1980), 297.

31. Chris Gosselin and Glenn Wilson, *Sexual Variations: Fetishism, Sadomasochism and Transvestism* (New York: Simon & Schuster, 1980), 60.

32. Grace Tiffany, *Erotic Beasts and Social Monsters: Shakespeare, Jonson, and Comic Androgyny* (Newark, N.J.: University of Delaware Press, 1995), 17.

33. Laura Beraha, "The Fixed Fool: Raising and Resisting Picaresque Mobility in Vladimir Vojnovič's *Čonkin* Novels," *Slavic and East European Journal* 40 (1996): 487.

34. According to O'Flaherty (*Women, Androgynes, and Other Mythical Beasts*, 284), the transvestite is probably most accurately regarded as a pseudo-androgyne.

35. Halimur Khan, "Folklore and Fairy-Tale Elements in Vladimir Voinovich's Novel *The Life and Extraordinary Adventures of Private Ivan Chonkin*," *Slavic and East European Journal* 40 (1996): 506.

36. My generalization here is limited to European Russian culture. As Marjorie Mandelstam Balzer has shown ("Sacred Genders in Siberia. Shamans, Bear festivals, and Androgyny," in Ramet, *Gender Reversals and Gender Cultures*), in the shamanistic traditions of Siberia "gender transformations perceived according to some European standards as deviant become instead sacred" (164).

37. Matthew Cullerne Bown, *Art under Stalin* (New York: Holmes & Meier, 1991); Boris Groys, *The Total Art of Stalinism*, trans. Charles Rougle (Princeton, N.J.: Princeton University Press, 1992).

38. In Blake's poetry, e.g., Jesus Christ represents "the androgynous ideal . . . the second Adam who has the power to reinstitute the androgynous harmony of the original creation." Diane Long Hoeveler, *Romantic Androgyny: The Women Within* (University Park: Pennsylvania State University Press, 1990), 215.

39. Wolfgang Holz, "Allegory and Iconography in Socialist Realist Painting," in *Art of the Soviets: Painting, Sculpture and Architecture in a One-Party State, 1917–1992,* ed. Matthew Cullerne Bown and Brandon Taylor (Manchester, Eng.: Manchester University Press, 1993), 77.

40. This song has erroneously been attributed to Vladimir Vysotsky, and the notoriety associated with it may have helped launch his career. See Kevin Windle, "Iuz Aleshkovski's 'Pesnia o Staline' and 'Sovetskaia paskhalnaia': A Study of Competing Versions," *Slavonic and East European Review* 74 (January 1996): 19 –37; Karl-heinz Kasper, "Ein literarischer Text für die Abiturstufe," *Mitteilungen für die Lehrer slawischer Fremdsprachen* 64 (December 1992): 17 –24.

41. Leonid Zhukhovitskii, "BOMZh vo frake: V Moskve vyshel trekhtomnik Iuza Aleshkovskogo," *Literaturnaia gazeta,* 31 July 1996, 6.

42. Yuz Aleshkovsky et al., "Writers in Exile: A Conference of Soviet and East European Dissidents," *Partisan Review* 4 (1983): 508.

43. Edward J. Brown, "Zinoviev, Aleshkovsky, Rabelais, Sorrentino, Possibly Pynchon, Maybe James Joyce, and Certainly *Tristram Shandy*: A Comparative Study of a Satirical Mode," *Stanford Slavic Studies* 1 (1987): 320.

44. Priscilla Meyer, "*Skaz* in the Work of Juz Aleškovskij," *Slavic and East European Journal* 28 (Winter 1984): 459.

45. Iuz Aleshkovskii, *Kenguru* (Voronezh: AMKO, 1992), 97. Subsequent citations from this edition are acknowledged parenthetically in the text.

46. R. Arsenidze, "Iz vospominanii o Staline," *Novyi zhurnal* 72 (1963): 223.

47. Rosalind Marsh, *Images of Dictatorship: Portraits of Stalin in Literature* (London: Routledge, 1989), 132.

48. M. Keith Booker and Dubravka Juraga, *Bakhtin, Stalin, and Modern Russian Fiction: Carnival, Dialogism, and History* (Westport, Conn.: Greenwood Press, 1995), 119.

49. Jacques Sarano, *The Meaning of the Body,* trans. James H. Farley (Philadelphia: Westminster Press, 1966), 50–51.

50. Sigmund Freud, "The Sexual Aberrations," in *The Basic Writings of Sigmund Freud,* trans. and ed. A. Brill (New York: Random House, 1938), 567.

51. Daniel Rancour-Laferriere, *The Mind of Stalin: A Psychoanalytic Study* (Ann Arbor, Mich.: Ardis, 1988), 63.

52. Isaac Babel, "My First Goose," in *Collected Stories,* trans. David McDuff (London: Penguin, 1994), 119.

53. Marsh, *Images of Dictatorship,* 132.

54. B. A. Uspenskii, "Mifologicheskii aspekt russkoi ekspressivnoi frazeologii," in *Izbrannye trudy,* vol. 2, *Iazyk i kul'tura* (Moscow: Iazyki russkoi kul'tury, 1996), 78 –80.

55. Freud ("The Sexual Aberrations") explains the mechanism of fetishism in some detail: "Another contribution to the explanation of the fetichistic [*sic*] preference of the foot is found in the Infantile Sexual Theories. The foot replaces the

penis, which is so much missed in the woman. In some cases of foot fetichism [*sic*] it could be shown that the desire for looking originally directed to the genitals, which strove to reach its object from below, was stopped on the way by prohibition and repression, and, therefore, adhered to the foot or shoe as a fetich [*sic*]. In conformity with infantile expectation, the female genital was hereby imagined as a male genital" (568).

56. Tim Scholl, "Queer Performance: 'Male' Ballet," in *Consuming Russia: Popular Culture, Sex, and Society since Gorbachev*, ed. Adele Marie Barker (Durham, N.C.: Duke University Press, 1999), 305.

57. Marjorie Garber, *Vested Interests: Cross-Dressing and Cultural Anxiety* (New York: Routledge, 1992), 17.

Chapter 4. The Monster Lurks Within

1. Aristotle, *Generation of Animals*, trans. A. L. Peck (Cambridge, Mass.: Harvard University Press, 1942), 425, 419.

2. Michael Palencia-Roth, "Enemies of God: Monsters and the Theology of Conquest," in *Monsters, Tricksters, and Sacred Cows: Animal Tales and American Identities*, ed. A. James Arnold (Charlottesville: University Press of Virginia, 1996), 24.

3. Jeffrey Jerome Cohen, "Monster Culture (Seven Theses)," in *Monster Theory: Reading Culture*, ed. Jeffrey Jerome Cohen (Minneapolis: University of Minnesota Press, 1996), 6.

4. David Williams, *Deformed Discourse: The Function of the Monster in Mediaeval Thought and Literature* (Exeter, Eng.: University of Exeter Press, 1996), 177.

5. Peter Mason, *Deconstructing America: Representations of the Other* (London: Routledge, 1990), 7; Palencia-Roth, "Enemies of God," 26.

6. Cohen, "Monster Culture," 8.

7. Ibid., 20.

8. M. Slonimskii et al., *My znali Evgeniia Shvartsa* (Leningrad: Iskusstvo, 1966).

9. Efim Dobin, "Dobryi volshebnik," *Neva* 11 (1988): 207. See also Felicia Hardison Londré, "Evgeny Shvarts and the Uses of Fantasy in the Soviet Theatre," *Research Studies* 47 (September 1979): 133.

10. Al. Dymshits, "V prokrustovom lozhe," *Literaturnaia gazeta*, 16 October 1968, 4; S. Tsimbal, "Fantaziia i real'nost' (Iz arkhiva Evgeniia Shvartsa)," *Voprosy literatury* 9 (1967): 159.

11. Irina H. Corten, "Evgenii Shvarts as an Adapter of Hans Christian Andersen and Charles Perrault," *Russian Review* 37 (January 1978): 52.

12. S. Borodin, "Vrednaia skazka," *Literaturnaia gazeta*, 25 March 1944, 3.

13. Amanda J. Metcalf, *Evgenii Shvarts and His Fairy-Tales for Adults* (Birmingham, Eng.: Dept. of Russian Language & Literature, University of Birmingham, 1979), 58.

14. The revival of Shvarts's plays in the sixties gave rise to a polemic about the function of the fairy-tale genre. *The Dragon* was decried as harmful by some critics

(Evgenii Binevich, "Dobryi i umnyi talant," *Literaturnoe obozrenie* 1 [1987]: 107), while others asserted that the genre is by its very nature allegorical and that to interpret fairy tales literally is to do violence to their intent (A. Lebedev, "Skazka est' skazka," *Teatr* 4 [1968]: 39–40).

15. Metcalf, *Evgenii Shvarts and His Fairy-Tales for Adults*, 66.

16. V. E. Golovnicher (*Epicheskii teatr Evgeniia Shvartsa* [Tomsk: Izdatel'stvo Tomskogo universiteta, 1992], 177) suggests that Zakharov damaged the internal organization of the play by inserting extraneous elements, probably because he could not find suitable cinematic equivalents.

17. Metcalf, *Evgenii Shvarts and His Fairy-Tales for Adults*, 47–48.

18. Veniamin Kaverin, "Shvarts i soprotivlenie," *Literaturnoe obozrenie* 2 (1989): 76.

19. Evgenii Shvarts, *Drakon*, in *Drakon, Klad, Ten', Dva klena, Obyknovennoe chudo i drugie proizvedeniia* (Moscow: Gud'ial, 1998), 275–76. Subsequent citations from this edition are indicated parenthetically in the text.

20. Metcalf, *Evgenii Shvarts and His Fairy-Tales for Adults*, 56.

21. Kaverin, "Shvarts i soprotivlenie," 77.

22. J. Douglas Clayton, "The Theatre of E. L. Shvarts: An Introduction," *Slavic and East European Studies* 19 (1974): 37.

23. L. V. Polikovskaia and E. M. Binevich, "Legenda i byl'," in *Zhitie skazochnika: Evgenii Shvarts* (Moscow: Knizhnaia palata, 1991), 8.

24. Clayton, "The Theatre of E. L. Shvarts: An Introduction," 37.

25. Norris Houghton, *Return Engagement* (New York: Holt, Rinehart and Winston, 1962), 47.

26. Quoted in Evg. Binevich, "Iz perepiski Evgeniia Shvartsa," *Voprosy literatury* 6 (1977): 228.

27. Kaverin, "Shvarts i soprotivlenie," 75.

28. Lev Loseff, *On the Beneficence of Censorship: Aesopian Language in Modern Russian Literature* (Munich: Otto Sagner, 1984), 136–37.

29. Vera Smirnova (*Sovremennyi portret. Stat'i* [Moscow: Sovetskii pisatel', 1964]) asks rhetorically: "Isn't it true that [the communiqués] poisonously, almost verbatim echo Hitler's communiqués from the front?" (273). Loseff, on the other hand, locates the source of Shvarts's verbal parody in the announcements of the Soviet Information Bureau (*On the Beneficence of Censorship*, 140).

30. Particularly important in this regard is Stalin's 1913 article "Marxism and the Nationalities Problem," which was written under Lenin's direct supervision. The article expresses strongly Russo-centric sentiments. See Ronald Hingley, *Joseph Stalin: Man and Legend* (London: Hutchinson, 1974), 72–73.

31. C. G. Jung, *Nietzsche's Zarathustra*, ed. James L. Jarrett, vol. 1 (Princeton, N.J.: Princeton University Press, 1988), 749.

32. The Dragon's association with these mushrooms links him with death through the root *grob*, "coffin."

33. Joyce Tally Lionarons's caveat concerning the interpretation of dragons (*The Medieval Dragon: The Nature of the Beast in Germanic Literature* [Enfield Lock, Middlesex, Eng.: Hisarlik Press, 1998], should be mentioned: "Contemporary linguistic and literary theory has taught us that it is dangerous to treat any word—even one which has a physical referent in the natural world—as if it were a transparent medium for the communication of a single, monologically determined meaning. This danger is compounded when we try to discover the meaning of a word like 'dragon' in its literary-historical context, for the dragon—in myth, in literature, and in history—has always been a purely imaginary, and thus primarily a linguistic, phenomenon.... The meaning of a particular usage of the word 'dragon' in a particular work of literature can therefore be determined only within that work's specific discursive context. We do not always already know what a dragon is" (1–2.).

34. Ernest Ingersoll, *Dragons and Dragon Lore* (New York: Payson & Clarke, 1928), 182.

35. Sheila R. Canby, "Dragons," in *Mythical Beasts*, ed. John Cherry (San Francisco: Pomegranate Artbooks, 1995), 20.

36. Williams, *Deformed Discourse*, 202.

37. This is in contrast to Chinese tradition, where the dragon is a positive symbol.

38. Canby, "Dragons," 35–36.

39. Ibid., 40.

40. The Christian nations of the Balkans have preserved the legend of Saint George in its popular version. For a discussion of this variant, see Edwin Sidney Hartland, *The Legend of Perseus: A Study of Tradition in Story, Custom and Belief*, vol. 3 (London: David Nutt in the Strand, 1896), 41. He is also revered by Muslims, who identify him with the Prophet Elijah.

41. Hartland, *The Legend of Perseus*, 38. According to Hartland, this conflation of the religious and secular figures may have been due to a misunderstanding of an encomium on the saint written in the tenth century (44–45).

42. Tsimbal, "Fantaziia i real'nost'," 178.

43. Emil A. Gutheil, *The Handbook of Dream Analysis* (New York: Liveright, 1951), 103–4, 153n.

44. Jung, *Nietzche's* Zarathustra, 261.

45. Ibid., 264.

46. Lionel Robert Simard, "The Life and Works of Evgenii Shvarts" (Ph.D. diss., Cornell University, 1970), 95.

47. St. Rassadin, *Obyknovennoe chudo: Kniga o skazkakh dlia teatra* (Moscow: Detskaia literatura, 1964), 84.

48. Ewa M. Thompson, *Understanding Russia: The Holy Fool in Russian Culture* (Lanham, Md.: University Press of America, 1987), 10.

49. Vasilii Aksenov, "Slozhnye otnosheniia s Rodinoi," interview by Ol'ga Kuchkina, *Kosomol'skaia pravda*, 12 August 1993, 6.

50. A. Mirchev, *15 interv'iu* (New York: Izdatel'stvo im. A. Platonova, 1989), 7.

51. Priscilla Meyer, "Aksenov and Stalinism: Political, Moral, and Literary Power," *Slavic and East European Journal* 30 (1986): 510. For his own account of this affair, see Vasilii Aksenov, "Kak Nikita possorilsia s pisateliami," *Argumenty i fakty* 45 (November 1991): 6.

52. L. A. Fink, "Besstrashie," in *Vasilii Aksenov: Literaturnaia sud'ba* (Samara: Samarskii universitet, 1994), 8.

53. For a brief account of the *Metropole* affair, see Arnold McMillin, "Vasilii Aksenov's Writing in the USSR and the USA," *Irish Slavonic Studies* 10 (1989): 4.

54. Vasilii Aksenov, "O sotsializme, prostite, govorit' ne budu . . . ," interview by Viktoriia Shokhina, *Nezavisimaia gazeta*, 20 July 1991, 5. See also Vasilii Aksenov, "Na ostatok zhizni ia osiadu v Rossii," interview by Iurii Kovalenko, *Izvestiia*, 16 June 1992, 7; Aksenov, "Slozhnye otnosheniia s Rodinoi," 6.

55. Vassily Aksyonov, *The Island of Crimea*, trans. Michael Henry Heim (New York: Random House, 1983), 241–42.

56. Vassily Aksyonov, *The Burn*, trans. Michael Glenny (London: Hutchison, 1984), 35–36.

57. According to Per Dalgård (*The Function of the Grotesque in Vasilij Aksenov*, trans. Robert Porter [Aarhus, Denmark: Arkona, 1982], 6), these terms are Aksenov's own.

58. Lena Karpov, introduction to *The Destruction of Pompeii and Other Stories*, by Vassily Aksyonov (Ann Arbor, Mich.: Ardis, 1991), viii.

59. John J. Johnson, Jr., "Introduction: The Life and Works of Aksenov," in *The Steel Bird, and Other Stories*, by Vasily Aksenov (Ann Arbor, Mich.: Ardis, 1979), xx.

60. Anatolii Gladilin, "Stal'naia ptitsa," *Kontinent* 14 (1977): 359.

61. M. Keith Booker and Dubravka Juraga, *Bakhtin, Stalin, and Modern Russian Fiction: Carnival, Dialogism, and History* (Westport, Conn.: Greenwood Press, 1995), 31.

62. Nina Efimov, "Religious Motifs in Vasilii Aksenov's Works" (Ph.D. diss., Florida State University, 1991), 65.

63. Konstantin Kustanovich, *The Artist and the Tyrant: Vassily Aksenov's Works in the Brezhnev Era* (Columbus, Ohio: Slavica, 1992), 67.

64. Vasilii Aksenov, *Stal'naia ptitsa*, in *Glagol*, vol. 1 (Ann Arbor, Mich.: Ardis, 1977), 47. Subsequent citations from this edition are acknowledged parenthetically in the text.

65. Dalgård, *The Function of the Grotesque in Vasilij Aksenov*, 34.

66. Efimov, *Religious Motifs in Vasilii Aksenov's Works*, 67.

67. Margaret Ziolkowski, *Literary Exorcisms of Stalinism: Russian Writers and the Soviet Past* (Columbia, S.C.: Camden House, 1998), 22–23.

68. Ibid., 107; Williams, *Deformed Discourse*, 150.

69. Ziolkowski, *Literary Exorcisms of Stalinism*, 114.

70. Dalgård, *The Function of the Grotesque in Vasilij Aksenov*, 40. Daniel Rancour-Laferriere ("The Boys of Ibansk: A Freudian Look at Some Recent Russian

Satire," *Psychoanalytic Review* 72 [Winter 1985]) asserts that Popenkov's illness is an intestinal disturbance and suggests that this detail contributes to "an essentially analized picture of Stalin" (645).

71. Efimov, *Religious Motifs in Vasilii Aksenov's Works*, 66.

72. Maria Kravchenko, *The World of the Russian Fairy Tale* (Bern, Switz.: Peter Lang, 1987), 76.

73. The representation of the soul through bird imagery is quite universal. Because it is a creature not confined to the earth, the bird effectively represents the spiritual. See Beryl Rowland, *Birds with Human Souls: A Guide to Bird Symbolism* (Knoxville: University of Tennessee Press, 1978), xiv. For a refutation of this point, see P. M. C. Forbes Irving, *Metamorphosis in Greek Myths* (Oxford: Clarendon Press, 1990), 113–14.

74. Aksenov, "O sotsializme, prostite, govorit' ne budu . . . ," 5.

75. Ronald Vroon, *Velimir Xlebnikov's Shorter Poems: A Key to the Coinages* (Ann Arbor: Dept. of Slavic Languages and Literatures, University of Michigan, 1983), 20–21.

76. Vadim Linetskii, "Aksenov v novom svete," *Neva* 8 (1992): 247.

77. A. M. Bowie, *Aristophanes: Myth, Ritual and Comedy* (Cambridge: Cambridge University Press, 1993), 153, 171.

78. Douglas M. MacDowell, *Aristophanes and Athens: An Introduction to the Plays* (Oxford: Oxford University Press, 1995), 202.

79. Irving, *Metamorphosis in Greek Myths*, 103–4.

80. Ibid., 111.

81. Bowie, *Aristophanes*, 158.

82. Aksenov has used the image of a steel bird in several other works, always with the connotation of tyranny. In the 1963 play *Vsegda v prodazhe* (*Always on Sale*) the neo-Stalinist Kistochkin is a steel bird. In the 1966 story "Na ploshchadi i za rekoi" ("On the Square and Beyond the River") Hitler flies off in the form of a metallic bird. A steel bird is the antagonist in the 1967 play *Chetyre temperamenta* (*The Four Temperaments*). The character Memozov in *Zolotaia nasha zhelezka* (*Our Golden Hardware*) (1980) resembles a steel bird. In *The Burn* the image of the steel bird is closely linked to the invasion of Czechoslovakia. As D. Barton Johnson has shown ("Vasilij Aksionov's Aviary: *The Heron* and *The Steel Bird*," *Scando-Slavica* 33 [1987]: 61), in Aksenov's oeuvre the steel bird tends to represent negative qualities, in opposition to those positive values embodied in the heron.

83. Rosalind Marsh, *Images of Dictatorship: Portraits of Stalin in Literature* (London: Routledge, 1989), 13.

84. Edward Mozejko, "*The Steel Bird* and Aksënov's Prose of the Seventies," in *Vasiliy Pavlovich Aksënov: A Writer in Quest of Himself*, ed. Edward Mozejko (Columbus, Ohio: Slavica, 1984), 205.

85. Mason, *Deconstructing America*, 113.

86. Booker and Juraga, *Bakhtin, Stalin, and Modern Russian Fiction*, 30.

87. Ludomír Dolozel, "Kafka's Fictional World," *Canadian Review of Comparative Literature* 11 (March 1984): 64.

88. Mozejko, "*The Steel Bird* and Aksënov's Prose of the Seventies," 213.

89. It is interesting that Aleksandr Kazintsev ("Pridvornye dissidenty i 'pogibshee pokolenie,'" *Nash sovremennik* 3 [1991]: 175) castigates Aksenov for blaming the Russian people for the excesses of Stalinism. While Kazintsev's assertion is unsupported and simplistic, it does demonstrate that this is a cardinal issue in Aksenov's work.

90. Dalgård, *The Function of the Grotesque in Vasilij Aksenov*, 37.

91. Aksenov's concern with the intelligentsia's failure to resist Stalinism informs much of his oeuvre. In his 1965 novel *Pora, moi drug, pora!* (*It's Time, My Friend, It's Time!*) the intelligentsia is portrayed as ambivalent. "Pobeda" ("Victory"), written the same year, depicts the *intelligent* protagonist (a chess grandmaster) as weak and evasive. In *The Burn* the intelligentsia is debauched and morally corrupt.

92. Marina Raskina ("The Emergence of Fantasmagoric Realism in Contemporary Russian, Hebrew, and British Literatures: Vasily Aksenov, Amos Oz, and Kingsley Amis" [Ph.D. diss., Purdue University, 1988]) calls Nikolaev a "worshipper of Stalin" (23). This characterization of the house manager is overstated; fear is an important factor in his behavior.

Chapter 5. The Devil Made Us Do It

1. Simon Franklin, "Nostalgia for Hell: Russian Literary Demonism and Orthodox Tradition," in *Russian Literature and Its Demons*, ed. Pamela Davidson (New York: Berghahn, 2000), 33.

2. Rosalind Marsh, "Literary Representations of Stalin and Stalinism as Demonic," in *Russian Literature and Its Demons*, ed. Pamela Davidson (New York: Berghahn, 2000), 477.

3. See, e.g., the following: Linda J. Ivanits, *Russian Folk Belief* (Armonk, N.Y.: M. E. Sharpe, 1989); Adam Weiner, *By Authors Possessed: The Demonic Novel in Russia* (Evanston, Ill.: Northwestern University Press, 1988); Julian W. Connolly, *The Intimate Stranger: Meetings with the Devil in Nineteenth-Century Russian Literature* (New York: Peter Lang, 2001); Pamela Davidson, ed., *Russian Literature and Its Demons* (New York: Berghahn Books, 2000).

4. Bernard McGinn, *Antichrist: Two Thousand Years of the Human Fascination with Evil* (New York: HarperCollins, 1994), 263.

5. Marsh, "Literary Representations of Stalin," 476.

6. Gregory C. Jenks, *The Origins and Early Development of the Antichrist Myth* (Berlin: Walter de Gruyter, 1991), 51.

7. McGinn, *Antichrist*, 33.

8. Michael Cherniavsky, "The Old Believers and the New Religion," in *The Structure of Russian History: Interpretive Essays*, ed. Michael Cherniavsky (New York: Random House, 1970), 148.

9. James E. Abbe, *I Photograph Russia* (N.p.: National Travel Club, 1934), 62.

10. Achmed Amba, *I Was Stalin's Bodyguard*, trans. Richard and Clara Winston (London: Frederick Muller, 1952), 83.

11. Roman Brackman, *The Secret File of Joseph Stalin: A Hidden Life* (London: Frank Cass, 2001), 6.

12. David Tutaev, trans. and ed., *The Alliluyev Memoirs: Recollections of Svetlana Stalina's Maternal Aunt Anna Alliluyeva and Her Grandfather Sergei Alliluyev* (New York: G. P. Putnam's Sons, 1968), 179.

13. A. H. Keane, *The Antichrist Legend*, trans. W. Bousset (London: Hutchison, 1896), 157.

14. Brackman, *The Secret File of Joseph Stalin*, 4, 11.

15. Edward Ellis Smith, *The Young Stalin: The Early Years of an Elusive Revolutionary* (New York: Farrar, Straus and Giroux, 1967), 24.

16. McGinn, *Antichrist*, 16.

17. Ibid., 15.

18. C. G. Jung, *Aion: Researches into the Phenomenology of the Self*, trans. R. F. C. Hull (Princeton, N.J.: Princeton University Press, 1959), 42.

19. For detailed accounts of Bulgakov's one-sided correspondence with Stalin and the famous telephone call of 18 April 1930, see the following: Andrew Barratt, *Between Two Worlds: A Critical Introduction to* The Master and Margarita (Oxford: Clarendon, 1987); A. Colin Wright, *Mikhail Bulgakov: Life and Interpretations* (Toronto: University of Toronto Press, 1978); J. A. E. Curtis, *Manuscripts Don't Burn: Mikhail Bulgakov; A Life in Letters and Diaries* (London: Bloomsbury, 1991); Lesley Milne, *Mikhail Bulgakov: A Critical Biography* (Cambridge: Cambridge University Press, 1990); and Anatoly Smeliansky, *Is Comrade Bulgakov Dead? Mikhail Bulgakov at the Moscow Arts Theatre*, trans. Arch Tait (London: Methuen, 1993).

20. Smeliansky, *Is Comrade Bulgakov Dead?* 170.

21. Ibid., 172.

22. Mariia Shneerson, "Sila mastera i bessilie vlastilina (Bulgakov i Stalin)," *Grani* 167 (1993): 120.

23. A. Smelianskii, "Ukhod," *Teatr* 12 (1988): 111; Shneerson, "Sila mastera i bessilie vlastilina," 141.

24. Marietta Chudakova, *Zhizneopisanie Mikhaila Bulgakova* (Moscow: Kniga, 1988), 427–28. See also Leslie Louise Chekin, "Dialogue with Stalin: Aesthetic Response to Stalin in the Works of Russian Writers of the Thirties (Tvardovskii, Pasternak, Bulgakov)" (Ph.D. diss., Cornell University, 1995), 188.

25. Anatolii Shvarts, "Zametki o Bulgakove," *Novoe russkoe slovo*, 17 May 1991, 26.

26. Smeliansky, *Is Comrade Bulgakov Dead?* 296.

27. Ellendea Proffer, *Bulgakov: Life and Work* (Ann Arbor, Mich.: Ardis, 1984), 522.

28. Maiia Kaganskaia and Zeev Bar-Sella, *Master Gambs i Margarita* (Tel Aviv: Milev General Systems Corp., 1984), 85–86.

29. Chudakova (*Zhizneopisanie Mikhaila Bulgakova*) seems to suggest that Elena Sergeevna's motivation in urging her husband to write a play about Stalin was based on self-interest, or at least misguided: "Later the notes in Elena Sergeevna's diary about work on this play will invariably be celebratory. Her dream was coming true"; and, later, "With special diligence Elena Sergeevna collects good reviews about this play" (460, 465).

30. Miron Petrovskii, "Delo o 'Batume,'" *Teatr* 2 (1990): 162.

31. Curtis, *Manuscripts Don't Burn*, 125.

32. Mikhail Bulgakov, *Batum*, in *Neizdannyi Bulgakov: Teksty i materialy*, ed. Ellendea Proffer (Ann Arbor, Mich.: Ardis, 1977), 163.

33. Petrovskii, "Delo o 'Batume,'" 164–68.

34. Bulgakov, *Batum*, 199.

35. Smelianskii, "Ukhod," 110.

36. Shneerson, "Sila mastera i bessilie vlastilina," 133. Andrzej Drawicz (*The Master and the Devil: A Study of Mikhail Bulgakov*, trans. Kevin Windle [Lewiston, N.Y.: Edwin Mellen, 2001]) also finds an Aesopian reading unconvincing: "It seems unlikely, however, that with the knowledge Bulgakov then possessed he could have introduced such effects consciously" (281n41).

37. Chekin, "Dialogue with Stalin," 171.

38. Judith M. Mills, "Of Dreams, Devils, Irrationality and *The Master and Margarita*," in *Russian Literature and Psychoanalysis*, ed. Daniel Rancour-Laferriere (Amsterdam: John Benjamins, 1989), 321.

39. For a concise summary of the convoluted publication history of *The Master and Margarita*, see Proffer, *Bulgakov*, 530, 636n8.

40. *Mikhail Bulgakov: Belaia gvardiia; Teatral'nyi roman; Master i Margarita* (Moscow: Khudozhestvennaia literatura, 1973). Subsequent citations from this edition are acknowledged parenthetically in the text.

41. Abram Terts, "Literaturnyi protsess v Rossii," *Kontinent* 1 (1974): 160.

42. Mills, "Of Dreams, Devils, Irrationality," 320.

43. D. G. B. Piper, "An Approach to Bulgakov's *The Master and Margarita*," *Forum for Modern Language Studies* 7 (April 1971): 153.

44. Andrei Sinyavsky, *Soviet Civilization: A Cultural History*, trans. Joanne Turnbull (New York: Arcade, 1988), 105.

45. G. Krugovoi, "Gnosticheskii roman M. Bulgakova," *Novyi zhurnal* 134 (1979): 67.

46. Rosalind Marsh, *Images of Dictatorship: Portraits of Stalin in Literature* (London: Routledge, 1989), 48.

47. Sinyavsky, *Soviet Civilization*, 105.

48. Lesley Milne, *The Master and Margarita: A Comedy of Victory* (Birmingham, Eng.: Dept. of Russian Language & Literature, University of Birmingham, 1977), 19.

49. Piper's extended analysis of Woland ("An Approach to Bulgakov's *The Master and Margarita*") illustrates the limitations of this approach. While many of the

parallels he shows are valid and persuasive, his claim for the exclusivity of the reading is weak.

50. There is an isolated exception to this in chapter 18—specifically the episode involving Dr. Kuzmin. See Barratt, *Between Two Worlds*, 149.

51. Ewa M. Thompson, "The Artistic World of Michail Bulgakov," *Russian Literature* 5 (1973): 59.

52. Merritt Clifton, "Rough-out of a Russian Devil," *Gypsy Scholar* 3 (1973): 82–83. A very interesting exception is the similarity of Woland to Mark Twain's Satan in his story "The Mysterious Stranger," published in 1916. As Ia. S. Lur'e points out ("M. Bulgakov i Mark Tven," in *Izvestiia Akademii Nauk SSSR*, Seriia literatury i iazyka, 6 [November–December 1987]: 565–66), Woland and Twain's Satan share key characteristics and are similarly attractive figures. Perhaps most significant for my purpose is the identity of the devil in both texts as a stranger, an outsider who is not a part of the culture he visits.

53. Another possible Russian source of this vision of the devil as banal is V. A. Chaianov's *Venediktov, or the Memorable Events of My Life* (*Venediktov, ili Dostopamiatyne sobytiia zhizni moei*). See Riitta H. Pittman, *The Writer's Divided Self in Bulgakov's* The Master and Margarita (New York: St. Martin's, 1991), 31.

54. Much has been written on the Faustian subtext of *The Master and Margarita*. See, e.g., Barratt, *Between Two Worlds*; Wright, *Mikhail Bulgakov*; and especially J. A. E. Curtis, *Bulgakov's Last Decade: The Writer as Hero* (Cambridge: Cambridge University Press, 1987).

55. Curtis, *Bulgakov's Last Decade*, 169.

56. Milne, The Master and Margarita: *A Comedy of Victory*, 20–22; Vladimir Lakshin, "Mikhail Bulgakov's *The Master and Margarita*," in *Twentieth-Century Russian Literary Criticism*, ed. Victor Erlich (New Haven, Conn.: Yale University Press, 1975), 260.

57. Iurii Borev, *Staliniada* (Moscow: Sovetskii pisatel', 1990).

58. Edward E. Ericson, Jr., *The Apocalyptic Vision of Mikhail Bulgakov's* The Master and Margarita (Lewiston, N.Y.: Edwin Mellen, 1991), 37.

59. David M. Bethea, *The Shape of Apocalypse in Modern Russian Fiction* (Princeton, N.J.: Princeton University Press, 1989), 194.

60. Elena N. Mahlow (*Bulgakov's* The Master and Margarita: *The Text as a Cipher* [New York: Vantage, 1975], 87) suggests that Berlioz is an Antichrist figure and that he is Woland's double in the novel. Berlioz's nihilism, his denial of any supernatural authority, is indeed in the tradition of Antichrist, but Mahlow's argument for doubling in the text is strained, depending as it does on similarities in appearance and a few descriptive terms.

61. Milne, *Mikhail Bulgakov: A Critical Biography*, 255.

62. Iurii Smirnov, "Mistika i real'nost' sataninskogo bala," *Pamir* 9 (1988): 146.

63. Marsh, "Literary Representations of Stalin and Stalinism as Demonic," 486.

64. Ronald H. Preston and Anthony T. Hanson, *The Revelation of Saint John the Divine: The Book of Glory* (London: SCM Press, 1962), 87; Annette Yoshiko Reed, *Fallen Angels and the History of Judaism and Christianity: The Reception of Enochic Literature* (Cambridge: Cambridge University Press, 2005).

65. A. C. Wright, "Satan in Moscow: An Approach to Bulgakov's *The Master and Margarita*," *PMLA* 88 (October 1973): 1163.

66. A. Vulis, "Posleslovie," *Moskva* 11 (1966): 129.

67. Barratt, *Between Two Worlds*, 170.

68. M. Chudakova, "*The Master and Margarita:* The Development of a Novel," *Russian Literature Triquarterly* 15 (1976): 204.

69. Ruth Zernova, "Song Poetry of the 1960's–1980's in the USSR," in *Proceedings: Summer 1986 Intensive Workshop in Chinese and Russian* (Eugene, Ore.: Department of Russian, University of Oregon, 1987), 197.

70. Iu. Krotkov, "A. Galich," *Novyi zhurnal* 130 (March 1978): 242.

71. Gerry Smith, "Whispered Cry: The Songs of Alexander Galich," *Index on Censorship* 3 (1974): 12.

72. These are enumerated by Gerry Smith in "Whispered Cry" (14n6) and described by Gene Sosin in "Alexander Galich: Russian Poet of Dissent," *Midstream* 20 (April 1974): 36.

73. Sviatoslav Pedenko, "'Erika' beret chetyre kopii: Vozvrashchenie A. Galicha," *Voprosy literatury* 4 (1989): 106.

74. I. Grekova, "Ob Aleksandre Galiche," *Znamia* 6 (June 1988): 62.

75. Al'bert Opul'skii, "Aleksandr Galich," *Grani* 119 (1981): 269; D. Andreeva, "Rossii serdtse ne zabudet . . . (O tvorchestve Aleksandra Galicha)," *Grani* 109 (1978): 228.

76. Stanislav Rassadin, "'Boiat'sia avtoru nechego,' ili Ispytanie glasnost'iu," *Oktiabr'* 4 (1988): 149.

77. M. Kniazevaia and A. Arkhangel'skaia, "Aleksandr Galich: Letopis' zhizni i tvorchestva," in Aleksandr Galich, *Sochineniia*, vol. 1 (Moscow: Lokid, 1999), 16.

78. Aleksandr Galich, *General'naia repetitsiia*, in *Vozvrashchenie: Stikhi, Pesni, Vospominaniia* (Leningrad: Muzyka, 1990), 208, 244.

79. A. Galich, "Ballada o tom, kak edva ne soshel s uma direktor," in *Pokolenie obrechennykh* (Frankfurt: Posev, 1972), 248.

80. Opul'skii, "Aleksandr Galich," 274.

81. Smith, "Whispered Cry," 15.

82. McGinn, *Antichrist*, 17.

83. Aleksandr Galich, "Poema o Staline," in *Sochineniia*, vol. 1 (Moscow: Lokid, 1999), 103. Subsequent citations from this edition are acknowledged parenthetically in the text.

84. Marsh, *Images of Dictatorship*, 110. Rosette C. Lamont ("Horace's Heirs: Beyond Censorship in the Soviet Songs of the *Magnitizdat*," *World Literature Today* 53 [Spring 1979]: 222, 225) sees Galich's treatment of Stalin and Christ in this work as

evidence of his conversion to Christianity. This interpretation is somewhat facile; in fact Christ's presence in this work is as problematic as his presence in Blok's poem.

85. Marsh, *Images of Dictatorship*, 111.

86. Lev Kopelev, "Pamiati Aleksandra Galicha," *Kontinent* 16 (1978): 338.

87. I am indebted to an anonymous reader for the University of Wisconsin Press for this insight.

88. Ivanits, *Russian Folk Belief*, 46.

89. Smith ("Whispered Cry," 15) suggests that Stalin's presence at the Nativity places him in the role of Herod, but there seems to be little evidence to support this interpretation.

90. Michael Seidel, *Satiric Inheritance: Rabelais to Sterne* (Princeton, N.J.: Princeton University Press, 1979), 34.

91. Chamberlin, *Antichrist and the Millennium*, 17.

92. McGinn, *Antichrist*, 2.

93. A. Galich, "Bez nazvaniia," in *Pokolenie obrechennykh* (Frankfurt: Posev, 1972), 41–42.

94. Galich, *General'naia repetitsiia*, 192.

95. Smith, "Whispered Cry," 19.

96. A. Galich, "Staratel'skii val'sok," in *Pokolenie obrechennykh* (Frankfurt: Posev, 1972), 13.

97. Smith, "Whispered Cry," 18; Kopelev, "Pamiati Aleksandra Galicha," 337.

98. Aleksandr Galich, "Ballada o chistykh rukakh," in *Pesni russkikh bardov*, vol. 2 (Paris: YMCA Press, 1977), 144.

99. Fazil' Iskander, "Ot avtora," in *Sandro iz Chegema*, vol. 1 (Moscow: Eksmo, 1999), 8.

100. The Russian volumes were published by Ardis Press. The translations, by Susan Brownsberger, are titled *Sandro of Chegem* and *The Gospel According to Sandro*. Both were published by Vintage.

101. Fazil' Iskander, *Sandro iz Chegema: Roman* (Moscow: Moskovskii rabochii, 1989).

102. Fazil' Iskander, *Sandro iz Chegema*, *Znamia*, no. 9 (1988): 13–75. The next issue contains the stories *Diadia Sandro i ego liubimets* and *Rasskaz mula starogo Khabuga*.

103. Milovan Djilas, *Conversations with Stalin*, trans. Michael B. Petrovich (New York: Harcourt, Brace & World, 1962), 76.

104. Fazil' Iskander, *Piry Valtasara*, in *Sandro iz Chegema*, vol. 1 (Moscow: Eksmo, 1999), 255. Subsequent citations from this edition are acknowledged parenthetically in the text.

105. Abbe, *I Photograph Russia*, 59.

106. Norman W. Porteous, *Daniel: A Commentary* (Philadelphia: Westminster Press, 1965), 76, 81.

107. Ibid., 77.

108. Belshazzar is a fitting model for Iskander's condemnatory portrait of Stalin, but there is even deeper significance in this analogy. Daniel is one of the major sources of the Antichrist myth. Here Antichrist (though unnamed) is the Little Horn on a ten-horned beast that uproots the others for space to grow until it over-shadows the earth. He utters blasphemies and persecutes the children of God until he is finally slain and cast into the flames. By explicitly using Daniel as a source Iskander adds an apocalyptic dimension to his satirical treatment of Stalin.

109. Ibid., 122.

110. Helen Rappaport, *Joseph Stalin: A Biographical Companion* (Santa Barbara, Calif.: ABC-CLIO, 1999), 261.

111. Jenks, *The Origins and Early Development of the Antichrist Myth*, 95.

112. Iurii Krokhin, "Fazil Iskander: Ideas and Images," *Moscow News*, 25 February–3 March 1994, 11.

Chapter 6. The Corpse and the Revenant

1. Iurii Borev, *Staliniada* (Moscow: Sovetskii pisatel', 1990), 359, 361; Catherine Merridale, *Night of Stone: Death and Memory in Russia* (London: Granta, 2000), 329; Helen Rappaport, *Joseph Stalin: A Bibliographical Companion* (Santa Barbara, Calif.: ABC-CLIO, 1999), 261.

2. Rappaport, *Joseph Stalin*, 262.

3. In the initial period after Stalin's death, there was some discussion of a grander display of dead Soviet leaders along the lines of a pantheon. It was suggested that a continuously flowing "fountain of tears" might be constructed alongside this building. See Merridale, *Night of Stone*, 334.

4. Andrei Sinyavsky, *Soviet Civilization: A Cultural History*, trans. Joanne Turnbull (New York: Arcade, 1988), 104.

5. Nina Tumarkin, *Lenin Lives! The Lenin Cult in Soviet Russia* (Cambridge, Mass.: Harvard University Press, 1983), 198–99.

6. Peter Metcalf and Richard Huntington, *Celebrations of Death: The Anthropology of Mortuary Ritual* (Cambridge: Cambridge University Press, 1991), 163, 171. Metcalf and Huntington point out that in many societies the leader's body is a natural and powerful symbol of the legitimacy of the political order. Thus, the death and subsequent decay of the physical body may endanger the health of the body politic.

7. Sinyavsky, *Soviet Civilization*, 113; Merridale, *Night of Stone*, 195.

8. Quoted in Tumarkin, *Lenin Lives!* 190.

9. George M. Young, Jr., *Nikolai F. Fedorov: An Introduction* (Belmont, Mass.: Nordland, 1979), 103.

10. Irene Masing-Delic, *Abolishing Death: A Salvation Myth of Russian Twentieth-Century Literature* (Stanford, Calif.: Stanford University Press, 1992), 85.

11. Masing-Delic, *Abolishing Death*, 102–3.

12. Tumarkin, *Lenin Lives!* 181.

13. D. K. Zelenin, *Izbrannye trudy,* vol. 2 of *Ocherki russkoi mifologii: Umershie neestestvennoiu smert'iu i rusalki* (Moscow: Indrik, 1995), 43–44; Paul Barber, *Vampires, Burial, and Death: Folklore and Reality* (New Haven, Conn.: Yale University Press, 1988), 36.

14. Maurice Bloch and Jonathan Parry, *Death and the Regeneration of Life* (Cambridge: Cambridge University Press, 1982), 4.

15. Arnold van Gennep, *The Rites of Passage,* trans. Monika B. Vizedom and Gabrielle L. Caffee (Chicago: University of Chicago Press, 1960), 160.

16. Christine Quigley, *The Corpse: A History* (Jefferson, N.C.: McFarland, 1996), 18.

17. Barber, *Vampires, Burial, and Death,* 37.

18. Zelenin, *Ocherki russkoi mifologii,* 45.

19. Barber, *Vampires, Burial, and Death,* 30.

20. Yevgeny Yevtushenko, *A Precocious Autobiography,* trans. Andrew R. MacAndrew (New York: E. P. Dutton, 1963), 19.

21. Yevtushenko, *A Precocious Autobiography,* 16.

22. Ibid., 17.

23. Evgenii Evtushenko, "Zelenye rostki v zloveshchei teni," *Literaturnaia gazeta,* 28 March 1990.

24. Max Oppenheimer Jr., "How Angry Is Evtushenko?" *South Atlantic Bulletin* 28 (May 1963): 1.

25. E. Sidorov, *Evgenii Evtushenko: Lichnost' i tvorchestvo* (Moscow: Khudozhestvennaia literatura, 1987), 203.

26. Andrei Sinyavsky, "In Defense of the Pyramid (On Yevtushenko's Poetry)," in *For Freedom of Imagination,* trans. Laszlo Tikos and Murray Peppard (New York: Holt, Rinehart and Winston, 1971), 175.

27. Yevtushenko, *A Precocious Autobiography,* 101–2.

28. Ibid., 83.

29. Ibid., 17.

30. Sinyavsky, "In Defense of the Pyramid," 193.

31. Yevtushenko, *A Precocious Atuobiography,* 43.

32. Ibid., 81.

33. Evtushenko, "Zelenye rostki v zloveshchei teni."

34. Ilya Zbarsky and Samuel Hutchinson, *Lenin's Enbalmers,* trans. Barbara Bray (London: Harvill, 1998), 167–68.

35. Evgenii Evtushenko, "Nasledniki Stalina," in *Stikhotvoreniia i poemy,* vol. 1 (Moscow: Sovetskaia Rossiia, 1987), 343. Subsequent citations from this edition are acknowledged parenthetically in the text.

36. V. P. Anikin, *Russkii fol'klor* (Moscow: Vysshaia shkola, 1987), 250; Y. M. Sokolov, *Russian Folklore,* trans. Catherine Ruth Smith (Hatboro, Pa.: Folklore Associates, 1966), 225.

37. Lenin also inhabited this liminal space, for his body was not buried but kept permanently on display. From the time when the decision was made to preserve his corpse, there has been discomfort expressed—sotto voce in the Soviet period, much more loudly in the post-Soviet period—with this treatment of Lenin's body. Yet the cult of Lenin focused on his spiritual immortality rather than the possibility of his return as a revenant. The creation of the cult of Lenin, its eclipse by the cult of Stalin, and its revival in the Thaw period is detailed by Nina Tumarkin in her book *Lenin Lives! The Lenin Cult in Soviet Russia.*

38. Anatoly Gladilin, *The Making and Unmaking of a Soviet Writer: My Story of the "Young Prose" of the Sixties and After,* trans. David Lapeza (Ann Arbor, Mich.: Ardis, 1979), 72.

39. Ibid., 136.

40. Ibid., 79.

41. Vladimir Abashev, review of *Repetitsiia v piatnitsu,* by Anatolii Gladilin, *Iunost'* 2 (1991): 68.

42. Anatolii Gladilin, *Repetitsiia v piatnitsu,* in *Repetitsiia v piatnitsu: Povest' i rasskazy* (Paris: Tret'ia volna, 1978), 25–26. The English translation of this passage does not convey the humorous effect of Stalin's accent, in particular the unpalatalized consonants characteristic of his speech. Subsequent citations from this edition are acknowledged parenthetically in the text.

43. Zbarsky and Hutchinson, *Lenin's Embalmers,* 118, 120.

44. Margaret Ziolkowski, *Literary Exorcisms of Stalinism: Russian Writers and the Soviet Past* (Columbia S.C.: Camden House, 1998), 23.

45. The original embalming of Lenin's corpse in the months following his death took place in a cold cellar beneath the temporary mausoleum; this space was eventually converted into the permanent residence of the body. See Zbarsky and Hutchinson, *Lenin's Enbalmers,* 118, 120.

46. Alison Jones, *Larousse Dictionary of World Folklore* (New York: Larousse, 1995), 193.

47. Michel Ragon, *The Space of Death: A Study of Funerary Architecture, Decoration, and Urbanism,* trans. Alan Sheridan (Charlottesville, Va.: University Press of Virginia, 1983), 58.

48. Zelenin, *Ocherki russkoi mifologii,* 48.

49. Maximilian Rudwin, *The Devil in Legend and Literature* (Chicago: Open Court, 1931), 2.

50. Gladilin, *The Making and Unmaking of a Soviet Writer,* 136.

51. Ziolkowski (*Literary Exorcisms of Stalinism*) notes that this speech is "larded with the trite expressions typical of the worst Soviet officialese" (29).

52. Catharine Theimer Nepomnyashchy, *Abram Tertz and the Poetics of Crime* (New Haven, Conn.: Yale University Press, 1995), 2. For another good biographical account of Sinyavsky's career, see Margaret Dalton, *Andrei Siniavskii and Julii Daniel': Two Soviet "Heretical" Writers* (Würzburg: Jal-verlag, 1973).

53. Catharine Theimer Nepomnyashchy, "An Interview with Andrei Sinyavsky," *Formations* 6 (Spring 1991): 8.

54. Richard Lourie, *Letters to the Future: An Approach to Sinyavsky-Tertz* (Ithaca, N.Y.: Cornell University Press, 1975), 26.

55. Nepomnyashchy, *Abram Tertz and the Poetics of Crime*, 3.

56. Sinyavsky believed that his identity was revealed to the KGB by the CIA. See Nepomnyashchy, *Abram Tertz and the Poetics of Crime*, 322–23; Joseph Frank, "The Triumph of Abram Tertz," *New York Review of Books* 38 (27 June 1991): 38.

57. Dm. Eremin, "Perevertyshi," *Izvestiia*, 13 January 1966.

58. Sholokhov's speech to the Twenty-third Party Congress is analyzed in detail in Nepomnyashchy, *Abram Tertz and the Poetics of Crime*, 19–21.

59. Nepomnyashchy, "An Interview with Andrei Sinyavsky," 7. See also the interview with Sinyavsky and Rozanova in *Conversations in Exile: Russian Writers Abroad*, ed. John Glad and trans. Richard and Joanna Robin (Durham, N.C.: Duke University Press, 1993), 150.

60. Nepomnyashchy, *Abram Tertz and the Poetics of Crime*, 37.

61. Andrei Siniavskii, "Siniavskii o sebe," in *The Third Wave: Russian Literature in Emigration*, ed. Olga Matich and Michael Heim (Ann Arbor, Mich.: Ardis, 1984), 108.

62. Abram Terts, "On Socialist Realism," in The Trial Begins and On Socialist Realism, trans. George Dennis (Berkeley: University of California Press, 1960), 216.

63. *Spokoinoi nochi* was published in Russia in 1998.

64. This book appeared both in the West and in Russia under the authorship of Abram Terts. I will use Sinyavsky's name as author of this work here for the sake of consistency. Sara Fernander ("Author and Autocrat: Tertz's Stalin and the Ruse of Charisma," *Russian Review* 58 [April 1999]) notes the "peculiar structure of authorship": "Tertz's name appears on the cover of the book which tells the story of his own origins. Andrei Sinyavsky appears as the novel's protagonist; Tertz himself, present as narrator, also makes fleeting appearances. The novel's narrative voice shifts almost imperceptibly between Sinyavsky and Tertz, each of whom lays claim to the first person" (294).

65. Abram Terts, *Spokoinoi nochi* (Moscow: Zakharov, 1998), 17, 228. Subsequent citations refer to this edition and are acknowledged parenthetically in the text.

66. Beth Holmgren, "The Transfiguring of Context in the Work of Abram Terts," *Slavic Review* 50 (Winter 1991): 974.

67. Stalin's human counterpart in the text is the character of Serezha, an acquaintance of the author's youth. Serezha is both tremendously talented and diabolical, willing to further his career by any means and lacking any moral compunctions. For more connections with Dostoevsky, see Olga Matich, "*Spokojnoj noči*: Andrej Sinjavskij's Rebirth as Abram Terc," *Slavic and East European Journal* 33 (Spring 1989): 56.

68. Abram Terz (Andrei Sinyavsky), "The Literary Process in Russia," trans. Michael Glenny, in *Kontinent 1: The Alternative Voice of Russia and Eastern Europe* (London: André Deutsch, 1976), 86. See also Matich, *Spokoinoi noči*, 232.

69. Matich "*Spokojnoj noči*: Andrej Sinjavskij's Rebirth as Abram Terc," 54.

70. Nepomnyashchy, *Abram Tertz and the Poetics of Crime,* 288.

71. Ibid., 291.

72. Abram Terts (Andrei Sinyavsky), *Strolls with Pushkin,* trans. Catharine Theimer Nepomnyashchy and Slava I. Yastremski (New Haven, Conn.: Yale University Press, 1993), 84.

73. Jesse Clardy and Betty Shalom, "Andrei Sinyavsky and Aleksandr Solzhenitsyn: Two Halves of One Brain," *Australian Slavonic and East European Studies* 7 (1993): 25.

74. Nepomnyashchy, *Abram Tertz and the Poetics of Crime,* 297.

75. Matich, "*Spokojnoj noči*: Andrej Sinjavskij's Rebirth as Abram Terc," 57.

76. Eremin, "Perevertyshi."

77. Terz, "The Literary Process in Russia," 93–94.

78. Andrey Sinyavsky, *Unguarded Thoughts,* trans. Manya Harari (London: Collins, Harvill, 1972), 38.

79. Sinyavsky's argument is based on euphonic affinities between the words *sovetskii* and *svoi.* See Terz, "The Literary Process in Russia," 95.

80. Terz, "The Literary Process in Russia," 106.

Bibliography

Abashev, Vladimir. Review of *Repetitsiia v piatnitsu,* by Anatolii Gladilin. *Literaturnoe obozrenie* 10 (1991): 68.

Abbe, James E. *I Photograph Russia.* N.p.: National Travel Club, 1934.

Adrianova-Perets, V. P., ed. *Narodno-poeticheskaia satira.* Leningrad: Sovetskii pisatel', 1960.

Agurskii, Mikhail. "Dvulikii Stalin." *Vremia i my* 18 (1977): 133 –46.

Akinin, V. P. *K mudrosti stupen'ka: O russkikh pesniakh, skazkakh, poslovitsakh, zagadkakh, narodnom iazyke.* Moscow: Detskaia literatura, 1988.

Aksenov, Vasilii. "Kak Nikita possorilsia s pisateliami." *Argumenty i fakty* 45 (November 1991): 6.

———. "Na ostatok zhizni ia osiadu v Rossii." Interview by Iurii Kovalenko. *Izvestiia,* 16 June 1992.

———. "O sotsializme, prostite, govorit' ne budu . . ." Interview by Viktoriia Shokhina. *Nezavisimaia gazeta,* 20 July 1991.

———. "Slozhnye otnosheniia s Rodinoi." Interview by Ol'ga Kuchkina. *Komsomol'skaia pravda,* 12 August 1993.

———. *Stal'naia ptitsa.* In *Glagol,* vol. 1, 25 –95. Ann Arbor, Mich.: Ardis, 1977.

Albertus Magnus. *Man and the Beasts.* Trans. J. J. Scanlan. Binghamton, N.Y.: Medieval and Renaissance Texts and Studies, 1987.

Aleshkovskii, Iuz. *Kenguru.* Voronezh: AMKO, 1992.

Allan, Nina. *Madness, Death and Disease in the Fiction of Vladimir Nabokov.* Birmingham, Eng.: University of Birmingham, 1994.

Amba, Achmed. *I Was Stalin's Bodyguard.* Trans. Richard and Clara Winston. London: Frederick Muller, 1952.

Amis, Martin. *Koba the Dread: Laughter and the Twenty Million.* New York: Hyperion, 2002.

Ambartsumov, Yevgeny. "Zinovyev, Kamenev, Others Rehabilitated." *Currrent Digest of the Soviet Press* 15 (1988): 7.

Anikin, V. P. *Russkii fol'klor.* Moscow: Vysshaia shkola, 1987.

Antonov-Ovseyenko, Anton. *The Time of Stalin: Portrait of a Tyranny.* Trans. George Saunders. New York: Harper & Row, 1981.

Arens, W. *The Man-Eating Myth: Anthropology and Anthropophagy.* New York: Oxford University Press, 1979.

Aristotle. *Generation of Animals.* Trans. A. L. Peck. Cambridge, Mass.: Harvard University Press, 1942.

Arsenidze, R. "Iz vospominanii o Staline." *Novyi zhurnal* 72 (1963): 218 –36.

Atkinson, Dorothy, Alexander Dallin, and Gail Warshofsky Lapidus, eds. *Women in Russia.* Stanford, Calif.: Stanford University Press, 1977.

Babel, Isaac. *Collected Stories.* Trans. David McDuff. London: Penguin, 1994.

Barber, Paul. *Vampires, Burial, and Death: Folklore and Reality.* New Haven, Conn.: Yale University Press, 1988.

Barratt, Andrew. *Between Two Worlds: A Critical Introduction to* The Master and Margarita. Oxford: Clarendon, 1987.

Beraha, Laura. "The Fixed Fool: Raising and Resisting Picaresque Mobility in Vladimir Vojnovič's *Čonkin* Novels." *Slavic and East European Journal* 40 (1996): 475 –93.

Bethea, David M. *The Shape of Apocalypse in Modern Russian Fiction.* Princeton, N.J.: Princeton University Press, 1989.

Binevich, Evgenii. "Dobryi i umnyi talant." *Literaturnoe obozrenie* 1 (1987): 107 –12.

———. "Iz perepiski Evgeniia Shvartsa." *Voprosy literatury* 6 (1977): 217 –32.

Birkenmayer, Sigmund S. *Nikolaj Nekrasov: His Life and Poetic Art.* The Hague: Mouton, 1968.

Bloch, Maurice, and Jonathan Parry. *Death and the Regeneration of Life.* Cambridge: Cambridge University Press, 1982.

Bloom, Edward A., and Lillian D. Bloom. *Satire's Persuasive Voice.* Ithaca, N.Y.: Cornell University Press, 1979.

Bode, Andreas. "Humor in the Lyrical Stories for Children of Samuel Marshak and Korney Chukovsky." *The Lion and the Unicorn* 13 (December 1989): 34 –55.

Booker, M. Keith, and Dubravka Juraga. *Bakhtin, Stalin, and Modern Russian Fiction: Carnival, Dialogism, and History.* Westport, Conn.: Greenwood Press, 1995.

Borev, Iurii. *Staliniada.* Moscow: Sovetskii pisatel', 1990.

Borodin, S. "Vrednaia skazka." *Literatura i iskusstvo,* 25 March 1944.

Bousset, Wilhelm. *The Antichrist Legend: A Chapter in Christian and Jewish Folklore.* Trans. A. H. Keane. London: Hutchinson, 1896.

Bowie, A. M. *Aristophanes: Myth, Ritual and Comedy.* Cambridge: Cambridge University Press, 1993.

Bown, Matthew Cullerne. *Art under Stalin.* New York: Holmes & Meier, 1991.

Bown, Matthew Cullerne, and Brandon Taylor, eds. *Art of the Soviets: Painting, Sculpture and Architecture in a One-Party State, 1917–1992.* Manchester, Eng.: Manchester University Press, 1993.

Brackman, Roman. *The Secret File of Joseph Stalin: A Hidden Life.* London: Frank Cass, 2001.

Briggs, Katharine M. *Nine Lives: Cats in Folklore.* London: Routledge, 1980.

Brinker-Gabler, Gisela, ed. *Encountering the Other(s).* Albany: State University of New York Press, 1995.

Brooks, Jeffrey. "The Young Kornei Chukovsky, 1905–1914: A Liberal Critic in Search of Cultural Unity." *Russian Review* 33 (1974): 50–62.

Brown, Edward. *Russian Literature since the Revolution.* Cambridge, Mass.: Harvard University Press, 1982.

———. "Solženicyn's Cast of Characters." *Slavic and East European Journal* 15 (1971): 153–66.

———. "Zinoviev, Aleshkovsky, Rabelais, Sorrentino, Possibly Pynchon, Maybe James Joyce, and Certainly *Tristram Shandy:* A Comparative Study of a Satirical Mode." *Stanford Slavic Studies* 1 (1987): 307–25.

Bulgakov, Mikhail. *Belaia gvardiia; Teatral'nyi roman; Master i Margarita.* Moscow: Khudozhestvennaia literatura, 1973.

Bychowski, Gustav. *Dictators and Disciples: From Caesar to Stalin; A Psychoanalytic Interpretation of History.* New York: International Universities Press, 1948.

———. "Joseph V. Stalin: Paranoia and the Dictatorship of the Proletariat." In *The Psychoanalytic Interpretation of History,* ed. Benjamin B. Wolman, 115–49. New York: Basic Books, 1971.

Chamberlin, E. R. *Antichrist and the Millennium.* New York: E. P. Dutton, 1975.

Chapple, Richard L. "Fazil Iskander's *Rabbits and Boa Constrictors:* A Soviet Version of George Orwell's *Animal Farm.*" *Germano-Slavica* 5 (1985): 33–47.

Chekin, Leslie Louise. "Dialogue with Stalin: Aesthetic Response to Stalin in the Works of Russian Writers of the Thirties (Tvardovskii, Pasternak, Bulgakov)." Ph.D. diss., Cornell University, 1995.

Cherniavsky, Michael, ed. *The Structure of Russian History.* New York: Random House, 1970.

Cherry, John, ed. *Mythical Beasts.* San Francisco: Pomegranate Artbooks, 1995.

Chester, Pamela. "Engaging Sexual Demons in Marina Tsvetaeva's 'Devil': The Body and the Genesis of the Woman Poet." *Slavic Review* 53 (1994): 1025–45.

Chichibabin, Boris. "Slovo o Bulate." In *Kol'tso A,* vol. 1. ed. Tat'iana Kyzovleva, 12–13. Moscow: Moskovskii rabochii, 1993–94.

Chudakova, M. "*The Master and Margarita:* The Development of a Novel." *Russian Literature Triquarterly* 15 (1976): 177–209.

———. *Zhizneopisanie Mikhaila Bulgakova.* Moscow: Kniga, 1988.

Chukovsky, Kornei. *The Poet and the Hangman: Nekrasov and Muravyov.* Trans. R. W. Rotsel. Ann Arbor, Mich.: Ardis, 1977.

———. *Sobranie sochinenii v shesti tomakh.* Moscow: Khudozhestvennaia literatura, 1965.

———. *Stikhi.* Moscow: Khudozhestvennia literatura, 1961.

Clifton, Merritt. "Rough-out of a Russian Devil." *Gypsy Scholar* 3 (1973): 77–83.

Clardy, Jesse, and Betty Shalom. "Andrei Sinyavsky and Aleksandr Solzhenitsyn: Two Halves of One Brain." *Australian Slavonic and East European Studies* 7 (1993): 15–29.

Clark, Willene B., and Meradith T. McMunn, eds. *Beasts and Birds of the Middle Ages: The Bestiary and Its Legacy.* Philadelphia: University of Pennsylvania Press, 1989.

Clayton, J. Douglas. "The Theatre of E. L. Shvarts: An Introduction." *Slavic and East-European Studies* 19 (1974): 23–43.

Cohen, Jeffrey Jerome, ed. *Monster Theory: Reading Culture.* Minneapolis: University of Minnesota Press, 1996.

Connery, Brian A., and Kirk Combe. "Theorizing Satire. A Retrospective and Introduction." In *Theorizing Satire: Essays in Literary Criticism*, ed. Brian A. Connery and Kirk Combe, 1–15. New York: St. Martin's Press, 1995.

Connolly, Julian W. *The Intimate Stranger: Meetings with the Devil in Nineteenth-Century Russian Literature.* New York: Peter Lang, 2001.

Corbey, Raymond, and Joep Leerssen. *Alterity, Identity, Image: Selves and Others in Society and Scholarship.* Amsterdam: Rodopi, 1991.

Cornwell, P. B. *The Cockroach.* Vol. 1, *A Laboratory Insect and an Industrial Pest.* London: Hutchinson, 1968.

Corten, Irina H. "Evgenii Shvarts as an Adapter of Hans Christian Andersen and Charles Perrault." *Russian Review* 37 (1978): 51–67.

Curtis, J. A. E. *Bulgakov's Last Decade: The Writer as Hero.* Cambridge: Cambridge University Press, 1987.

———. *Manuscripts Don't Burn: Mikhail Bulgakov; A Life in Letters and Diaries.* London: Bloomsbury, 1991.

Dalgård, Per. *The Function of the Grotesque in Vasilij Aksenov.* Trans. Robert Porter. Aarhus, Denmark: Arkona, 1982.

Dalton, Margaret. *Andrei Siniavskii and Julii Daniel': Two Soviet "Heretical" Writers.* Würzburg: Jal-verlag, 1973.

Davidson, Pamela, ed. *Russian Literature and Its Demons.* New York: Berghahn Books, 2000.

De Beauvoir, Simone. *The Second Sex.* Trans. H. M. Parshley. New York: Vintage, 1989.

Dewhirst, Martin, and Robert Farrell. *The Soviet Censorship.* Metuchen, N.J.: Scarecrow Press, 1973.

Djilas, Milovan. *Conversations with Stalin.* Trans. Michael B. Petrovich. New York: Harcourt, Brace & World, 1962.

Dobin, Efim. "Dobryi volshebnik." *Neva* 11 (1988): 205–7.

Dolzhenko, Oleg. "Den' zhizni otlichat' ot nochi." In *Khronograf: Ezhegodik 89.* Moscow: Moskovskii rabochii, 1989.

Drawicz, Andrzej. *The Master and the Devil: A Study of Mikhail Bulgakov.* Trans. Kevin Windle. Lewiston, N.Y.: Edwin Mellen, 2001.

Du Plessix Gray, Francine. *Soviet Women: Walking the Tightrope*. New York: Doubleday, 1989.

Dymshits, Al. "V prokrustovom lozhe." *Literaturnaia gazeta*, 16 October 1968.

Efimov, Nina A. "Religious Motifs in Vasilii Aksenov's Works." Ph.D. diss., Florida State University, 1991.

Eremin, Dm. "Perevertyshi." *Izvestiia*, 13 January 1966.

Ericson, Edward E., Jr. *The Apocalyptic Vision of Mikhail Bulgakov's* The Master and Margarita. Lewiston, N.Y.: Edwin Mellen, 1991.

Ermolaev, Herman. *Censorship in Soviet Literature, 1917–1991*. Lanham, Md.: Rowman & Littlefield, 1997.

Evans, Dylan. *An Introductory Dictionary of Lacanian Psychoanalysis*. London: Routledge: 1996.

Evtushenko, Evgenii. *Stikhotvoreniia i poemy*. Moscow: Sovetskaia Rossiia, 1987.

———. "Zelenye rostki v zloveshchei teni." *Literaturnaia gazeta*, 28 March 1990.

Feiler, Lily. "Marina Cvetaeva's Childhood." In *Marina Tsvetaeva: Trudy 1-ogo mezhdunarodnogo simpoziuma (Lozanna, 30.VI–3.VII.1982)*, ed. Robin Remball, 37–45. Bern, Switz.: Peter Lang, 1991.

———. "Tsvetaeva's God/Devil." In *Marina Tsvetaeva 1892–1992*, vol. 2, ed. Svetlana Elnitsky and Efim Etkind, 34–42. Northfield, Vt.: The Russian School of Norwich University, 1992.

Filips-Juswig, K. "New Chapters for Solženicyn's *V kruge pervom*: Indirect Modes of Expression." *Russian Language Journal* 29 (1975): 95–106.

Fink, L. A. "Besstrashie." In *Vasilii Aksenov: Literaturnaia sud'ba*, ed. V. P. Skobelev and L. A. Fink, 5–10. Samara, Russia: Samarskii universitet, 1994.

Fischer, Louis. *The Life and Death of Stalin*. New York: Harper, 1952.

Fletcher, M. D. *Contemporary Political Satire: Narrative Strategies in the Post-Modern Context*. Lanham, Md.: University Press of America, 1987.

Fontenrose, Joseph. *Python: A Study of Delphic Myth and Its Origins*. New York: Biblio & Tannen, 1974.

Forbes Irving, P. M. C. *Metamorphosis in Greek Myths*. Oxford: Clarendon, 1990.

Foucault, Michel. *Madness and Civilization: A History of Insanity in the Age of Reason*. Trans. Richard Howard. New York: Vintage, 1988.

Frank, Joseph. "The Triumph of Abram Tertz." *New York Review of Books*, 27 June 1991.

Freud, Sigmund. "The Sexual Aberrations." In *The Basic Writings of Sigmund Freud*, trans. and ed. A. A. Brill, 553–79. New York: Random House, 1938.

———. "The 'Uncanny.'" In *Psychological Writings and Letters*, trans. Alix Strachey, ed. Sander L. Gilman, 120–53. New York: Continuum, 1995.

Frumkin, Vladimir. *Bulat Okudzhava: 65 Songs*. Vols. 1 and 2. Ann Arbor, Mich.: Ardis, 1980, 1986.

Frye, Roland Mushat, ed. *The Reader's Bible: A Narrative*. Princeton, N.J.: Princeton University Press, 1965.

Galich, Aleksandr. *Pesni russkikh bardov*. Paris: YMCA-Press, 1977.

————. *Pokolenie obrechennykh*. Frankfurt: Posev, 1972.

————. *Sochineniia*. Moscow: Lokid, 1999.

————. *Vozvrashchenie: Stikhi, Pesni, Vospominaniia*. Leningrad: Muzyka, 1990.

Girard, René. *The Scapegoat*. Trans. Yvonne Freccero. Baltimore, Md.: Johns Hopkins University Press, 1986.

Girgus, Sam B. "The Devil and the Demon Woman: Symbols of Freedom in Isaac Bashevis Singer." *Angloamericana* 6 (1985): 131–50.

Glad, John, ed. *Conversations in Exile: Russian Writers Abroad*. Durham, N.C.: Duke University Press, 1993.

Gladilin, Anatolii. *The Making and Unmaking of a Soviet Writer: My Story of the "Young Prose" of the Sixties and After*. Trans. David Lapeza. Ann Arbor, Mich.: Ardis, 1979.

————. *Repetitsiia v piatnitsu: Povest' i rasskazy*. Paris: Tret'ia volna, 1978.

————. Review of *Stal'naia ptitsa*, by Vasilii Aksenov. *Kontinent* 14 (1977): 356–59.

Glazov, Yuri. *The Russian Mind since Stalin's Death*. Dordrecht, Neth.: D. Reidel, 1985.

Glen, Robert. "Man or Beast? English Methodists as Animals in 18th Century Satiric Prints." *Connecticut Review* 14 (1992): 83–100.

Gollerbakh, Evgenii. "Neprilichnyi anekdot: O proze Vladimira Voinovicha." *Novyi zhurnal*, nos. 184–85 (1991): 324–43.

Golovchenko, Zhanna. "Otstupleniia byt' ne dolzhno." *Sovetskii ekran* 14 (1988): 5.

Golovchiner, V. E. *Epicheskii teatr Evgeniia Shvartsa*. Tomsk: Izdatel'stvo Tomskogo Universiteta, 1992.

Goossens, J., and T. Sodmann, eds. *Proceedings: Third International Beast Epic, Fable and Fabliau Colloquium, Muenster, 1979*. Cologne: Böhlau, 1981.

Gorky, Maxim. *My Childhood*. Trans. Ronald Wilks. London: Penguin, 1966.

Gosselin, Chris, and Glenn Wilson. *Sexual Variations: Fetishism, Sadomasochism and Transvestism*. New York: Simon & Schuster, 1980.

Grekova, I. "Ob Aleksandre Galiche." *Znamia* 6 (1988): 61–62.

Groys, Boris. *The Total Art of Stalinism*. Trans. Charles Rougle. Princeton, N.J.: Princeton University Press, 1992.

Gutheil, Emil A. *The Handbook of Dream Analysis*. New York: Liveright, 1951.

Hamel, Frank. *Human Animals: Werewolves and Other Transformations*. New Hyde Park, N.Y.: University Books, 1969.

Hanson, Philip. "Alexander Zinoviev on Stalinism: Some Observations on *The Flight of Our Youth*." *Soviet Studies* 40 (1988): 125–35.

Hartland, Edwin Sidney. *The Legend of Perseus: A Study of Tradition in Story, Custom and Belief*. London: David Nutt in the Strand, 1896.

Hershman, D. Jablow, and Julian Lieb. *A Brotherhood of Tyrants: Manic Depression and Absolute Power*. Amherst, Mass.: Prometheus, 1994.

Highet, Gilbert. *The Anatomy of Satire*. Princeton, N.J.: Princeton University Press, 1962.

Hingley, Ronald. *Joseph Stalin: Man and Legend*. London: Hutchinson, 1974.

Hochschild, Adam. *The Unquiet Ghost: Russians Remember Stalin*. New York: Viking, 1994.

Hodgart, Matthew. *Satire*. New York: McGraw-Hill, 1969.

Hoeveler, Diane Long. *Romantic Androgyny: The Woman Within*. University Park: Pennsylvania State University Press, 1990.

Holmgren, Beth. "The Transfiguring of Context in the Work of Abram Terts." *Slavic Review* 50 (1991): 965 –77.

Houghton, Norris. *Return Engagement*. New York: Holt, Rinehart and Winston, 1962.

Howey, M. Oldfield. *The Cat in the Mysteries of Religion and Magic*. New York: Castle Books, 1956.

——. *The Encircled Serpent: A Study of Serpent Symbolism in All Countries and Ages*. New York: Arthur Richmond, 1955.

Hutton, J. Bernard. *Stalin, the Miraculous Georgian*. London: Neville Spearman, 1961.

Hyde, H. Montgomery. *Stalin: The History of a Dictator*. New York: Farrar, Straus and Giroux, 1971.

Ingersoll, Ernest. *Dragons and Dragon Lore*. New York: Payson & Clarke, 1928.

Irigary, Luce. "The Question of the Other." Trans. Noah Guynn. *Yale French Studies* 87 (1995): 7 –19.

Iskander, Fazil'. *Kroliki i udavy*. Ann Arbor, Mich.: Ardis, 1982.

——. *Poety i tsary (Sbornik)*. Moscow: Ogonek, 1991.

——. *Pshada. Znamia* 8 (1993): 3 –36.

——. *Rabbits and Boa Constrictors*. Trans. Ronald E. Peterson. Ann Arbor, Mich.: Ardis, 1989.

——. *Sandro iz Chegema*. Ann Arbor, Mich.: Ardis, 1979.

——. *Sandro iz Chegema*. Moscow: Eksmo, 1999.

Ivanov, Sergei. "O 'maloi proze' Iskandera, ili chto mozhno sdelat' iz nastoiashchei mukhi." *Novyi mir* 1 (1989): 252–56.

Ivanova, Natal'ia. "Smekh protiv strakha." In *Kroliki i udavy*, by Fazil' Iskander, 3 – 10. Moscow: Knizhnaia palata, 1988.

——. *Smekh protiv strakha, ili Fazil' Iskander*. Moscow: Sovetskii pisatel', 1990.

Ivanits, Linda J. *Russian Folk Belief*. Armonk, N.Y.: M. E. Sharpe, 1989.

Iverni, Violetta. "Kazhdyi raven svoemu vyboru . . ." *Grani* 116 (1980): 184 –92.

——. "Komediia nesovmestimosti." *Kontinent* 5 (1975): 427 –54.

Jakobson, Roman. "Marginalia to Vasmer's Russian Etymological Dictionary (Р-Я)." *International Journal of Slavic Linguistics* 1–2 (1959): 266 –78.

Janson, Charles. "Zinoviev on Paradoxes of Stalinism." *Soviet Analyst*, 28 September 1983.

Jenks, Gregory C. *The Origins and Early Development of the Antichrist Myth*. Berlin: Walter de Gruyter, 1991.

Johnson, D. Barton. "Vasilij Aksionov's Aviary: *The Heron* and *The Steel Bird.*" *Scando-Slavica* 33 (1987): 45–61.

Johnson, John J., Jr. "Introduction: The Life and Works of Aksenov." In *The Steel Bird, and Other Stories*, by Vasily Aksenov, ix–xxvii. Ann Arbor, Mich.: Ardis, 1979.

Jones, Alison. *Larousse Dictionary of World Folklore.* New York: Larousse, 1995.

Jung, C. G. *Aion: Researches into the Phenomenology of the Self.* Trans. R. F. C. Hull. Princeton, N.J.: Princeton University Press, 1959.

———. *Nietzsche's* Zarathustra: *Notes of the Seminar Given in 1934–1939 by C. G. Jung.* Ed. James L. Jarrett. Princeton, N.J.: Princeton University Press, 1988.

Juvenal. *The Satires.* Trans. Niall Rudd. Oxford: Clarendon, 1991.

Kaganskaia, Maiia, and Zeev Bar-Sella. *Master Gambs i Margarita.* Tel-Aviv: Milev General Systems, 1984.

Karpov, Lena. Introduction to *The Destruction of Pompeii and Other Stories*, by Vassily Aksyonov, 7–10. Ann Arbor, Mich.: Ardis, 1991.

Kasper, Karlheinz. "Ein literarischer Text für die Abiturstufe." *Mitteilungen für die Lehrer slawischer Fremdsprachen* 64 (1992): 17–24.

Kaverin, Veniamin. "Pridvornye dissidenty i 'pogibshee pokolenie.'" *Nash sovremennik* 3 (1991): 171–76.

———. "Shvarts i soprotivlenie." *Literaturnoe obozrenie* 2 (1989): 75–77.

Kearney, Richard. *Strangers, Gods and Monsters: Interpreting Otherness.* London: Routledge, 2003.

Keith, Tomas. *Man and the Natural World: A History of the Modern Sensibility.* New York: Pantheon, 1983.

Kemp-Welch, A. *Stalin and the Literary Intelligentsia, 1928–39.* Houndmills, Eng.: Macmillan, 1991.

Kern, Gary. "Solzhenitsyn's Portrait of Stalin." *Slavic Review* 33 (1974): 1–22.

Khan, Halimur. "Folklore and Fairy-Tale Elements in Vladimir Voinovich's Novel The Life and Extraordinary Adventures of Private Ivan Chonkin." *Slavic and East European Journal* 40 (1996): 494–518.

Kirkwood, Michael. *Alexander Zinoviev: An Introduction to His Work.* Houndmills, Eng.: Macmillan, 1993.

———. "Alexander Zinoviev: Seer or Scientist?" In *Ideology in Russian Literature*, ed. Richard Freeborn and Jane Grayson, 174–87. Houndmills, Eng.: Macmillan, 1990.

———. "Elements of Structure in Zinov'ev's *Zheltyi dom.*" *Essays in Poetics* 7 (1982): 86–118.

Klingender, Francis. *Animals in Art and Thought to the End of the Middle Ages.* Cambridge, Mass.: M.I.T. Press, 1971.

Klishina, Svetlana. "Stalin na prieme u psikhoanalitika." *Moskovskie novosti*, 22 February–1 March 1998.

Kniazevaia, M., and A. Arkhangel'skaia (Galich). "Aleksandr Galich: Letopis' zhizni i tvorchestva." In *Sochineniia*, by Aleksandr Galich, vol. 1, 11–28. Moscow: Lokid, 1999.

Kopelev, Lev. "Pamiati Aleksandra Galicha." *Kontinent* 16 (1978): 334–43.

Korzhavin, N. "Poeziia Bulata Okudzhavy." In *Proza i poeziia*, by Bulat Okudzhava. Frankfurt: Posev, 1984.

Kozlovskii, Vladimir. "I. V. Stalin v russkoi zhargonnoi leksike." *SSSR: Vnutrennie protivorechiia* 3 (1982): 104–11.

Krasnov, Vladislav. *Solzhenitsyn and Dostoevsky: A Study in the Polyphonic Novel.* Athens: University of Georgia Press, 1980.

Krasnov-Levitin, Anatolii. *Dva pisatelia.* Paris: Poiski, 1983.

———. "Vl. Maksimov." In *V literaturnom zerkale: O tvorchestve Vladimira Maksimova*, 124–96. Paris: Third Wave, 1986.

Kravchenko, Maria. *The World of the Russian Fairy Tale.* Bern, Switz.: Peter Lang, 1987.

Kristeva, Julia. *Strangers to Ourselves.* Trans. Leon S. Roudiez. New York: Columbia University Press, 1991.

Krokhin, Yuri. "Fazil Iskander: Ideas and Images." *Moscow News*, 25 February–3 March 1994.

Krotkov, Iu. "A. Galich." *Novyi zhurnal* 130 (March 1978): 242–45.

Krugovoi, G. "Gnosticheskii roman M. Bulgakova." *Novyi zhurnal* 134 (1979): 47–81.

Kustanovich, Konstantin. *The Artist and the Tyrant: Vassily Aksenov's Works in the Brezhnev Era.* Columbus, Ohio: Slavica, 1992.

Lakshin, Vladimir. "Mikhail Bulgakov's *The Master and Margarita*." In *Twentieth-Century Russian Literary Criticism*, ed. Victor Erlich, 247–83. New Haven, Conn.: Yale University Press, 1975.

Lamont, Rosette C. "Horace's Heirs: Beyond Censorship in the Soviet Songs of the *Magnitizdat*." *World Literature Today* 53 (1979): 220–27.

Laqueur, Walter. *Stalin: The Glasnost Revelations.* New York: Charles Scribner's Sons, 1990.

Layton, Susan. "The Mind of the Tyrant: Tolstoj's Nicholas and Solženicyn's Stalin." *Slavic and East European Journal* 23 (1979): 479–90.

Lebedev, A. "Skazka est' skazka." *Teatr* 4 (1968): 38–44.

Leighton, Lauren G. "Homage to Kornei Chukovsky." *Russian Review* 31 (1972): 38–48.

Levinas, Emmanuel. *Time and the Other and Additional Essays.* Trans. Richard A. Cohen. Pittsburgh, Pa.: Duquesne University Press, 1987.

———. *Totality and Infinity: An Essay on Exteriority.* Trans. Alphonso Lingis. Pittsburgh, Pa.: Duquesne University Press, 1969.

Leyburn, Ellen Douglass. *Satiric Allegory: Mirror of Man.* New Haven, Conn.: Yale University Press, 1956.

Lindsay, Jack. *The Origins of Alchemy in Graeco-Roman Egypt*. New York: Barnes & Noble, 1970.

Linetskii, Vadim. "Aksenov v novom svete." *Neva* 8 (1992): 246–51.

Lionarons, Joyce Tally. *The Medieval Dragon: The Nature of the Beast in Germanic Literature*. Enfield Lock, Eng.: Hisarlik, 1998.

Lipovetskii, Mark. "Usloviia igry." *Literaturnoe obozrenie* 7 (1988): 46–49.

Londré, Felicia Hardison. "Evgeny Shvarts and the Uses of Fantasy in the Soviet Theatre." *Research Studies* [Pullman, Wash.] 47 (1979): 131–44.

Loseff, Lev. *On the Beneficence of Censorship: Aesopian Language in Modern Russian Literature*. Munich: Otto Sagner, 1984.

Lotman, Iurii M., and Boris A. Uspenskii. "Binary Models in the Dynamics of Russian Culture (to the End of the Eighteenth Century)." In *The Semiotics of Russian Cultural History*, trans. and ed. Alexander D. Nakhimovsky and Alice Stone Nakhimovsky, 30–66. Ithaca, N.Y.: Cornell University Press, 1985.

Lourie, Richard. *Letters to the Future: An Approach to Sinyavsky-Tertz*. Ithaca, N.Y.: Cornell University Press, 1975.

Lovejoy, Arthur O. *The Great Chain of Being: A Study of the History of an Idea*. Cambridge, Mass.: Harvard University Press, 1950.

Lur'e, Ia. S. "M. Bulgakov i Mark Tven." *Izvestiia Akademii Nauk SSSR. Seriia literatury i iazyka* 46 (1987): 564–71.

MacDowell, Douglas M. *Aristophanes and Athens: An Introduction to the Plays*. Oxford: Oxford University Press, 1995.

McGinn, Bernard. *Antichrist: Two Thousand Years of the Human Fascination with Evil*. New York: HarperCollins, 1994.

McMillin, Arnold. "Vasilii Aksenov's Writing in the USSR and the USA." *Irish Slavonic Studies* 10 (1989): 1–16.

Mahlow, Elena N. *Bulgakov's* The Master and Margarita: *The Text as a Cipher*. New York: Vantage Press, 1975.

Maksimov, Vladimir. "Literatura tam, gde est' bol'." *Literaturnaia gazeta*, 9 March 1994.

———. *Sobranie sochinenii*. Frankfurt: Posev, 1979.

———. "Vladimir Maximov's Visa: An Interview in London." *Encounter* 42 (1974): 51–55.

Mandelstam, Nadezhda. *Hope Abandoned*. Trans. Max Hayward. New York: Atheneum, 1981.

Marreo, Mara Négron. "Crossing the Mirror to the Forbidden Land (Lewis Carroll's *Alice in Wonderland* and Marina Tsvetaeva's *The Devil*)," trans. Susan Sellers. In *Writing Differences: Readings from the Seminar of Hélène Cixous*, ed. Susan Sellers, 66–70. Milton Keynes, Eng.: Open University Press, 1988.

Marsh, Rosalind. *Images of Dictatorship: Portraits of Stalin in Literature*. London: Routledge, 1989.

———. "Introduction: New Perspectives on Women and Gender in Russian Literature." In *Gender and Russian Literature: New Perspectives*, ed. Rosalind Marsh, 1–37. Cambridge: Cambridge University Press, 1996.

Masing-Delic, Irene. *Abolishing Death: A Salvation Myth of Russian Twentieth-Century Literature*. Stanford, Calif.: Stanford University Press, 1992.

Mason, Peter. *Deconstructing America: Representations of the Other*. London: Routledge, 1990.

Matich, Olga. "*Spokojnoi noči*: Andrej Sinjavskij's Rebirth as Abram Terc." *Slavic and East European Journal* 33 (1989): 50–63.

Matich, Olga, and Michael Heim, eds. *The Third Wave: Russian Literature in Emigration*. Ann Arbor, Mich.: Ardis, 1984.

Medvedev, Roi. *Sem'ia Tirana: Mat' i syn; Smert' Nadezhdy Alliluevoi*. Nizhnii Novgorod: Leta, 1993.

Medvedev, Roy A. *Let History Judge: The Origins and Consequences of Stalinism*. Trans. Colleen Taylor. New York: Alfred A. Knopf, 1971.

Medvedev, Zhores. "Russia under Brezhnev." *New Left Review* 117 (1979): 3–29.

Medzhakov-Koriakiin, I. I. "Osobennosti romantizma v poezii Bulata Okudzhavy." *Melbourne Slavonic Studies* 7 (1972): 58–83.

Merridale, Catherine. *Night of Stone: Death and Memory in Russia*. London: Granta Books, 2000.

Metcalf, Amanda J. *Evgenii Shvarts and His Fairy-Tales for Adults*. Birmingham, Eng.: Dept. of Russian Language & Literature, University of Birmingham, 1979.

Metcalf, Peter, and Richard Huntington. *Celebrations of Death: The Anthropology of Mortuary Ritual*. Cambridge: Cambridge University Press, 1991.

Meyer, Priscilla. "Aksenov and Stalinism: Political, Moral, and Literary Power." *Slavic and East European Journal* 30 (1986): 509–25.

———. "*Skaz* in the Work of Juz Aleškovskij." *Slavic and East European Journal* 28 (1984): 455–61.

Mikhailov, O. "Korol' bez korolevstva." In *Istreblenie tiranov*, by Vladimir Nabokov, 3–16. Minsk: Mastatskaia litaratura, 1989.

Miller, Frank J. *Folklore for Stalin: Russian Folklore and Pseudofolklore of the Stalin Era*. Armonk, N.Y.: M. E. Sharpe, 1990.

Mills, Judith M. "Of Dreams, Devils, Irrationality and *The Master and Margarita*." In *Russian Literature and Psychoanalysis*, ed. Daniel Rancour-Laferriere, 303–27. Amsterdam: John Benjamins, 1989.

Milne, Lesley. "Fazil' Iskander: From 'Petukh' to *Pshada*." *Slavic and East European Review* 74 (1996): 445–63.

———. The Master and Margarita: *A Comedy of Victory*. Birmingham, Eng.: Dept. of Russian Language & Literature, University of Birmingham, 1977.

———. *Mikhail Bulgakov: A Critical Biography*. Cambridge: Cambridge University Press, 1990.

Mirchev, A. *15 Interv'iu.* New York: Izdatel'stvo im. A. Platonova, 1989.

Moldavskii, Dm. *Russkii lubok XVII–XIX vv.* Moscow: Gosudarstvennoe izdatel'stvo izobrazitel'nogo iskusstva, 1962.

Morton, Donald E. *Vladimir Nabokov.* New York: Frederick Ungar, 1978.

Mozejko, Edward. "*The Steel Bird* and Aksënov's Prose of the Seventies." In *Vasiliy Pavlovich Aksënov: A Writer in Quest of Himself*, ed. Edward Mozejko, 205–23. Columbus, Ohio: Slavica, 1984.

Nabokov, Vladimir. *Speak, Memory: An Autobiography Revisited.* New York: Vintage, 1989.

———. *Tyrants Destroyed and Other Stories.* New York: McGraw-Hill, 1975.

———. *Vesna v Fial'te i drugie rasskazy.* New York: Izdatel'stvo imeni Chekhova, 1956.

Nepomnyashchy, Catharine Theimer. *Abram Tertz and the Poetics of Crime.* New Haven, Conn.: Yale University Press, 1995.

———. "An Interview with Andrei Sinyavsky." *Formations* 6 (1991): 6–23.

Nietzsche, Frederick W. *Thus Spoke Zarathustra: A Book for Everyone and No One.* Trans. R. J. Hollingdale. Harmondsworth, Eng.: Penguin, 1969.

Nivat, Georges. "Solzhenitsyn's Different *Circles*: An Interpretive Essay." In *Solzhenitsyn in Exile: Critical Essays and Documentary Materials*, ed. John B. Dunlop, Richard S. Haugh, and Michael Nicholson, 211–28. Stanford, Calif.: Hoover Institution Press, 1985.

O'Flaherty, Wendy Doniger. *Women, Androgynes, and Other Mythical Beasts.* Chicago: University of Chicago Press, 1980.

Okudzhava, Bulat. "Ia vnov' povstrechalsia s nadezhdoi." Interview by Il'ia Medovoi. *Moskovskie novosti*, 31 May 1987.

———. "Iz liricheskoi tetradi." *Druzhba narodov* 1 (1988): 114–19.

———. "My iz shkoly XX veka." Interview by Larisa Mikhailova. *Literaturnoe obozrenie* 5–6 (1994): 12–17.

———. *Proza i poeziia.* Frankfurt: Posev, 1984.

Oppenheimer, Max, Jr. "How Angry Is Evtushenko?" *South Atlantic Bulletin* 28 (1963): 1–3.

Opul'skii, Al'bert. "Aleksandr Galich." *Grani* 119 (1981): 264–76.

Ovid. *Metamorphoses.* Trans. Rolfe Humphries. Bloomington: Indiana University Press, 1955.

Palencia-Roth, Michael. "Enemies of God: Monsters and the Theology of Conquest." In *Monsters, Tricksters, and Sacred Cows: Animal Tales and American Identities*, ed. A. James Arnold, 23–49. Charlottesville: University of Virginia Press, 1996.

Pedenko, Sviatoslav. "'Erika' beret chetyre kopii. Vozvrashchenie A. Galicha." *Voprosy literatury* 4 (1989): 80–112.

Perrie, Maureen. *The Image of Ivan the Terrible in Russian Folklore.* Cambridge: Cambridge University Press, 1987.

Perryman, Sally Anne. "Vladimir Voinovich: The Evolution of a Satirical Soviet Writer." Ph.D. diss., Vanderbilt University, 1981.

Pesch, Helmut W. "The Sign of the Worm: Images of Death and Immortality in the Fiction of E. R. Eddison." In *Death and the Serpent: Immortality in Science Fiction and Fantasy,* ed. Carl B. Yoke and Donald M. Hassler, 91–101. Westport, Conn.: Greenwood Press, 1985.

Petro, Peter. "Hašek, Voinovich, and the Tradition of Anti-Militarist Satire." *Canadian Slavonic Papers* 22 (1980): 116–21.

Petrovskii, Miron. "Delo o *Batume.*" *Teatr* 2 (1990): 161–68.

———. *Kniga o Kornee Chukovskom.* Moscow: Sovetskii pisatel', 1966.

Phillips, William, et al. "Writers in Exile: A Conference of Soviet and East European Dissidents." *Partisan Review* 4 (1983): 487–525.

Piper, D. G. B. "An Approach to Bulgakov's *The Master and Margarita.*" *Forum for Modern Language Studies* 7 (1971): 134–57.

Pittman, Riitta H. *The Writer's Divided Self in Bulgakov's* The Master and Margarita. New York: St. Martin's Press, 1991.

Polikovskaia, L., and E. Binevich. "Legenda i byl'." In *Zhitie skazochnika: Evgenii Shvarts,* 5–16. Moscow: Knizhnaia palata, 1991.

Pollard, Arthur. *Satire.* London: Methuen, 1970.

Pomper, Philip. "Nechaev, Lenin, and Stalin: The Psychology of Leadership." *Jahrbücher für Geschichte Osteuropas* 26 (1978): 11–30.

Pope, Alexander. *Epistles to Several Persons (Moral Essays).* Ed. James E. Wellington. Miami, Fla.: University of Miami Press, 1963.

Porteous, Norman W. *Daniel: A Commentary.* Philadelphia: Westminster Press, 1965.

Porter, Robert. "Vladimir Voinovich and the Comedy of Innocence." *Forum for Modern Language Studies* 16 (1980): 97–108.

Preston, Ronald H., and Anthony T. Hanson. *The Revelation of Saint John the Divine: The Book of Glory.* London: SCM Press, 1949.

Prince, Charles. "A Psychological Study of Stalin." *Journal of Social Psychology* 22 (1945): 119–40.

Proffer, Ellendea. *Bulgakov: Life and Work.* Ann Arbor, Mich.: Ardis, 1984.

———, ed. *Neizdannyi Bulgakov: Teksty i materialy.* Ann Arbor, Mich.: Ardis, 1977.

Pulsipher, D. Curtis. "The Use of the Fantastic, Neo-Fantastic, Animals and Humor as Vehicles for Satire in the Works of Juan Jose Arreola and Marilo Rubiao." Ph.D. diss., University of Illinois at Urbana-Champaign, 1985.

Quigley, Christine. *The Corpse: A History.* Jefferson, N.C.: McFarland, 1996.

Radzinsky, Edvard. *Stalin.* London: Hodder & Stoughton, 1996.

Ragon, Michel. *The Space of Death: A Study of Funerary Architecture, Decoration, and Urbanism.* Trans. Alan Sheridan. Charlottesville: University Press of Virginia, 1983.

Ramet, Sabrina Petra, ed. *Gender Reversals and Gender Cultures: Anthropological and Historical Perspectives.* London: Routledge, 1996.

Rancour-Laferriere, Daniel. "The Boys of Ibansk: A Freudian Look at Some Recent Russian Satire." *Psychoanalytic Review* 72 (1985): 639–56.

———. "The Deranged Birthday Boy: Solzhenitsyn's Portrait of Stalin in *The First Circle." Mosaic* 18 (1985): 61–72.

———. "From Incompetence to Satire: Voinovich's Image of Stalin as Castrated Leader of the Soviet Union in 1941." *Slavic Review* 50 (1991): 36–47.

———. *The Mind of Stalin: A Psychoanalytic Study.* Ann Arbor, Mich.: Ardis, 1988.

Rappaport, Helen. *Joseph Stalin: A Biographical Companion.* Santa Barbara, Calif.: ABC-CLIO, 1999.

Rassadin, Stanislav. " 'Boiat'sia avtoru nechego,' ili Ispitanie glasnost'iu." *Oktiabr'* 4 (1988): 149–51.

———. *Obyknovennoe chudo: Kniga o skazkakh dlia teatra.* Moscow: Detskaia literatura, 1964.

Raskina, Marina. "The Emergence of Fantasmagoric Realism in Contemporary Russian, Hebrew, and British Literatures: Vasily Aksenov, Amos Oz, and Kingsley Amis." Ph.D. diss., Purdue University, 1988.

Ravich, Petr. "Nachala eposa." In *V literaturnom zerkale: O tvorchestve Vladimira Maksimova,* ed. Dzhemma Kvachevskaia, 58–60. Paris: Third Wave, 1986.

Reck, Vera T., trans. and ed. "Excerpts from the Diaries of Korney Chukovsky Relating to Boris Pilnyak." *California Slavic Studies* 11 (1980): 187–99.

Reed, Annette Yoshiko. *Fallen Angels and the History of Judaism and Christianity: The Reception of Enochic Literature.* Cambridge: Cambridge University Press, 2005.

Rogers, Katharine M. *The Troublesome Helpmate: A History of Misogyny in Literature.* Seattle: University of Washington Press, 1966.

Rowland, Beryl. *Animals with Human Faces.* Knoxville: University of Tennessee Press, 1973.

———. *Birds with Human Souls: A Guide to Bird Symbolism.* Knoxville: University of Tennessee Press, 1978.

Rudwin, Maximilian. *The Devil in Legend and Literature.* Chicago: Open Court, 1931.

Rutherford, Brent M. "Psychopathology, Decision-Making, and Political Involvement." *Journal of Conflict Resolution* 10 (1966): 387–407.

Ryan-Hayes, Karen. *Contemporary Russian Satire: A Genre Study.* Cambridge: Cambridge University Press, 1995.

Sale, Roger. *Fairy Tales and After: From Snow White to E. B. White.* Cambridge, Mass.: Harvard University Press, 1978.

Sarano, Jacques. *The Meaning of the Body.* Trans. James H. Farley. Philadelphia: Westminster Press, 1966.

Scammell, Michael. *Solzhenitsyn: A Biography.* New York: Norton, 1984.

Scherr, Barry P. *Maxim Gorky.* Boston: Twayne, 1988.

Scholl, Tim. "Queer Performance: 'Male' Ballet." In *Consuming Russia: Popular Culture, Sex, and Society since Gorbachev,* ed. Adele Marie Barker, 303–17. Durham, N.C.: Duke University Press, 1999.

Seeman, Klaus Dieter. "Bulat Okudžavas 'Černyi kot' als antistalinistische Parodie." *Die Welt der Slaven* 31 (1986): 139 –46.

Seidel, Michael. *Satiric Inheritance: Rabelais to Sterne.* Princeton, N.J.: Princeton University Press, 1979.

Shakespeare, William. *Hamlet.* In *Four Tragedies,* ed. David Bevington, 25 –171. Toronto: Bantam Books, 1988.

Shneerson, Mariia. "Sila mastera i bessilie vlastitelina (Bulgakov i Stalin)." *Grani* 167 (1993): 99 –145.

Shusterman, Richard. "Understanding the Self's Others." In *Cultural Otherness and Beyond,* ed. Chhanda Gupta and D. P. Chattopadhyaya, 107 –14. Leiden, Neth.: Brill, 1998.

Shvarts, A. "Zametki o Bulgakove." *Novoe russkoe slovo,* 17 May 1991.

Shvarts, Evgenii. *Drakon, Klad, Ten', Dva klena, Obyknovennoe chudo i drugie proizvedeniia.* Moscow: Gud'ial, 1998.

Sidorov, E. *Evgenii Evtushenko: Lichnost' i tvorchestvo.* Moscow: Khudozhestvennaia literatura, 1987.

Simard, Lionel Robert. "The Life and Works of Evgenii Shvarts." Ph.D. diss., Cornell University, 1970.

Simon, Hilda. *Snakes: The Facts and the Folklore.* New York: Viking, 1973.

Sinyavsky, Andrei. "In Defense of the Pyramid (On Yevtushenko's Poetry)." In *For Freedom of Thought and Imagination,* trans. Laszlo Tikos and Murray Peppard, 167 –95. New York: Holt, Rinehart and Winston, 1971.

———. *Soviet Civilization: A Cultural History.* Trans. Joanne Turnbull. New York: Arcade, 1988.

———. *Unguarded Thoughts.* Trans. Manya Harari. London: Collins, Harvill, 1972.

Slonimskii, M., et al. *My znali Evgeniia Shvartsa.* Leningrad: Iskusstvo, 1966.

Smelianskii, A. "Ukhod." *Teatr* 12 (1988): 88 –115.

Smeliansky, Anatoly. *Is Comrade Bulgakov Dead? Mikhail Bulgakov at the Moscow Art Theatre.* Trans. Arch Tait. London: Methuen, 1993.

Smirnov, Iurii. "Mistika i real'nost' sataninskogo bala." *Pamir* 9 (1988): 139 –63.

Smirnova, Vera. *Sovremennyi portret: Stat'i.* Moscow: Sovetskii pisatel', 1964.

Smith, Edward Ellis. *The Young Stalin: The Early Years of an Elusive Revolutionary.* New York: Farrar, Straus and Giroux, 1967.

Smith, G. S. "Whispered Cry: The Songs of Alexander Galich." *Index on Censorship* 3 (1974): 11 –28.

Smith, Kathleen E. *Remembering Stalin's Victims: Popular Memory and the End of the USSR.* Ithaca, N.Y.: Cornell University Press, 1996.

Sokolov, Y. M. *Russian Folklore.* Trans. Catherine Ruth Smith. Detroit, Mich.: Folklore Associates, 1966.

Solzhenitsyn, Aleksandr. *The Oak and the Calf: Sketches of Literary Life in the Soviet Union.* Trans. Harry Willetts. New York: Harper & Row, 1980.

———. *Sobranie sochinenii.* Paris: YMCA-Press, 1978.

Sosin, Gene. "Alexander Galich: Russian Poet of Dissent." *Midstream* 20 (1974): 29 –37.

Spring, Derek. "Stalinism—The Historical Debate." In *Stalinism and Soviet Cinema*, ed. Richard Taylor and Derek Spring, 1–14. London: Routledge, 1993.

Suny, Ronald Grigor. "Beyond Psychohistory: The Young Stalin in Georgia." *Slavic Review* 50 (1991): 48 –58.

Svirski, Grigori. *A History of Post-War Soviet Writing: The Literature of Moral Opposition*. Trans. Robert Dessaix and Michael Ulman. Ann Arbor, Mich.: Ardis, 1981.

Sytova, Alla. *The Lubok: Russian Folk Pictures, 17th to 19th Century*. Leningrad: Aurora, 1984.

Tarasova, N. "Bulat Okudzhava—sovremennyi baian." In *Bud' zdorov, shkoliar: Stikhi*, by Bulat Okudzhava, vii–xiv. Frankfurt: Posev, 1966.

Terts, Abram [Andrei Sinyavsky]. "The Literary Process in Russia." Trans. Michael Glenny. In *Kontinent 1: The Alternative Voice of Russia and Eastern Europe*, ed. Vladimir Maximov, 73 –110. London: André Deutsch, 1976.

———. "Literaturnyi protsess v Rossii." *Kontinent* 1 (1974): 143 –90.

———. "On Socialist Realism." In The Trial Begins *and* On Socialist Realism, trans. George Dennis, 147–219. Berkeley: University of California Press, 1960.

———. *Spokoinoi nochi*. Moscow: Zakharov, 1998.

———. *Strolls with Pushkin*. Trans. Catharine Theimer Nepomnyashchy and Slava I. Yastremski. New Haven, Conn.: Yale University Press, 1993.

Thomas, Keith. *Man and the Natural World: A History of the Modern Sensibility*. New York: Pantheon Books, 1983.

Thompson, Ewa M. "The Artistic World of Michail Bulgakov." *Russian Literature* 5 (1973): 54 –64.

———. *Understanding Russia: The Holy Fool in Russian Culture*. Lanham, Md.: University Press of America, 1987.

Thompson, Kristin. "*Ivan the Terrible* and Stalinist Russia: A Reexamination." *Cinema Journal* 17 (1977): 30 –43.

Tiffany, Grace. *Erotic Beasts and Social Monsters: Shakespeare, Jonson, and Comic Androgyny*. Newark, N.J.: University of Delaware Press, 1995.

Todorov, Tzvetan. *The Conquest of America: The Question of the Other*. Trans. Richard Howard. New York: Harper & Row, 1984.

———. *On Human Diversity: Nationalism, Racism, and Exoticism in French Thought*. Trans. Catherine Porter. Cambridge, Mass.: Harvard University Press, 1993.

Troll', Iuliia. "'Kroliki i udavy' Fazilia Iskandera." *Novyi zhurnal* 151 (1983): 301–4.

Trotsky, Leon. *Stalin: An Appraisal of the Man and His Influence*. Trans. and ed. Charles Malamuth. New York: Stein & Day, 1967.

Tsimbal, S. "Fantaziia i real'nost' (Iz arkhiva Evgeniia Shvartsa)." *Voprosy literatury* 11 (1967): 158 –81.

Tucker, Robert C. "The Dictator and Totalitarianism." *World Politics* 17 (1965): 555 –83.

———. *Stalin as Revolutionary, 1879–1929: A Study in History and Personality.* New York: Norton, 1973.

Tumarkin, Nina. *Lenin Lives! The Lenin Cult in Soviet Russia.* Cambridge, Mass.: Harvard University Press, 1983.

Tutaev, David, trans. and ed. *The Alliluyev Memoirs: Recollections of Svetlana Stalina's Maternal Aunt Anna Alliluyeva and Her Grandfather Sergei Alliluyev.* New York: G. P. Putnam's Sons, 1968.

Ulam, Adam B. "The Price of Sanity." In *Stalinism: Its Impact on Russia and the World*, ed. G. R. Urban, 100–145. London: Maurice Temple Smith, 1982.

———. *Stalin: The Man and His Era.* New York: Viking, 1973.

Uspenskii, B. A. "Mifologicheskii aspekt russkoi ekspressivnoi frazeologii." In *Izbrannye trudy*, vol. 2, *Iazyk i kul'tura*, 67–161. Moscow: Iazyki russkoi kul'tury, 1996.

Van Gennep, Arnold. *The Rites of Passage.* Trans. Monika B. Vizedom and Gabrielle L. Caffee. Chicago: University of Chicago Press, 1960.

Vasiuchenko, Irina. "Chtia vozhdia i armeiskii ustav." *Znamia* 10 (1989): 214–16.

Veselaia, Elena. "Esli ostanovimsia, nas poneset nazad." *Moskovskie novosti*, 12 March 1989.

Voinovich, Vladimir. *The Anti-Soviet Soviet Union.* Trans. Richard Lourie. San Diego: Harcourt Brace Jovanovich, 1986.

———. *Zhizn' i neobychainye prikliucheniia soldata Ivana Chonkina: Litso neprikosnovennoe.* Ann Arbor, Mich.: Ardis, 1985.

Von Ssachno, Helen. "Zinoviev's Paradoxes." *Encounter* 52 (1979): 84–86.

Vroon, Ronald. *Velimir Xlebnikov's Shorter Poems: A Key to the Coinages.* Ann Arbor: Dept. of Slavic Languages and Literatures, University of Michigan, 1983.

Vulis, A. "Posleslovie." *Moskva* 11 (1966): 127–30.

Weiner, Adam. *By Authors Possessed: The Demonic Novel in Russia.* Evanston, Ill.: Northwestern University Press, 1988.

Williams, David. *Deformed Discourse: The Function of the Monster in Mediaeval Thought and Literature.* Exeter, Eng.: University of Exeter Press, 1996.

Willis, Roy. "The Meaning of the Snake." In *Signifying Animals: Human Meaning in the Natural World*, ed. R. G. Wills, 246–52. London: Unwin Hyman, 1990.

Windle, Kevin. "Iuz Aleshkovskii's 'Pesnia o Staline' and 'Sovetskaia paskhalnaia': A Study of Competing Versions." *Slavonic and East European Review* 74 (1996): 19–37.

Wright, A. C. *Mikhail Bulgakov: Life and Interpretations.* Toronto: University of Toronto Press, 1978.

———. "Satan in Moscow: An Approach to Bulgakov's *The Master and Margarita.*" *PMLA* 88 (1973): 1162–72.

Yevtushenko, Yevgeny. *A Precocious Autobiography.* Trans. Andrew R. MacAndrew. New York: E. P. Dutton, 1963.

Young, George M., Jr. *Nikolai F. Fedorov: An Introduction.* Belmont: Nordland, 1979.

Zbarsky, Ilya, and Samuel Hutchinson. *Lenin's Embalmers.* Trans. Barbara Bray. London: Harvill, 1998.

Zelenin, D. K. *Izbrannye trudy.* Vol. 2, *Ocherki russkoi mifologii: Umershie neestest-vennoiu smert'iu i rusalki.* Moscow: Indrik, 1995.

Zernova, Ruth. "Song Poetry of the 1960's–1980's in the USSR." In *Proceedings: Summer 1986 Intensive Workshop in Chinese and Russian.* Eugene, Ore.: Department of Russian, University of Oregon, 1987.

Zhukhovitskii, Leonid. "BOMZh vo frake: V Moskve vyshel trekhtomnik Iuza Aleshkovskogo." *Literaturnaia gazeta,* 31 July 1996.

Zinov'ev, Aleksandr. "From Yawning Heights to Radiant Future." *Survey* 23 (1977–78): 1–11.

———. *My i zapad.* Lausanne: L'Age d'Homme, 1981.

———. *Nashei iunosti polet.* Lausanne: L'Age d'Homme, 1983.

———. *Zheltyi dom.* Lausanne: L'Age d'Homme, 1980.

Ziolkowski, Margaret. *Literary Exorcisms of Stalinism: Russian Writers and the Soviet Past.* Columbia, S.C.: Camden House, 1998.

———. "A Modern Demonology: Some Literary Stalins." *Slavic Review* 50 (1991): 59–69.

Index

www.ingramcontent.com/pod-product-compliance
Lightning Source LLC
Chambersburg PA
CBHW061725270326
41928CB00011B/2112